# Prophetic Translation

Edinburgh Studies in Modern Arabic Literature
Series Editor: Rasheed El-Enany

*Writing Beirut: Mappings of the City in the Modern Arabic Novel*
Samira Aghacy

*Autobiographical Identities in Contemporary Arab Literature*
Valerie Anishchenkova

*The Iraqi Novel: Key Writers, Key Texts*
Fabio Caiani and Catherine Cobham

*Sufism in the Contemporary Arabic Novel*
Ziad Elmarsafy

*Gender, Nation, and the Arabic Novel: Egypt 1892–2008*
Hoda Elsadda

*The Unmaking of the Arab Intellectual: Prophecy, Exile and the Nation*
Zeina G. Halabi

*Post-War Anglophone Lebanese Fiction: Home Matters in the Diaspora*
Syrine Hout

*Prophetic Translation: The Making of Modern Eyptian Literature*
Maya I. Kesrouany

*Nasser in the Egyptian Imaginary*
Omar Khalifah

*Conspiracy in Modern Egyptian Literature*
Benjamin Koerber

*War and Occupation in Iraqi Fiction*
Ikram Masmoudi

*Literary Autobiography and Arab National Struggles*
Tahia Abdel Nasser

*The Arab* Nahḍah*: The Making of the Intellectual and Humanist Movement*
Abdulrazzak Patel

*Sonallah Ibrahim: Rebel with a Pen*
Paul Starkey

*Minorities in the Contemporary Egyptian Novel*
Mary Youssef

edinburghuniversitypress.com/series/smal

# Prophetic Translation

## The Making of Modern Egyptian Literature

Maya I. Kesrouany

EDINBURGH
University Press

*To my mother and father,*
*Alia and Issam,*
*for always looking beyond their worlds and encouraging me to venture there.*

Edinburgh University Press is one of the leading university presses in the UK. We publish academic books and journals in our selected subject areas across the humanities and social sciences, combining cutting-edge scholarship with high editorial and production values to produce academic works of lasting importance. For more information visit our website: edinburghuniversitypress.com



Edinburgh University Press Ltd
The Tun – Holyrood Road
12 (2f) Jackson's Entry
Edinburgh EH8 8PJ

First published in hardback by Edinburgh University Press 2019

Typeset in 11/15 Adobe Garamond by
Servis Filmsetting Ltd, Stockport, Cheshire, and
printed and bound by CPI Group (UK) Ltd

A CIP record for this book is available from the British Library

ISBN 978 1 4744 0740 3 (hardback)
ISBN 978 1 4744 7450 4 (paperback)
ISBN 978 1 4744 0741 0 (webready PDF)
ISBN 978 1 4744 0742 7 (epub)

# Contents

# Series Editor's Foreword

Edinburgh Studies in Modern Arabic Literature is a new and unique series that will, it is hoped, fill in a glaring gap in scholarship in the field of modern Arabic literature. Its dedication to Arabic literature in the modern period, that is, from the nineteenth century onwards, is what makes it unique among series undertaken by academic publishers in the English-speaking world. Individual books on modern Arabic literature in general or aspects of it have been and continue to be published sporadically. Series on Islamic studies and Arab/Islamic thought and civilisation are not in short supply either in the academic world, but these are far removed from the study of Arabic literature qua literature, that is, imaginative, creative literature as we understand the term when, for instance, we speak of English literature or French literature. Even series labelled 'Arabic/Middle Eastern Literature' make no period distinction, extending their purview from the sixth century to the present, and often including non-Arabic literatures of the region. This series aims to redress the situation by focusing on the Arabic literature and criticism of today, stretching its interest to the earliest beginnings of Arab modernity in the nineteenth century.

The need for such a dedicated series, and generally for the redoubling of scholarly endeavour in researching and introducing modern Arabic literature to the Western reader, has never been stronger. Among activities and events heightening public, let alone academic, interest in all things Arab, and not least Arabic literature, are the significant growth in the last decades of the translation of contemporary Arab authors from all genres, especially fiction, into English; the higher profile of Arabic literature internationally since the award of the Nobel Prize in Literature to Naguib Mahfouz in 1988; the growing number of Arab authors living in the Western diaspora and writing both in English and Arabic; the adoption of such authors and others by mainstream, high-circulation publishers, as opposed to the academic publishers of the past; the establishment of prestigious prizes, such as the International Prize for Arabic Fiction (IPAF) (the Arabic Booker), run by the Man Booker Foundation, which brings huge publicity to the shortlist and winner every year, as well as translation contracts into English and other languages; and, very recently, the events of the Arab Spring. It is therefore part of the ambition of this series that it will increasingly address a wider reading public beyond its natural territory of students and researchers in Arabic and world literature. Nor indeed is the academic readership of the series expected to be confined to specialists in literature in the light of the growing trend for interdisciplinarity, which increasingly sees scholars crossing field boundaries in their research tools and coming up with findings that equally cross discipline borders in their appeal.

There is no shortage of studies that make a link between the rising national consciousness and resistance to British colonial rule in Egypt in the early decades of the twentieth century on the one hand, and the emergence of new narrative genres in Arabic literature, particularly the novel, on the other. The novel as literary form offered itself to writers as an ideal vehicle for giving voice to a new-found sense of national identity previously overshadowed by the pan-Islamic identity of the Ottoman caliphate and later the hegemony of foreign colonial powers. But intellectual endeavour to forge, or perhaps more accurately to articulate, an Egyptian identity was not limited to the writing of novels. That endeavour naturally took many other forms, of which one (perhaps not entirely unrelated to writing novels) was translation of fiction and non-fiction from European languages, especially French and English. Interestingly, some of those very translators also wrote their own novels as well as non-fiction works, while some were even directly involved in the political and not only intellectual life of the country. It is not therefore inconceivable that whatever grand national project or quest motivated their novel writing and/or political pursuits also motivated their translations: the choices of authors and texts that they translate and the political and social thought they contain and its relevance to Egyptian reality at the time. In a time of social and political transformation, it is not inconceivable either that the strategies adopted in translation and adaptation and the degree of 'faithfulness' to the original were also dictated consciously or unconsciously by the same ulterior motives that lay behind the writing of novels. Important as the subject is, studies of the phenomenon have been scarce. Whereas critics and scholars have for decades devoted a fair amount of attention to researching the early Egyptian novel in relation to rising national consciousness and the birth of the nation-state, they have been less forthcoming on the matter of the many concomitant translations of the same period.

It is into this little-trodden terrain that the current book offers to venture, bringing the latest developments in translation theory and postcolonial approaches to bear on some little-studied translations from European languages by major Egyptian authors in the early decades of the twentieth century.

*Professor Rasheed El-Enany, Series Editor,*
*Emeritus Professor of Modern Arabic Literature,*
*University of Exeter*

# Acknowledgements

Most of this book was written in the streets of Beirut in 2014, although it addressed the alleys of Cairo. The earlier decades of the twentieth century brought the two cities into a different encounter than the previous century and the current one. Both cities lived such singular revolutionary moments and seemed to tell their historical stories in different languages. But both remained conflicted about their relationships to Arabic, made to speak in French and English until they became enamoured with both. Early twentieth-century writers craved European literature, again for different reasons and to different ends, but the love affair went beyond a desire for the other to a passion for words. The experience of the two cities and their writers echoed mine, and translation seemed to be the metaphor for my own existence, and that of the writers I admired and envied throughout my education. Although well studied, the Egyptian translators I chose – Muṣṭafā Luṭfī al-Manfalūṭī (1876–1924), Muḥammad al-Sibāʿī (1881–1931), Muḥammad Ḥusayn Haykal (1888–1956), and Ṭāhā Ḥusayn (1889–1973) – were misunderstood. I was drawn to how they negotiated their memories, heritage, and modernity and made the literary text into history through their creative adaptations of Western literature.

In reading their works, I became a translator myself – retranslating their own translations – and, along the way, I developed a deep appreciation for the impossible task of translation. Walter Benjamin once said, 'It is the task of the translator to release in his own language that pure language that is under the spell of another, to liberate the language imprisoned in a work in his re-creation of that work' ('The Task of the Translator', 1923, p. 80). The spell of the other language was less of an abstract pursuit for my translators and more of an active digging to recall and reinvent a past that appeared to speak a different language but be under the spell of their own. In another text, Benjamin described memory as 'not an instrument for surveying the past but its theater. . . . He who seeks to approach his own buried past must conduct himself like a man digging' ('Excavation and Memory', 1932, p. 576). And I went digging with them, hoping that they would teach me something about the past, the present, and perhaps the future. And they did. The past is precisely the theatre of memory, the present is the scriptwriter, and the future, well, is yet another fictional theatre waiting for its performers. I am grateful for those lessons, and to the people who helped me read them.

I would especially like to thank Professor Roger Allen who has been the most gracious mentor: offering to read my manuscript, responding to my emails within minutes and encouraging me all along.

I cannot express enough gratitude to Professor Robert Young, whose faith in me has restored my own faith in this project, Professor Justin Stearns who read my entire manuscript in only two weeks and helped me see beyond my words, and Professor Toral Gajarawala who sat with me for hours to talk book and life.

I am infinitely grateful for my intellectual community at New York University in Abu Dhabi (NYUAD), United Arab Emirates – I am so fortunate to have the friendship of some of the most brilliant people I have ever met. I have also been privileged enough to meet so many wonderful and generous thinkers who came to visit NYUAD from different parts of the world; our conversations have shaped so much of this book.

I always tell people how fortunate I was with my professors at Emory University, Atlanta, Georgia, USA – Professor Elissa Marder, my mentor, my primary reader, and my most trusted intellectual force, I am thankful to her commitment to me in every way; Professor Devin Stewart, whose eclectic brilliance and support brought me to a deeper understanding of Arabic literature and its tradition; and Professor Geoffrey Bennington whose brilliance is only paralleled by his composure, a combination that made French philosophical thought a lived part of my everyday.

I would like to thank Professor Jeffrey Sacks – who has never met me – and yet agreed to read my manuscript and give me such generous and engaged feedback.

I am thankful to Professor Rasheed El-Enany, the series editor, for his support and patience at every step of this project, and the editors and project managers at Edinburgh University Press who not only respond immediately but also take the time to check in.

My time as a Mellon fellow at the Arts and Humanities Center in 2014–2015 at the American University of Beirut in Lebanon was one of the happiest times of my academic career. The intellectual environment, the communal support, and the back alleys of Beirut brought this project back to life.

I want to thank the Barjeel Art Foundation in Sharjah, UAE, for generously allowing me to use Egyptian painter George Bahgoury's (b. 1932) *The Scribe* (2009) – dedicated to Ṭāhā Ḥusayn, as some of this book is – as the book's cover image. Bahgoury also straddled two worlds: living in Paris for three decades and adopting French cubism to record Egyptian cultural history. When describing his painting of Umm Kolthoum in an interview with *Al Ahram* newspaper (May 2009, Issue No. 946), Bahgoury echoes my translators' task: 'With every stroke of the brush I recall an Egypt that I don't want to disappear.'

And, finally, to my friends and family who constantly distracted me, pulled me away from the book and into the real world, made me late on deadlines, and reminded me to snap out of it; for that I am most grateful.

# Introduction
# Prophetic Tendencies: Egyptian Translators of the Twentieth Century

It were as wise to cast a violet into a crucible, that you might discover the formal principles of its colour and odor, as to seek to transfer from one language into another the creations of a poet.

Percy Bysshe Shelley (1792–1882)[1]

The form (of the story) crystallised in the newly arrived seed and a contemporary style was readied for it. But there remained above and beyond both a mysterious thing which I call the intuitive feel for the soul of narrative art, its rhythm, and its temperament. These were available exclusively to writers intimate with Western culture. Stories written by others, despite fulfilling all the [formal] requirements, still lacked that secret scent which makes story [writing] an art. This phenomenon persists to this day [1960]. There is no harm, therefore, in admitting that the story came to us from the West and that its foundations here were laid by pioneering individuals who had been influenced by European, especially French literature. For even though some English masterpieces had been translated into Arabic, the origins of the story in our culture are rooted in French literature. The Egyptian temperament at that time felt no alienation from France as it did from England – perhaps because of the cultural similarity among the peoples of the Mediterranean basin. Another factor may have also contributed to that, namely the fact that some French writers had played important political roles in the history of their country. The names of these writers became widely known as symbols of liberation

> movements. [Victor] Hugo, whose *Les Misérables* Ḥāfiẓ [Ibrāhīm] translated, was such a writer; al-Manfalūṭī followed suit and rendered in Arabic only texts of French literature.
>
> Yaḥya Ḥaqqī (1905–92)[2]

The Arabic novel has yet to tell its own story. Accused of being a purely borrowed form, it has been compelled to follow other stories unfolding in other places. As a form, the Arabic novel was in fact always partially on loan from European traditions, but this loan came packaged in translation. Traditionally, translation implied the translator's submission to an outside power: either the original source or divine inspiration. It is not surprising that in the history of Western literature, translation was always bound to revealed religions; it was expected to reproduce the original word intact in singular vernaculars. The paradoxical task of translation was thus born: religious meaning always eludes perfect translation at the same time that it *demands* it. Translation proceeds as though the transmission of meaning in a new language is possible without much loss, while the experience of revelation, the original religious meaning as it were, is reserved for those with faith in the divine source. This onerous task befalls the translator as she becomes a channel, ideally a clear vessel, that mediates the passage of the original word to its target text. What becomes of this expectation in a colonial setting, when such mediation is already framed in unequal power relations, between two antagonistic idioms, and two very different worlds, reductively referred to as European and Arab? What becomes of the translator when she finds herself in a colonial situation that wants to speak not just for her but also through her?

*Prophetic Translation: The Making of Modern Egyptian Literature* explores such acts of literary translation in colonial Egypt in the early twentieth century. It approaches them within the colonial moment that shapes their production and circulation, but also thinks through how to read them as prophetic texts, not in the sense of foretelling a future, but as texts that expose the complicated relationship between colonial discourse and tradition, literature and religion. The prophetic emerges on three levels: first, the translators saw themselves as modernist prophets and agents of change. Second, they wrote various religious narratives such as biographies of the prophet. Third, under the spell of romanticism, the prophetic becomes a narrative position produced in their theories and practice of translation. Releasing the translation from any obligation to recognise the original, these texts reveal their worlds as colonial representations and carve out new spaces of interpretation by desecrating both original texts and accounts of origins. They arrest the colonial logic of representation in the process, calling attention to the present text precisely as a *new* text – a transformation of received and traditional genres – that could bear witness to a changing Arab moment. This *new* text is not new because it is modern – in fact, reading it in and as translation confirms its deviation from another borrowed colonial narrative, that of liberal nationalism. Rather, prophetic translation points specifically to how competing local and colonial discourses transform from representations to realities in colonial Egypt. The prophetic, moreover, is *not* a secular project that replaces religion with literature – it does not *pretend* to rid us of the divine. Rather, the prophetic emerges in the space between sacred and secular, original and translation, being neither here nor there. In this way *Prophetic Translation* moves beyond the question of fidelity in translation and the compatibility between fictional imagination and Islam, as well as the 'novelty of the novel', and towards understanding the significance of the proliferation of experimental, 'translated' narrative forms at the turn of the century. In undoing the relationship to the origin, prophetic translation also undoes a teleological narrative that carries us from a starting point to a destination. No longer is it possible when reading these texts to answer where they come from and where they may be headed, for prophetic translation becomes a *mode* of close reading that constantly interrupts both the original and its translation.

Muṣṭafā Luṭfī al-Manfalūṭī (1876–1924) understood that potential well when in the introduction to his adaptation of Edmond Rostand's *Cyrano de Bergerac* (1897) as *al-Shāʿir* (The Poet) (1921), he confessed: 'I have tried to abide by the original in its entirety, and controlled myself to only remove sentences that were of no importance or added only expressions that were necessary for the context.' His 'Arabised version' is 'the actual French original', and he only 'changed it from a play into a short story so that the reader can see it on paper as the audience sees it in the theatre'.[3] In those few lines, al-Manfalūṭī, who knew no foreign languages and based his adaptations on his acquaintances' rough, mostly non-literary, and often oral, renditions of French literature, identifies the three pivots of literary translation in early twentieth-century Egypt: fidelity, context, and genre. Translation of European literature took on various forms – such as *iqtibās* (paraphrase), *ta<sup>c</sup>rīb* (Arabisation), and *naql* (copying) – with various degrees of tampering with the original. While some critics have argued that translation becomes more literal with the turn of the century, *Prophetic Translation* invests in the inevitable betrayal of all forms of literary translation and specifically in the promise of this betrayal to revising genealogies of the Arabic novel. By betrayal, I refer to the inevitable loss in the process of transferring meaning from one language and context into another. While several critics read these early translations of novels, short stories, and philosophical texts as failed emulations, this book treats them as early articulations of 'literariness' that interrupt the canonisation of the Arabic realist novel as the penultimate 'modern' genre.[4] Throughout I place the adjective 'modern' in quotation marks, wary of its teleological connotations in the Egyptian *nahḍa* or renaissance of the late nineteenth century and early twentieth, traditionally said to begin in 1798 with Napoleon's arrival in Alexandria, continue until 1914, and mark an awakening from the age of 'decadence' or *<sup>c</sup>aṣr al-inḥiṭāṭ*. I insist on close reading as interruptive of these teleological framings of a translated modernity in twentieth-century Egypt, shifting the focus from elite constructions of the modern to its articulations in exemplary translations from the period. This book reads the elite intelligentsia's translations of European romanticism and realism away from their national grammar, and towards mapping how literature emerges from the confluence of discourses in their translations. It examines various instances of translation, from plagiarism to accurate translation, and finally auto/biographical adaptations of the lives of European authors.

How do we read these translations of major reform-minded Egyptian intellectuals as performances of betrayal? Whom do these adaptations betray, and how do we approach this betrayal in mapping new literary histories? Muhammad Siddiq describes the 'most fatal blind spot' in the literary reform discourses of the *nahḍa* as 'the desperate belief that a sufficient number of desirable features of European modernity can be successfully grafted onto a carefully edited and updated core of Islamic curriculum' to fast-forward through years of 'stagnation' into 'modernity'.[5] But what if this 'fatal' blind spot were reframed within a close reading of perfect translation as a necessary failure since the copy could never be an exact replica of the original? This book examines closely both the theory and practice of literary translation of several prominent Egyptian writers to reassess this supposed blind faith in the 'emulation' of the Western master text. It reframes these early translations, even though they are elite cultural expressions, as moments of unrealised reformist aspirations and utterances that resist, even while pretending to copy, the logic of narrative representation. They bridge memories of a pre-colonial literary fantasy with the aspiration of producing literary texts that could recall Arabic as a truth-language.[6]

All the translators studied in this book have seemingly succumbed to that fatal blind spot. Al-Manfalūṭī, whose Arabic 'translations' were free adaptations, barely conceals the European garments under his Azharite dress, writes Abdelfattah Kilito (ᶜAbdulfattāḥ Kīlīṭū).[7] Muḥammad al-Sibāᶜī (1881–1931), known for his more 'accurate' and 'good' translations of British literature, has recently been described as complicit in a dangerous self-orientalism.[8] Muḥammad Ḥusayn Haykal (1888–1956) and Ṭāhā Ḥusayn (1889–1973) – whose translations varied from excerpted rewritings to full texts and critical biographies – are often the modernist gatekeepers, moderating the encounter between East and West from a comfortably conciliatory, or *tawfīqī,* position.[9] In revising these accusations, every chapter reads the intersection between translation theory, praxis, and literature.

But could these various models of translation – if we were to model 'translation as a becoming' as Lydia Liu suggests – complicate the reception of these authors and their works?[10] How did these adaptations of European fiction and philosophy influence modern Arabic narrative? This book explores the emergence of a narrative voice – not of the historical author but as a locus of discursive relationships that also includes the reader – that conceives of the poetic word as essentially performative, creating the world it references.[11] I insist on the creative dimension both as a legacy of romanticism but also as a resistant residue of the translators' Islamic education at the *kuttāb*, a traditional elementary school for boys, and al-Azhar, Egypt's oldest university associated with al-Azhar mosque. In many ways, literary translation presented itself as prophetic – promising new meanings and worlds that are *essentially* literary. All four translators reference prophecy in their literary and Islamic writings,[12] and the tension between literary genius and the Muslim prophet persists throughout their works.

The prophet Muḥammad becomes an important figure of emulation in the early twentieth century, in the throes of colonial occupation and within the struggle to author a native literary expression. Maḥmūd Taymūr described the prophet's 'personality' as 'a living translation of the Book of God . . . God intended . . . that Muḥammad should be the model for all human beings'.[13] Translation becomes an act of emulation and not mere mimicking of the original, and this act mirrors the emulation of the prophet as a human ideal of perfection. Both forms of emulation remain incomplete and unrealised. These translations do not pretend to 'represent' an immediate Egyptian present, recognising in their different ways that they come from elsewhere. Rather they conceive a *new* literary language that recalls a prehistory of 'modern' Arabic narrative – the latter supposedly a product of the nineteenth century – as it confronts premodern cultural forms with modern exigencies. In the process, they move us away from a nationalist discourse that champions the novel, and towards specific literary articulations that have participated in producing the 'modern'. They also compel us to revise dominant genealogies of the Egyptian novel that read its development through European conceptual categories, measuring its success as a literary capacity for 'representing' the world in a 'modern' Arabic language.[14] Read closely, these translations reveal themselves as sites of generic confusion and transformation and urge us to reexamine the comparative lens that translates *adab* as literature.[15]

Significantly, these texts were not exactly 'translations', if by translation here we mean an accurate copying of content from one language into another. Some are complete adaptations that do not mention the original title or author. Even those texts that pretend to be faithful to the original rewrite it in subtle ways to make it relevant to the translating culture's background. In some instances, as per the translator's whim, education, background, or intended audience, entire parts of the original are removed, names are changed, forms adapted, and plots drastically altered. Inevitably, some of these translations were plagiaristic: in some instances, the translations pretend to be the originals. In other cases, ideas are adapted or copied without mentioning the original source, and in yet others original ideas are intentionally and unintentionally attributed to other writers. That translation took mostly the form of adaptation tells us that Arabic literature in the early twentieth century was negotiating with rather than failing to emulate another model perfectly – and these 'failures' are the most productive sites of study. As Pierre Cachia puts it, from the beginning, 'Arab translators did not view their task as one of slavish transposition, but rather of adaptation to the needs of a new public'.[16]

Samah Selim draws a parallel between the 'story' of the *nahḍa* and that of the Arabic novel, both beginning in translation and adaptation.[17] Focusing on entertainment fiction, Selim explores other *nahḍa*s that do not figure into the 'modern novelistic canon'.[18] When the novel as a genre was institutionalised, translations and popular fiction fell out of its literary trajectory. This process is complex, as some of the elites studied in this book pushed entertainment literature to the margins to establish a European-like canon that occasionally returned to the Arabic literary tradition. Using translation, this book complicates the canonisation of the Arabic novel: it explores whether there were aesthetic categories in the Arabic tradition that could determine the 'genre' and hence reading of these translations. Michael Allan finds none, and explains this lack in relation to how Orientalist scholarship translated *adab* as literature in a universal language of European humanism: in the process, 'modern' Arabic literature acquired its status outside of the historical moment that transformed it.[19] Roger Allen notes how universal literary values dictate the Arabic novel's maturation according to European criteria – the year 1988 marking Naguib Mahfouz's receipt of the Nobel Prize seals this teleology.[20] In a popular narrative that transposes such values onto the literary history of the Arabic novel, it is generally agreed that the Arabic novel moves from romanticism to realism to modernism and then to an experimental postmodernism. But this genealogy is only possible if we ignore the legacy of the simultaneous translation of realism and romanticism in the early twentieth century.

The transformation of *adab* into modern Arabic literature also demanded the 'modernisation' of the Arabic language. We find, for instance, that al-Manfalūṭī critiques and uses classical rhetorical devices, al-Sibāʿī's language marks a transitional phase between classical and modern standard Arabic, Haykal adopts a simpler *fuṣḥā* while Ḥusayn rejects the colloquial in favour of classical Arabic. The colloquial is a corrupted dialect, writes Ḥusayn, which would waste the heritage that only classical Arabic has preserved.[21] In colonial Egypt, Timothy Mitchell tells us, language use became abstract, pointing to a discursive violence that erased local differences by classifying them under general and familiar terms.[22] Jeffrey Sacks also describes Mitchell's abstraction as linguistic violence, as it endorsed 'a realm of "meaning" that is believed to exist quite apart from words themselves under the theological name of "language" or "truth" or "mind" or "culture"'.[23] Similarly, ᶜAbd al-Muḥsin Ṭāhā Badr adds translation to the mix: the popular and unfaithful literary translations initiated a troubling loss of linguistic reference or *dalāla*.[24]

*Prophetic Translation* reads the translations of romantic and realist texts closely to locate in them this changed relationship to language not just in specific instances of adaptation, but also in the transformed narrative voice that appeals to the prophetic potential of literature. Although it addresses the translators' Islamic writings, it locates the prophetic as a narrative capacity produced in their literary adaptations. The prophetic emerges as an analytical position rather than a transcendental one: it does not issue from the translators' will, but from overlapping discourses in their adaptations that move us away from the writer as the mouthpiece of the nation. The translations make room for a new narrative subjectivity – the subject's formation in the act of telling or writing – made possible precisely in the formal struggle between realism and romanticism, biography and autobiography. They include adaptations of novels, philosophical texts, and auto/biographies. In each case, I discuss the formation of this narrative subject in relation to the shifting use of personal pronouns, the critique of omniscient narration, and the radical uprooting of the original. What these translations expose is both realism's and romanticism's failed promises of representation. They inadvertently challenge social realism as a sure path to reform, as well as European romanticism's modes of subjectivity. Read beyond the reforming intentions of their translators, these translations offer a different approach to the literary history of modern Arabic narrative. Because the original historical and political contexts that fostered the birth of European romanticism and realism cannot be translated into colonial Egypt, this book suggests that these translations must necessarily fall out of hegemonic accounts that appeal to universal generic values of narrative. Instead, they stage the formation of the literary object through translation, and this construction is formal and aesthetic, as well as historical.

The translators produce a set of aesthetic criteria that come through their translations, mostly in their critical writings on the purpose of translation and literature. Each chapter explores the translator's specific task of translation, his translation performance, and finally the new set of aesthetic criteria that emerges from such a paralleling. In moving us from the realm of religious to literary interpretation, the translators do more than inculcate the secular as Shaden Tageldin, Muhsin al-Musawi, and others have argued. Rather, this shift from the religious to the literary registers how early twentieth-century Egyptian literature reconciled the moral with the aesthetic. In conversation with discussions in comparative literature, translation, and postcolonial studies, this book treats translation as formative of the literary in early twentieth-century Egypt. The literary is not simply a secular imitation of a Western text, but one that uses translation to interrupt as it borrows. While the social climate and the question of literacy are fundamental, the book's major ambition is to trace how aesthetic categories are produced in translation to offer a different way of reading the Egyptian novel's history and an alternate way of thinking about religion and literature. In a time when modern Arabic literature becomes complicit in the modernisation story of Egypt, through borrowing new literary forms in translation, this book explores how translation disrupts rather than endorses such modernisation accounts.

## English Renaissance Humanism, Romanticism and Literature

Muḥammad Ḥusayn Haykal was a lawyer, journalist, writer, and the Minister of Education in 1940s Egypt. Like Haykal, Ṭāhā Ḥusayn – the 'Dean of Arabic Literature' – also studied at the Sorbonne and was the Egyptian Minister of Education in the 1950s. Less formally educated than Haykal and Ḥusayn, ᶜAbbās Maḥmūd al-ᶜAqqād (1889–1964) actually began learning French when he was imprisoned in 1930 after insulting Prime Minister Ismāᶜīl Ṣidqī Pasha for suspending the constitution. Al-ᶜAqqād also notoriously plagiarised European romantic literature to establish modern Arabic poetics.[25] He was a formative member of the Dīwān group, one of three groups of Arab romantic poets, which takes its name from al-ᶜAqqād's treatise on modern Arabic poetry that he co-authored with Ibrāhīm al-Māzinī (1890–1949).

The other two groups were the Mahjar group, contemporary with the Dīwān group and made up of Syrian/Lebanese émigrés in North America, such as Gibran Khalil Gibran (1883–1931), and the Apollo group, named after the short-lived poetry magazine, the *Apollo* (1932–4). All three groups embraced European Renaissance, Enlightenment, and Romantic literature in the works of Shakespeare and Thomas Carlyle.

In the introduction to *ᶜAbqariyyat Muḥammad* (The Genius of Muḥammad) (first edition 1941; 1957), al-ᶜAqqād admits his debt to Carlyle's essay on the Hero as Prophet, an authority on the Prophet at the time,[26] although 'of course, the impressionistic portrait he draws of the Prophet is free from the occasional blemishes in Carlyle's treatment'.[27] In his review of Carlyle's *Sartor Resartus*, published in *Sāᶜāt bayn al-kutub* (Hours Spent among Books) (first edition 1929; 1969), al-ᶜAqqād uses Carlyle's Prometheus-like poet to establish 'the right of poets and artists to be called Sultans/Kings of this world because they depict for people new symbols and capture light for them from the sky that will guide them'.[28] Muhammad ᶜAbdul-Hai identifies those lines as 'the cultural translation in which the Prometheus-like poet assumes the function of a Qurᵓānic prophet'.[29] This poet-seer creates the meanings of symbols in a cultural translation that weds the emulation of the Muslim prophet to the new role of the romantic poet/writer.

The romantic legacy, especially in the adapted Carlylean figures of the hero-poet and hero-prophet as the poet-prophet, shapes the translators' prophetic aspirations. The four writers/translators knew Shakespeare and Carlyle in English and/or Arabic, and their search for the poet-prophet begins with Shakespeare. Through Shakespeare and Carlyle, they revolted against the Azharites' monopoly over religious interpretation and rejection of literature. Al-Sibāᶜī's faithful translation of *Coriolanus* in 1912 marked a new, more definitive phase in the solidification of romantic concepts. ᶜAbdul-Hai describes al-Sibāᶜī's translation of Carlyle's *On Heroes*,[30] especially the lecture on Hero as Poet, as 'the first romantic edification in Arabic of Shakespeare as poet-prophet with creative genius . . . a creative visionary and unacknowledged legislator of humanity'[31] and hence the 'image of the poet as visionary and prophet'.[32]

Ḥusayn campaigned to have all Shakespeare's plays translated when he was Minister of Education.[33] Haykal defended Shakespeare in *Tarājim miṣriyya wa gharbiyya* (Biographies of Western and Egyptian Personalities) (1929) as a prophet burdened by his own message to the point of burning. Shakespeare could overcome his dangerous imagination only by writing prolifically for only writing could quell Shakespeare's excessive desires.[34] Haykal locates in Shakespeare a revolutionary psychological probing of characters rather than a moralistic edification of readers. Shakespeare's imagination, according to Haykal, 'creates a whole world, similar to ours, with all its things, people and gods, a prophet, a rebellious spirit and a child of nature . . . as creative as nature herself'.[35] Similarly, al-Manfalūṭī finds comfort in Shakespeare's raw, uneducated genius. Unfamiliar with any foreign languages or literary traditions, al-Manfalūṭī could identify with the untutored Shakespeare, calling him the poet-prophet and, like Muḥammad, the 'unlettered prophet'. In addition to the influence of Shakespeare and Carlyle, there are two obvious strands to prophecy in modern Arabic literature: Gibran's *The Prophet* (1923) and the prophet Muḥammad.

The figure of the poet-prophet in the Arab world, however, looks different with the Lebanese diaspora or Mahjar poets of the early twentieth century writing in North America such as the Lebanese Gibran, on whom ᶜAbdul-Hai confers 'the status of a universal poet-prophet'.[36] Gibran's prophet borrowed from American transcendental thought and Nietzsche's *Zarathustra*, even if more in form than content.[37] And while his work found an audience in the Arab writers of the 1920s, it did not substantially impact the translators considered in this book. For example, in the 1955 article 'The Modern Renaissance of Arabic Literature' (written in English and published in *Books Abroad*, now *World Literature*), Ḥusayn finds Gibran's writing too foreign to be relevant to the Arab world. Gibran's Arabic works 'released' the subjective in Arabic literature, writes Salma Jayyusi, since what defines early twentieth-century literature is 'a greater or lesser tinge of Romanticism', when writers had 'to seek order within' against the chaos of colonialism, oppressive cultural influences, and war.[38] Appealing as the subjective impulse was, Gibran's prophet could not become a model of emulation because he (or she) thrived in romantic isolation and withdrawal from the world, and contemporaneous Egyptian romantic poetry was very much a product of its historical moment.[39]

In fact, the narrative prophetic voice in these translations is specifically not philosophical; rather, it comes about in the slippages of translation from the colonial master text and not in a philosophically charged adaptation of a Nietzschean superman. The romantic legacy in their works also engages Islamic prophecy.[40] In a talk in 1870 to Ottoman officials and *ᶜulamāʾ* (religious scholars), Jamāl al-Dīn al-Afghānī (1838–97) had set the tone for the intellectuals' literary reformist agenda when he confirmed the superiority of philosophers' eternal truths to prophets' contextual revelations.[41] Al-Afghānī's troubling comparison succumbs to the logic of colonial translation. Bernard S. Cohn best defines colonial translation when he describes how the British invaded India with 'their own forms of knowing and thinking', and the confidence that this new world could be represented as 'a series of facts'. When the facts of this new place did not correspond with theirs, they used 'translation' to conquer it: 'establishing correspondence could make the known and the strange knowable'.[42] For example, in his response to Ernest Renan's infamous lecture at the Sorbonne in 1883, 'L'islamisme et la science', al-Afghānī takes issue with Renan's dismissal of Islam's potential openness to scientific enquiry, but adopts his basic premise that religion must succumb to individual, critical enquiry. In the late nineteenth century, al-Afghānī and Muḥammad ᶜAbduh (1849–1905) – the 'modernist' reformers – campaigned for religious interpretation or *ijtihād* to become an individual endeavour, attacking the tradition of imitation or *taqlīd* – reference to earlier jurists' interpretations of Islamic law – as outmoded and lazy. As Indira Falk Gesink puts it, reviving *ijtihād* was also a definitional campaign for the modernists, shifting it from 'a legal method restricted to use by highly trained jurists to a principle of intellectual investigation'.[43]

Al-Afghānī's assertion of the philosopher's superiority to the prophet meets its sophisticated English confirmation in Thomas Carlyle's *On Heroes, Hero-Worship, and the Heroic in History* (1841), with an entire lecture dedicated to the Prophet of Islam. Carlyle's condescending dismissal of Islam as a lesser form of Christianity determines the lecture's overarching tone, but his portrayal of 'Mahomet' as one of 'a poor shepherd people, roaming unnoticed in . . . deserts since the creation of the world: a Hero-Prophet . . . sent down to [the Arabs] with a word they could believe', romantic as it sounds, locates the prophet's heroism in his humanity, sincerity, and impact on 'what the world meant and means with him'.[44] Al-Sibāᶜī translates the lecture into Arabic, alongside the one on the 'Hero as Poet', and the two heroes combined form the manifesto of Arab romanticism. While the romantic strain impelled the translators towards reimagining the boundaries of their worlds, the prophetic legacy gave their work authorial legitimacy outside the Western master text. After all, Haykal wrote an entire book on *Ḥayāt Muḥammad* (The Life of Muḥammad) (1934), and more importantly a book on his pilgrimage in 1937, *Fī manzil al-waḥy* (In the House of Inspiration and/or Revelation). Al-Manfalūṭī was an Azharite, well versed in Qurʾānic scripture, an education that shaped his adaptations of sentimental and romantic French fiction. Ḥusayn also studied at al-Azhar, and all four writers produced Islamic literature that varied from didactic articles and stories to biographies of the prophet. Such emulation, however, also figures as a radical separation between the Muslim prophet and the subjective aspirations of the writers who use translation to deliver literature as *creative* of alternate realities. My interest here is not specifically in the religious feeling behind these authors' individual relationships to Islam. Rather, the translations complicate al-Afghānī's adopted colonial logic of translation where he subdues Islam to the European master text. The literary adaptations expose the master text's narrative strategies for establishing its truth. As such, they undo the fantasy of translation of equivalences between the two cultural traditions and challenge the imposition of correspondences on the Arabic text. And in the process, they destabilise the threshold between premodern and modern in the critical labelling of the *nahḍa*.

## The *Nahḍa* Revisited

Considered a primary agent in catapulting the Arabs into modernity, the translation movement was instrumental in the retrospective critical construction of periods of *inḥiṭat* or decadence and *nahḍa* or renaissance. Perhaps no one defines that approach better than Hamilton Alexander Rosskeen Gibb:

> For the Muslim world, and especially its Arab lands, the nineteenth century ushered in an era of storm and stress, both from within and without. Napoleon's meteoric invasion of Egypt in 1798 tore aside the veil of apathy which had cut them off from Europe and gave the death-blow to medievalism.[45]

In response to Gibb's claim, Dror Ze'evi reminds us that modernity in the Middle East had started in the earlier seventeenth- and eighteenth-century 'internal shifts in power' that made Napoleon's invasion 'a change in pace' rather than a radical revolution.[46] The Moroccan historian Abdallah Laroui largely shaped the contemporary debate on the *nahḍa* when, in 1974, he insisted on using 'Arab cultural retardation' to indict colonialism.[47] His loaded language was a response to the traditionalism of his contemporaries, who were advocating a complete abdication of European critical traditions in their own *nahḍa*. Laroui espouses a Marxist historicist approach that focuses on colonial violence to reclaim the critical promise of the first *nahḍa* (the second one takes place from 1963 to 1965).[48] This historical narrative of renaissance finds its best ally in the cultural one. Arab cultural production has seemingly (according to normative critical accounts) followed a similar path of maturation or progress towards modernity[49] and the *nahḍa* figures prominently as an effort of literary renovation.[50] Recent studies, however, have challenged this view from cultural, historical, and economic perspectives.[51] A good example is the 2006 volume *Arabic Literature in the Post-Classical Period*, which explores Arabic cultural production before Napoleon's expedition in what Roger Allen names the 'post-classical' period, extending from 1150 to 1850, to compensate for 'an almost complete lack of sympathy for very different aesthetic norms'.[52] Some contemporary accounts of Arab cultural modernity still romanticise portions of the past to reimagine other beginnings of modernisation or *iḥdāth*, but these historical reimaginings continue to take off from clashes or encounters with cultural others.[53]

These periodisation accounts, however, also echo a Western teleological narrative of literary development.[54] Revisionist historical approaches of the period again frame events in the pre-Napoleonic Ottoman Empire within a Western notion of evolutionary time.[55] Ze'evi proposes that modernity is not temporal disruption so much as 'a mental construct forged in tandem with colonialism' and hence not a simple ingraining of a 'ready-made new culture' in the Arab Middle East. Such a move makes possible different versions of modernity when we remember that 'historical subjects' concepts of time and periodization are part of history itself'.[56] Unlike Bill Ashcroft's invitation to explore 'alternative modernities'[57] in colonial contexts, Ze'evi wants to eschew the term 'modernity', but he faults the native elites for bringing about a fatal point in the Islamic Middle East, effectively effacing traditions and ways of being that existed prior to the 'modern', and reifying their cultures into punctuating nodes in a Western narrative of progress.[58]

*Prophetic Translation* resists that last conclusion by espousing close reading to challenge our theoretical generalisations. The translations speak from their specific present moment, foregrounding narratives of progress, emulation and disenchantment that redress simple reproduction. Close reading shifts the focus from the elites as generators of discourse to what Stephen Sheehi describes as 'points of intersection, between material transformations and epistemological shifts'.[59] Despite the translators' own self-orientalism, their translations reveal a discomfort with the terms of European modernity in two ways: first, the translations disable a projected futurity complicit in a colonial project of modernisation, a complicity the intellectuals have apparently fully endorsed. Second, they expose how novel epistemologies come about to establish a 'normative narrative of reality'.[60] Their adaptations also resituate the confrontation between premodern and modern literary forms away from a traditional/modern binary and towards zones of negotiation between the two. Because the translations deny correspondence with the originals, they make possible an alternative reading of the modern.

## Somewhere between Here and There: Translation as Manipulation

That possibility emerges from the particular form that these translations take. Friedrich Schleiermacher in *Ueber die verschiedenen Methoden des Uebersezens* (On the Different Methods of Translating) (1813) proposes two methods of translation: the translator either approximates the original as much as possible or adapts the original to the reader's context. Schleiermacher preferred the first method, as it draws the reader into its linguistic and cultural otherness. Schleiermacher's distinction situated translation as a textual and formal transaction between writer and reader and did not address the cultural or historical context. In fact, translation studies only began to accommodate non-Western traditions as late as the 1990s due to the cultural turn that opened the discipline to an external critique. This is when Lawrence Venuti returns to Schleiermacher's two methods, naming them 'domesticating' (*einbürgernde*) and 'foreignising' (*verfremdende*). In a domesticating translation, the translator tries to remain as close to the original's style as possible, focusing on a fluency effect. Venuti finds this approach to be the normative translation process – a dangerous one at that, as it tends to surrender linguistic and cultural choices to the dominant language, usually leaving out marginal languages and genres. In a foreignising translation, the translator actively disrupts both linguistic and generic expectations of the target culture, highlighting the foreignness of the translated text, and making it possible for the 'translation to be read as a translation' in its departures from the target culture's values and linguistic norms.[61] The foreign is importantly not an 'essence' found in the original but 'a strategic construction whose value is contingent on the current situation in the receiving culture', such that a foreignising translation highlights the foreign text's differences while also 'disrupting the cultural codes that prevail in the target language'.[62]

Venuti's distinction between the two styles of translation also recalls Walter Benjamin's theory of translation, developed through his 1923 translation of Baudelaire's *Tableaux Parisiens*. Benjamin articulates the relationship between the original and translation in the language of intention, naming a strange demand for fidelity to the original. Venuti insists on foreignising translation as a way to remember the foreignness of the original and guard against fully domesticating it within existing power structures in the target culture. Benjamin's concern is different: fidelity is not the exact rendering of an original in the target language. Rather, and in quite ambiguous terms, Benjamin's imperative to be literal demands that the translator make changes to the translating or target language so it approximates the original's intended meaning as closely as possible.[63] The translator's task is to find the 'intended effect' on her own language that could 'echo' the original, while recognising the original's 'mode of signification' and bringing the original and translation together as part of a greater or pure language (*reine Sprache*).[64] A pure language exceeds contextual signification, for 'all information, all sense, and all intention finally encounter a stratum in which they are destined to be extinguished . . . a new and higher justification for free translation'. Although pure language is an abstraction that could only be glimpsed through good translation, Benjamin's task of translation in no way forgets the original. In fact, the translation only solidifies the original's status and does not usurp it. Good translations point to the pure language that is not there in the original but is nonetheless intended in the original – much as the foreign for Venuti is not an essential attribute of the original but a product of translation. At the end of the essay, Benjamin locates the ideal of translation in interlinear scriptural translation, that which is *not* written, because the meaning lies in the original intention and not in the words on the page.

Benjamin's thesis motivates poststructuralist philosophers to relate translation paradigmatically to epistemology and interpretation. Both Paul de Man and Jacques Derrida in reading Benjamin's essay locate an alienation between the original and translation that is embedded in language's inability to reflect reality or produce universal sense according to a referential model. This always-present condition of alienation and impossible transparency has informed this book's approach to various articulations of translation theory and praxis. For instance, de Man reverses the privileged position that Benjamin gives to the original, which ends up 'absorbing' the translation, moving us away from a similarity model towards a syntagmatic one. De Man treats the two texts as equals, so that Benjamin's mode of intention becomes less about identifying that of the original and more about comparing the two as an experience that unfolds in language. Now the original can appear in a foreign place and the target text assumes an in-between position, not completely original and not fully foreign. This third position (which does not appear in Schleiermacher's model) suggests a new language use that moves us away from questions of fidelity and towards ones of creative adaptation and critique.

Importantly, the translator does not actively determine this third position. De Man, for instance, finds that translation is an inevitable failure of language outside of the translator's agency.[65] Because of the already existing arbitrary relationship between signifier and referent, translations can never really refer back to an origin but must remain 'wandering, an errance, a kind of permanent exile'.[66] A literal translation unsettles the original's sense by rendering it word for word in a different language and 'introduce[s] in it a slippage' that makes control over that original meaning an illusion.[67] On the other hand, translation for sense implies that all languages have similar ways of producing meaning. Thus, the failure of all translations is rooted in the originals since translations approach original works as though 'freed of the illusion of meaning' and point to the failed attempt at making 'meaning' that was always there in the original. If the original is already in a state of permanent exile, then the translator's language is only doubly so, 'for there is no homeland, nothing from which one has been exiled'.[68]

Like de Man, Derrida recognises that the translation points to an original failure, because 'originally [the origin] was not there without fault, full, complete, total and identical to itself. From the origin of the original-to-be-translated, there is exile and fall'.[69] What de Man reads as a permanent exile of the translator's language, Derrida identifies as a promising change in the translating culture's language because the alien text *demands* translation. Because both original and translation ultimately fail to produce complete or perfect meaning, Derrida finds that they can in fact complement each other. In reading Shakespeare's *Merchant of Venice*, he relates a relationship of debt between the original and translation to the ultimately 'incommensurable' exchange-values of words because although 'translation is always an attempt at appropriation that aims to transport home, in its language' and 'in the most relevant way possible, the most proper meaning of the original text, this foreign meaning cannot be understood as a static construction'.[70] The Arabic translations may rewrite the original occasionally without citing it, but they still recognise a debt to the original's potential to transform their own language. The debt to the original emerges, as we will see, in revisionary moments that interrupt an otherwise complacent literary history of modernity that moves us from romanticism through realism to modernism. While genealogical accounts of the modern Arabic novel reproduce this teleology, the translations recognise the failures in the originals while paying their dues to produce more localised expressions of Egyptian literature's trajectory. De Man's inevitable failure has informed my reading of each translation. I examine the ways in which the translation fails to render the original's meaning while simultaneously exposing the original's failure to utter its own meaning. However, in reading the relationship between original and translation, my analysis is also indebted to Derrida's idea of complementarity such that every translation informs our reading of the original text. The translations under study are imitative translations to the extent that they adapt the original, even when some claim to be metaphrastic or word-for-word renditions. I focus on moments of adaptation as important moments of failures, in Paul de Man's sense, that move us away from fidelity towards a contextual understanding of these translations' aesthetic and historical intervention into existing epistemologies of reading.

The third position that these translations occupy – neither fully domesticating nor fully foreignising – resonates with the translators' own positions. As Gesink describes the debates between the religious modernists and conformists, neither side was a fully complicit agent in 'conceptual colonization' or a 'defender of tradition'. Against the urge to retroactively 'fetishise a "pure" precontact culture' in the confrontation with an evil colonialism, she continues, 'all these debates worked together as agents of hybridization, sculptors of the new cultural forms Islam would inhabit in the twentieth century'.[71] Importantly, she refers to the 'debates' and not the agents as hybrid. In my analysis, the translations are 'hybrid texts', in that they draw on the Western originals but also manipulate them. This is not an abstract postcolonial hybridity as these translation acts are historically embedded. The translators promote literary communication by incorporating individual understanding of the source texts and using new expressions and different literary genres. The translated text hangs in that in-between and rewriting becomes a powerful form of manipulation.[72]

De Man's failed translation recalls the labelling of early Arabic literary translations as failed (and aborted) efforts by several critics of modern Arabic fiction.[73] The deviations from the source text are not merely errors; rather, they point to how the relationship between the two texts is one of constant flux and to how self-understanding unfolds in the new language position that translation makes possible. However, in light of de Man, this failure points to the necessary failure of reference, and is not a negative, but always there in the original's broken promise to deliver referential meaning. In revealing this failure, the Arabic translations profane the original text: for instance, al-Manfalūṭī's translation forgets the original author and text, while Haykal's adaptation of Rousseau's life converts the latter into an Egyptian prophet. The failure of signification in translation reiterates the original's inevitable failure and makes way for the prophetic narrative voice. Although the deconstructive reading is alien to the Arabic tradition, the prolific translation and adaptation of Western texts makes reading Arabic translations deconstructively a productive way to explain the hesitant relationship to Classical Arabic in the early twentieth century. The failure to produce narrative subjectivities in the translators' adaptations is not simply a lack of ability on their part; rather, it points to the futility of absolute self-composition in narrative, especially in the context of colonial translation and under the influence of romantic symbolism. The inevitable failure of signification makes the constitution of a coherent narrative subjectivity impossible.

Neither Schleiermacher nor Benjamin consider the colonial context of translation, and even when Venuti is attentive to the structures of power that frame translation acts, he also falls short of proposing a truly encompassing model for foreignising translation. Venuti finds that domestication categorically refers to 'an ethnocentric reduction of the foreign text to target-language cultural values, bringing the author back home', whereas foreignisation places 'pressure on those (cultural) values to register the linguistic and cultural difference of the foreign text, sending the reader abroad'.[74] Foreignisation in translation is the only sure way to fight ethnocentrism. But what of colonial contexts? As Tejaswini Niranjana notes, such approaches often forget 'to account for the relationships between "unequal" languages', as translation studies work within a 'naively representational theory of language' that refuses 'to consider questions of power and historicity'.[75] Venuti is not unaware of such questions, but his absolute championing of a foreignising translation model to battle ethnocentrism is based on the choice of text to be translated and a 'conscious' choice of a translation trend. Venuti claims that the 'translator always exercises a choice concerning the degree and direction of the violence at work in his practice'.[76] The translator's conscious choice, however, is not necessarily the final measure; rather, the cultural background could account for the inevitable failure of translation and resultant complementarity between original and translation. The choice of the text-to-be-translated can either be based on a perceived similarity in the social situation of the origin and target cultures; or on its theme that can contribute to the 'creation of a specific discourse of nation in the translating culture'; or, finally, on the possibility of translating the foreign text with a discursive strategy popular in the translating culture. This active choosing of the master text makes possible the formation of national identity narratives. The original texts' foreignness is forgotten, Venuti continues, 'repressed in a fantastic identification with an apparently homogeneous national identity' – that is, the foreign one. This paradoxical 'conceptual economy' uses the 'irreducible foreignness' of alien texts to fuel its own desire for a 'unified nation that the translation cannot fulfill by virtue of those very differences'.[77] However, as Maria Tymoczko notes, Venuti proposes his parallel terms of domestication as fluency and foreignisation as resistance to be a 'universal standard of evaluation, with a sort of on/off quality rather than a sliding scale'[78] without specifying how much foreignisation is needed for a translation to qualify as such. Tymoczko finds that any translation that involves cultural resistance is potentially foreignising, regardless of its actual translation choices, although it is often difficult to agree on the terms of cultural resistance.

*Prophetic Translation* does not mean to deprive the translators of any form of agency. After all, each one has a unique background that makes his peculiar translative strategies possible. However, the romantic inheritance of the poet-prophet is not simply a preoccupation with the writer himself. Rather, the poet-prophet's voice struggles with reference (*dalāla*), making it necessary to read these performances of translation closely to reconfigure agency in relation to changing practices of reading and writing. In the Arabic adaptations, the process of 'fantastic identification' exaggerates the alien text's 'irreducible foreignness'. After all, some of the early translations into Arabic announced their status as translations but made no reference to original authors or titles, while others masqueraded as translations to avoid censorship when they were in fact native expressions. The choice of translations was quite random at the beginning, as these were intended to provide entertainment for the masses that were unexposed to Classical Arabic literature in a time of occupation and failed revolutions.

At about the turn of the twentieth century, translation began to participate more directly in nationalist discourse wherein the promise of producing fiction à la Rousseau, Voltaire, Balzac, and Zola provided the terms for a national literature. In other words, these creative translations[79] validate Venuti's idea that the nation was produced in translation, even when the translators were not always deliberately creating a nationalist discourse, for '[t]he formation of national identities can remain unconscious' as it unfolds 'in language that originates elsewhere, in the subject's relations to others, but that the subject perceives as his or her own self-expression'.[80] This identity is bound to the condition of exile that the foreign text and language bring to bear on the colonised culture. The inevitable alienation explains the significance of Benjamin's, Derrida's, and de Man's work on translation to this study.[81]

Rewriting is not simply the condition of creative translation; it is also bound to the historical moment. Liu warns that reading translation outside of its historical contingency 'is bound to lead to the reification of the idea, concept, or theory'.[82] In reading acts of translation in their historical moment, but also locating in them a prophetic capacity of literary creation, I insist on the untranslatability of the contexts of realism and romanticism. The prophetic thus becomes a contingent act of rupture both with the classical tradition and the European master text, and imagination as *khayāl* (imagination) and *waḥy* (inspiration and/or revelation) remains in conversation with the Arabic tradition but also posits its own terms.[83] Reading from this position helps frame the translators' approach to the 'modern' as interrupted reading. The historical contingency of these acts of translation anchors them in at least two very different contexts – the original and target cultures – all the time compromising the translators' pronounced intentions. As we will see, even what they perceive as radically new in their works is continuous when they least intend it to be.

The expectation of fidelity is pejorative in these translations, which occasionally credit the originals, but mostly embrace a liberating plagiarism not alien to an Arabic literary tradition (see Chapter Two). All four translators want to deliver a literary promise of totality in representation, and although this totality is a legacy of Western philosophical thinking brought into the colonial encounter as Niranjana asserts, for the Arab authors, the infatuation with a pure language is also a legacy of Classical Arabic. The previous legacy of metaphysical thinking merges with the romantic inheritance of the poet-prophet to consolidate the search of a pure literary language. In this search, these adaptations reinscribe the originals into that third space between foreignisation and domestication.

## The Prophetic, the Secular and the Profane

Manipulative translation compels us to approach interpretation as an inevitable act of betrayal. For Derrida, such betrayal brings secularisation and translation together, returning us to the opening paradox: the sacred text *demands* translation but loses its sacred status as original naming when obligated to communicate.[84] Both translation and 'secularisation' long for a pure language that would just mean and not have to denigrate itself by communicating or explaining. Both, however, predictably become impossible when they begin to speak – '*façon de parler*' – and no longer just *are*.[85] Derrida wonders where the 'appeal to guard oneself (from secularization) in order to safeguard the sacred language . . . takes place: is it in the sacred language or outside it? . . . Can one speak a sacred language as a foreign language?'[86] This limit between the two places is what I am naming the space of the profane that brings translation and religion together in a literary text that aspires for a language of its own while remaining bound to that very impossibility. In colonial settings, as Gauri Viswanathan explains, the institution of modern literary studies demands a similarly paradoxical relationship between power and religion. British colonial institutions in India, for example, established their superiority by dissociating from Christianity – the logic being that Christian texts presented themselves as truth texts, authorities in and of themselves with no need for self-justification.[87] The English Nation as equivalent to the Christian God is 'rewritten as (but emphatically not supplanted by)' another equivalence between that nation and 'new forms of knowledge' proven by historical progress.[88] Derrida describes the impossibility of such rewriting from a strictly linguistic point of view: both secularisation and translation have to present themselves in language, and that language ends up betraying their truth-claims at every step. Although historical colonial violence is undeniably a result of a power dynamic that pretended to be secular, I am proposing that literature in translation could expose the frailty of those language claims. For one, the Qurʾān makes a different truth claim (being arguably the most self-referential of Abrahamic scriptures): even while it promises one truth, textually it revels in multiple layers from commentaries to *aḥādīth*. The plurality of interpretation functioned differently in this context such that the British dominion over 'truth value' in Viswanathan's analysis was less absolute in Egyptian literary conversations on theology.[89]

Critics have long agreed on a problematic Islamic shift in the works of several *nahḍawī* intellectuals, notably Ḥusayn, al-Aqqād, and Haykal. Their Islamic narratives feed the 'viable language' of the nation-state, writes al-Musawi, especially since they separated religion from literature, and Islam as personal faith from the Muslim Brotherhood's doctrinal conflation of Islam and politics. They also adopted the orientalist 'reductive humanization of the character of Muhammad'.[90] However, the writer-prophet straddles both the aesthetic and historical – especially with the Islamic writings of Haykal and

Ḥusayn in the 1930s. As cultural prophets, they saw themselves producing something 'new', but their actual translations implicate the 'new' in Islamic discourse and Arabic literary tradition, complicating the 'secularity' of a colonial morality that separated between personal faith and doctrine. Talal Asad has taught us how the secular emerges from within religion in the colonial context; the elite figures considered in this book have repeatedly been read as complicit in the propagation of the secular. The translators were familiar with Orientalist representations of Islam, as is evident in al-Manfalūṭī's retort to Lord Cromer (Chapter Two), al-Sibāᶜī's rewriting of Carlyle (Chapter Three), Haykal's critique of Jean-Jacques Rousseau and Ḥusayn's conversation with André Gide (Chapter Four). Even though Islam is often abstracted in these responses, their translations maintain the tension between sacred and profane, making it difficult to identify them as absolutely secular.[91] *Prophetic Translation* reads their translations closely beyond their declared affiliations to explore how the secular becomes synonymous with modern constructions of *adab* as literature. Roberto Schwarz describes a similar situation for the Brazilian novel: when the novel form comes to Brazil, the inherent contradictions of European universality (erasing class struggle) after 1848 are passed on as paradoxes of liberalism. To catch this peculiar paradox, the Brazilian writer uncovers 'something singular' in literature, 'an emptying out of what is already hollow'.[92] In adapting the borrowed form of the novel to the new context, the Brazilian writer exposes the emptiness central to that form, precisely that which it pretends to erase or forget, in this case class difference and struggle. This original emptiness as it were – the 'already hollow' part of the original – becomes the territory of profanation in these translations. Beyond producing modern literature as secular, these translations reveal that which was never there in the original.

This literary profanity relates to Giorgio Agamben's notion of 'profanation', the way by which things are given a non-utilitarian function, not in a return to some original prior state, but to what has never existed.[93] Agamben finds a power in profanation that secularisation renders impotent, for while 'political secularization of theological concepts (the transcendence of God as a paradigm of sovereign power)' preserves the power of the 'heavenly monarchy' in the 'earthly' one, profanation 'neutralises what it profanes. Once profaned, that which was unavailable and separate loses its aura and is returned to use.' The profane also has the power to return to 'common use the spaces that power had seized, while the secular works to preserve power structures'.[94] The literary profane does not preserve the transcendental in the secular; rather, it reveals how colonial secularisation ingrains itself in the host culture through reading practices.[95] These literary translations do not simply shift the locus of power from God's word (through the Prophet's revelations) to their own utterances – and as such do not merely 'reproduce' the secular in a native idiom. Rather, they profane the separation between literary and religious interpretation, bringing the stakes of narrative representation to bear on European ideals of subjectivity and universal reason. Literature *does not become* the secular modern; rather, this book engages Islam and *adab* specifically in the ways they appear in the translations. Even when Islamic themes and ideas are borrowed, and the historicity of the Qurʾān questioned as it is by Ḥusayn, the literary is not simply secular. If literature in translation occupies a site of tension between divine and secular, then the prophetic narrative voice interrupts the presumed equivalences between literature and modernity. Translation becomes neither domesticating nor foreignising but a space where various representational claims are simultaneously adapted and contested. The prophetic narrative voice does not exist outside of language, but occupies different places within it so as to profane the logic of colonial language and the relegation of literature's role to moral instruction at al-Azhar.[96] Thus, 'religion' in this book emerges in the dialogue between translation and original.

Literary translation as an act of profanity makes way for the prophetic. Maurice Blanchot, without naming it profane, implicates literature with prophecy in *Le Livre à Venir* (The Book to Come) (French 1959; English 2003). In the earlier *L'espace littéraire* (The Space of Literature) (1955; 1982), Blanchot had marked Franz Kafka's entry into literature as a dispossession from meaning in substituting the impersonal 'it' or '*il*' for 'I'.[97] The '*il*' – a neutral pronoun – makes the subject speak from a place of emptiness that is not transcendent but emerges from within the text.[98] The 'it' (*il*) does not replace the subject, Blanchot insists, but is instead 'a mobile fragmentation' that challenges our understanding of place as 'fixed' or 'unique'.[99] The literary takes shape precisely in that non-space, at once within the text but not identifiable to one speaker within it.[100] Similarly, in *The Book to Come*, the prophet's words exist outside of common-use language because they stand in for God's word.[101] The message is not communicable, but 'wandering speech' (*parole errante*),[102] recalling Walter Benjamin's letter to Martin Buber (17 July 1916), 'I can only understand writing, as far as it effects matter, poetically prophetically . . . that is to say, immediately.'[103] Ian Balfour succinctly draws out the prophetic as 'mediated immediacy or immediate mediation . . . the . . . most definitive language'.[104] The question remains: if language is not communicating content, what exactly is it doing? Language as a performance of naming, as comes through in Benjamin's rereading of *Genesis*, is action; a word literally *acts* on the world in naming it. For Benjamin, this act of translation, of naming the world and rendering it legible, precedes the functional aspect of language as communication.

By displacing the originals into new contexts, the translations profane the originals' status as singular. The prophetic in this book emerges from this profanation in particular moments of adaptation of a foreign text, beyond the translator's conscious volition. In other words, it is the use of literary language that produces the prophetic as a legacy of both romantic symbolism and Qur'ānic language.[105] It also makes possible a different approach to translation that could help explain the nuances of colonial borrowings of genres under occupation beyond frameworks of resistance. The translators' narrative voice is prophetic but does not promise religious prophecy. It unknowingly borrows the intersection between the prophetic and literary in Blanchot's work. Beyond the secular, what emerges is profane translation that straddles the divine and secular but does not replace either. It also mobilises a new conception of literary language that is neither radically different from the *adab* tradition nor the product of a liberal, humanist, and national project. The literary text in and as translation develops a 'hollow' status as it claims to be coming from the space in between original and translation. In that sense, it comes to profane and not simply secularise both the tradition and the borrowed text.

Finally, it is important to distinguish between an Islamic text and what I am calling a prophetic voice.[106] Some critics have argued that an Islamic novel is impossible as the form's creativity is inherently irreconcilable with Islamic ideals. Even though the Arabic novel was an imitation of the European model, Edward Said finds the 'desire to create an alternative world' that motivates the Western text 'inimical to the Islamic world-view'. Since the Prophet 'has completed a world-view', Islam approaches the world as already perfect, requiring no amendment.[107] While Said's claim is contestable, since fictional narrative has always been a part of Arabic prose tradition, the teleological narrative of the European realist novel is new to Arabic literature.[108] Traditional forms of Arabic prose tend to be more episodic than teleological. My interest, however, is in the *promise* of the prophetic received in the translation of European literature.[109] The translations mark an important literary historical moment before Qurʾānic discourse (either as citation, commentary, or rewriting) becomes a creative intertext in the Arabic novel. Theology and literature continue to exist side by side and are approached in similar representational terms, but, significantly, one does not supplant the other.[110] Even though Egypt's religious landscape coupled with the translators' Azharite education impacts their articulations of prophecy, translation profanes this prophetic vocation. For example, al-ʿAqqād makes a distinction between genius and prophecy through the Prophet Muḥammad and allows for reproduction only of genius. Al-Manfalūṭī, on the other hand, transforms *waḥy* into *khayāl* (imagination) and declares himself a model to be emulated, placing himself in the line of illiterate prophets. It is in this particular sense of the prophetic and against stifling colonial dynamics of identification that the translations of the early twentieth century are able to craft a narrative voice unique to them.

In each instance of translation, the terms of identification vary according to particular formal and linguistic adaptations of the original. In every chapter I consider each translator's particular theory of translation alongside his actual translation to locate the prophetic in that space in-between the two, not as a religious capacity but specifically as a narrative one that challenges predictable linguistic reference. In various forms, the translators engaged contemporary discussions on the inadequate equivalences between languages. As Liu puts it, 'One does not translate between equivalents; rather one creates tropes of equivalence in the middle zone of interlinear translation between the host and guest languages.'[111] The dynamic of emulation, which echoes the impossibility of complete emulation of the Islamic prophet, enables the birth of the prophetic, which profanes the original and the tradition, without establishing a simple relationship of equivalence between the two.

The translators profane the originals in finding something of their own in the ideals of European romanticism and realism that was never really there. Even if we consider the rampant onslaught of colonial and imperial capitalism in early-twentieth-century Egypt, we can still identify in these translations a profanation that introduces a kind of literary reading – one that was never in use and foreign to the Arabic literary tradition – to common use. As common use, however, these translations end up claiming a place supposedly organic to that same tradition. This book draws upon Agamben's idea of the profane to think of prophecy as a narrative capacity opening up fissures in the narrative text and unsettling predictable temporalities of classical European literature (and by extension a classical European project of teleological enlightenment). Thus, the prophetic fulfils the promise of a literary voice that occupies many places and no place within language.

Literary translation as profane is *not* ahistorical, but rather interruptive; much like the '*il*' in Blanchot's analysis, the prophetic voice speaks from within the text, occupying different places and voices, repeatedly producing the literary object in an 'untrascendental contingency' (Derek Attridge's term).[112] The act of reading is repeated and singular every time, particular in speaking to its reader and context, while simultaneously appealing to literature's universalist humanism. In every chapter, I assess whether this promise is fulfilled, in what capacity, and in whose language, insisting that the prophetic, much like perfect translation, resides most powerfully in lack of fulfilment.

The works considered here include al-Manfalūṭī's 1923 translation of Bernardin de Saint-Pierre's *Paul et Virginie* (1788/9) and his 1915 adaptation of François-René de Chateaubriand's *René* (1802) and *Atala* (1801); Muḥammad al-Sibāʿī's 1911 translation of Thomas Carlyle's *On Heroes* (1841) and 1912 translation of Charles Dickens' *A Tale of Two Cities* (1859); Ṭāhā Ḥusayn's 1946 translation of André Gide's *Œdipe* (1930) and *Thésée* (1946), and Voltaire's *Zadig* (1747) in 1947; and Haykal's two-volume biography of Jean-Jacques Rousseau (1921; 1923). The literary prophetic emerges in each case in the free adaptation of the originals, and throughout, the prophetic voice is not consciously subversive. As I already mentioned, most Egyptian translators of the time engaged in self-orientalisation rather than outright subversive mimicry of the colonial text, as Shaden Tageldin explains: imagining themselves as equals to the coloniser in a relationship rapt in seduction.[113] While every chapter recognises this self-orientalising, the prophetic voice displaces it from the author's person into his text. As such, the prophetic complicates the idea that subjectivity and individuality are transacted and forged through the absolute copying of European forms. Rather, subjectivity remains incomplete, inasmuch as translation and emulation of the Muslim prophet remain incomplete. This incompleteness is not a 'failure' but, remarkably, a transaction with the original text. The literary prophetic, emerging and developing in plagiarised and creative translations, simultaneously annexes and radically separates the translator from the European master text, challenging our approach to translation as strictly domesticating or foreignising.

## Mirror, Mirror at Sea, Won't You Just Reflect Me?

Arguably, it was Napoleon Bonaparte's use of translation when he arrived in Alexandria in 1798 that instigated this double function of translation as annexing and radically severing the translated text from the original. Onboard his ship *L'Orient*, Napoleon printed his Arabic speech to the Egyptians, promising that he would liberate them from the oppressive rule of the Mamluks.[114] This promise proclaimed in a language he did not speak was made possible in and on French terms: the allegiance to France was the precondition for the people's liberation. Albert Hourani reads this paradox as beginning 'with the traditional Muslim invocation', but then citing a new idea, for 'this proclamation, it declared, was issued by the French Government, which was "built on the basis of freedom and equality"', and Napoleon 'proceeded to apply these principles to Egypt'.[115] Napoleon's declaration initiated secular translation politics – wherein the master text himself, Napoleon, was speaking in translation, announcing himself as the supplementary text to the Qur'ānic invocation.[116] Thus, even after he was defeated by Sir Horatio Nelson at the Battle of the Nile in 1801, this particular promise of translation, consolidated by the printing press, journals, and other institutions that he set up, persisted and became increasingly influential with the rise of Muḥammad ʿAlī to power as governor of Egypt and Sudan in 1805, and particularly after 1811, when the Mamluks were eliminated at the Citadel. And while the British colonial presence dominated Egyptian political life from 1882 until 1952, the French texts that Napoleon introduced in translation had the most tangible effect on the political, social, and cultural constitutions of the country.[117] Napoleon established the Institut d'Égypte, made up of French scholars, whereby the French invader (Napoleon) became at once the legislator who created a library, a health service, a botanical garden, an observatory, and a museum. The French scholars devised an Arabic–French dictionary and put together an Egypto-Coptic-Franco calendar. With the introduction of his own printing press, Napoleon supervised the publication and distribution of two journals in Cairo. Both compiled and edited by the Orientalist, Jean Joseph Marcel, the first, *La Décade égyptienne* (The Egyptian Decade), concerned itself primarily with literature and political economy, and the second – *Le Courrier de l'Égypte* (The Courier of Egypt) – took up mainly political issues.[118] The journals established the superiority of French knowledge and urged Muḥammad ᶜAlī as early as 1809 to send Egyptians on missions to France asking them to bring back as many French books as they could carry. About six hundred books came into Cairo at once in 1809,[119] because 'Muḥammad ᶜAlī considered that his means to achieve reform was copying [that is, translation] from the West'.[120] In 1835, Muḥammad ᶜAlī established the School of Languages (Madrasat al-alsun), which taught only foreign languages. Rifāᶜa Rāfiᶜ al-Ṭahṭāwī (1801–73), a pioneering Egyptian literary translator, headed the school until his banishment in 1850.[121]

Al-Ṭahṭāwī's work marked the beginning of a new phase of literary translation.[122] There were different and overlapping approaches to translation that ranged from completely free appropriations to more literal attempts, but throughout translation remained a creative act of adaptation.[123] Although distinctions between translation styles may hold in a more comprehensive overview of different literary translations, they are not entirely accurate. For one, the translations in this book range from very literal to complete adaptations and they are all published within the same period, from 1911 to 1949. Moreover, as mentioned earlier, many of these adaptations approached the originals freely, adapting or removing parts, changing the original's structure and in many cases intended meaning, and occasionally removing the original authors' names.

Thus, translation here implies a combination of all these styles, from literal proximity to original texts, to less faithful adaptation that accommodates the receiving culture, and finally to free rewriting of original texts and lives of authors in an effort to sculpt a new prophetic voice for the Egyptian writer. Translation during this period was synonymous with *taᶜrīb* and *iqtibās*, Arabisation and adaptation, and remained so until after World War II. For instance, al-Manfalūṭī develops a prophetic voice through his free rewritings of French fiction, while al-Sibāᶜī articulates his version of the hero-poet-prophet through a subtle rewriting of Carlyle's two eponymous lectures, and Haykal makes Rousseau into the Carlylean hero of historical biography. Approaching translation as a fusion of all these styles is more productive than treating it as a series of stylistic phases unfolding in some form of chronological development. The translations in this book are creative adaptations even when they pretend to complete fidelity, because they always manipulate the Western original.[124] Against Franco Moretti's 'distant reading', this book espouses a close reading that can account for the nuances in these different performances of adaptation.[125]

For instance, these 'creative translations', as Mattityahu Peled calls them, took on a more complex shape and urgent role during the later decades of the *nahḍa*. While in the previous phases of translation under Muḥammad ᶜAlī, the imperative was to be literal and copy European 'modernity' as accurately as possible, the later phases involve more literary adaptation as fiction becomes the space of political critique. During the *nahḍa*, translation of European literature took on the immense task of representing the new nation and by extension, the new authorial self. According to Selim, the *nahḍa* embraced translation to achieve a fast-paced modernity in the Arab world.[126] Tageldin clarifies that for the *nahḍawī* thinkers, 'becoming modern' was never about giving up Arabic; rather, the *nahḍa* 'unfolded in translation: it transported French or English into Arabic. Thus it appeared to "preserve" Arabic while "*translating* it"'.[127] The *nahḍawī* authors of the late nineteenth century paved the way for the twentieth-century translators, who found in translation a promise of literary freedom. Al-Manfalūṭī, al-Sibāᶜī, Haykal, and Ḥusayn write within and against this promise of translation. In every chapter, this 'preservation' of Arabic in translation is related to the duplicitous promise of translation to deliver absolute equivalence.

The translators' romantic leanings shaped that freedom: al-Manfalūṭī adapted Chateaubriand, al-Sibāᶜī translated Shakespeare and Carlyle, Haykal rewrote Rousseau's life, and Ḥusayn found himself in Gide. Romanticism here does not refer strictly to French or English traditions, even though the three groups of romantic Arab poets were educated in both. Rather, the adjective 'romantic' implies the opposite of what was understood to be realistic narration or mimetic representation. The chapter on al-Manfalūṭī deals with this polemic in more depth, as he became the target of the realist writers, and suggests that the 'escapist' tendencies promised by sentimental and romantic literature made possible a 'way out' of the tyranny of the coloniser's master text precisely in the prophetic voice and despite the author's affiliations. This reading is not meant to bestow a subversive potential on these authors that they do not possess. Rather, it approaches translation as a literary promise, resorting to other texts about and in other worlds, that betrays a certain allure for these thinkers; coupled with romanticism, the allure transforms into a narrative voice that manipulates language and genre.

This new narrative vocation, although subjective in its vision, is not to be confused with a fully developed narrative subjectivity. Under the influence of romanticism, it was not until the 1919 Nationalist Revolution against British occupation, confirms Selim, that the first fictional subjectivities begin to appear.[128] The national fiction of the 1930s competed with popular serialised fiction from the get-go. Literary subjectivity may have become more articulate in the 1930s, but it starts taking shape in an earlier dialogue with translations of al-Manfalūṭī, the poetic project of the Dīwānīs, and the auto/biographical translations of Haykal and Ḥusayn. *Prophetic Translation* reads the narrative function produced in plagiarised translation as a way to understand the later evolution of narrative subjectivities. For as there are periods of translation, there are corresponding periods of development of the Arabic novel.

## Genre, Literary History and Translation

A telling example is ᶜAbd al-Muḥsin Ṭāhā Badr's foundational *Taṭawwur al-riwāya al-ᶜArabiyya al-ḥadītha fī Miṣr (1870–1938)* (The Development of the Modern Arabic Novel in Egypt (1870–1938)). Badr categorises the novels published in Egypt from 1870 to 1938 into three currents: the first includes the didactic and entertainment novels popular from 1870 until 1919; the second and third phases coincide in the years from 1920 to 1938. These phases include all translators considered in this book, despite their very different translation styles. In this early phase of translation there was an interest in detective fiction and the works of Victor Hugo, Sir Walter Scott, and William Thackeray – and in a misunderstood and shallow version of romanticism, as these authors, Badr continues, turned to romantic literature believing it did not involve analysis.[129] The best examples are al-Manfalūṭī's peculiar adaptations of sentimental fiction marked by the absence of the original author's name and removal of 'unfamiliar' details like dialogue. In Badr's analysis, such translation occasioned a crisis in literary expression because knowledge of the precise reference of words (*dalāla*) became uncertain. In Chapter One, I argue that this is precisely the precondition of al-Manfalūṭī's adaptations of French fiction and ultimately the dimension of the prophetic as he articulates it in the first volume of the trilogy *Al-Naẓarāt* (Visions) (1910).

For Badr, the second phase is of the artistic novel (1920–38), which came into its own after 1919 under the influence of two translations: Johann Wolfgang von Goethe's *Werther* and Alexandre Dumas, fils's *La Dame aux Camélias*.[130] The last two translations introduced the middle-class hero and narrative subjectivity into Arabic literature. The artistic novel was more realistic in its depiction of Egyptian reality and includes Yaḥyā Ḥaqqī, Maḥmūd Taymūr, and ᶜĪsā ᶜUbayd.[131] Because of the simultaneous translation of romantic and realist European fiction, the writers of the artistic novel struggled to reconcile the politics and aesthetics of the novel, a crisis that significantly reaches its peak in the romantic translations in the interwar period (such as Aḥmad Ḥasan al-Zayyāt's 1925 translation of Alphonse de Lamartine's *Raphaël*). This current would tangentially include the translations of al-Sibāᶜī whose translation of Charles Dickens's *A Tale of Two Cities* in 1912 is one of the sincerest engagements of the realistic style in the history of the Arabic novel. Coexistent with this current is the novel of subjective translation, which includes Haykal, Ḥusayn, al-ᶜAqqād, al-Māzinī, and Tawfīq al-Ḥakīm. The subjective novel revolves around an inflated authorial self, although Badr leaves out the role of translation in the evolution of this self. After all, Haykal wrote a book on Rousseau; Ḥusayn translated French literature prolifically; and al-Māzinī translated collections of English fiction by Oscar Wilde, John Galsworthy, and H. G. Wells, to name a few.[132] Some of these translations were complete adaptations that did not mention the original's title or author; others mentioned the original author but completely changed the title; others completely changed the content; and others claimed to be translations of European texts when they were native and original novels. Pierre Cachia finds that the varied translation styles testify to an evolving taste and desire for different types of Western narratives and the emergence of a reading public.[133]

The prophetic narrative voice in early adaptations and emulations of European fiction troubles these neat genealogies of the Egyptian novel by confronting new styles with narrative traditions and recalling the legacy of the *maqāma*, *sīra*, *ḥadīth,* and the *One Thousand and One Nights*. Although brought about through translation, the prophetic narrative voice remains in conversation with older narrative forms, and carries in it traces of the Arab storyteller figure, such that the narrative voice maintains an oral address in the written text.[134]

Moreover, the history of translation into Arabic challenges a straightforward, teleological genealogy of the Arabic novel. For one, romantic, sentimental, and realist fiction was being translated and emulated at the same time. The aesthetic criteria of the three types of fiction, which developed chronologically in European literature, came into Arabic all at once, and gave rise to what Niranjana calls 'a conceptual economy'. Because Western philosophies of representation pretend to coincide with the reality out there, as she calls it, 'translation in the colonial context produces and supports a conceptual economy that works into the discourse of Western philosophy . . . as a philosopheme (a basic unit of philosophical conceptuality)'. This economy, a product of a hegemonic Western philosophy of representation imposed on the colonised, makes them 'beg for the English books' and produces representation as reality, making it even more compelling for the colonised to write like the coloniser.[135] Translations into Arabic certainly produce a 'conceptual economy' of representation that remains in conversation with the European text. It is important to reiterate that translation of European texts by native translators does not guarantee subversive appropriation of the originals. In fact, the translators of the early twentieth century were still in Franz Fanon's first phase of (post)colonial writing,[136] that of emulating the master text, and they were also under British colonial domination and Ottoman rule since 1517 (which collapsed in 1924), not to mention the powerful influence of the short-lived Napoleonic expedition (1798–1802). As such, in producing these translations, the translator did not purport subversively to adapt the master text.

Besides, in colonial Egypt, the translation of romantic and Enlightenment fiction overlapped with the lingering legacy of the *adab* tradition of communicating a moral. While Blanchot's prophetic word is radically cut off from sense, the historical situation of the literary text in twentieth-century Egypt placed a burden of didacticism on literature in what was seen as a national imperative to educate the masses. The translations, however, respond to the prophetic imperative in choosing a different source from immediate reality, and remaining cut off in that sense, such that translation is not secondary and derivative in a colonial system of dysfunctional equivalences. Instead of simply heeding the imperative to 'represent', and under the obligation to 'instruct', these translations produce the literary precisely as critique of discursive modalities of colonial modernity. Literature comes to both document and *be* the historical, as we find that many of these texts were literally put on trial and the translators sent to prison or exile. The prophetic invective to create the world in language entails the very real ways in which these writers interrupt political histories and the cultural time of modernity, as their texts become punctuating events that both reflect and produce historical moments. As Ḥusayn writes in '*al-Adab wa-l-ḥayāt*' (Literature and Life) (1955), 'literature is a source of human history, and perhaps in comparison to some nations, or some of their epochs, the most dangerous historical source'.[137] From within the texts emerge the discursive and non-discursive practices in which historical time becomes the text's present moment – its publication, circulation, and reception. Because these translations revise the original, and refer it to the receiving context, they also point to how the modern comes about in the equivalence between colonial secularism and literary discourse. For example, the ways in which the translations confront various linguistic registers (the *ʿāmmiyya* and *fuṣḥā*, romanticism and realism) capture the tension between divine and profane when the author situates his text as a contingent act of reading. Instead of maintaining distinctions between high and low forms, I ask: how do these translations re-present dominant ideological structures?

I read these translations closely to rethink their relationship to Islam as a discourse and a lived religion on the one hand, and their place in genealogical accounts on the other. Such double reading helps identify the shift they occasion from religious to literary interpretation, such that the emulation of the prophet Muḥammad as model-human parallels the emulation of the original; translation as intervention, however, supercedes authorial intention. In examining other *nahḍa*s through popular fiction that habitually falls outside popular accounts of the Arabic novel's origins, Selim challenges 'the hegemony of the European liberal concept of the subject' as a locus of 'authorship and copyright in the literary domain'.[138] Only popular translations in her view escape 'the Romantic conventions of authorship that the Nahda appropriated and carnivalised'.[139] The translators' historically situated acts of translation critique the liberal individual's 'I', the objectively contained 'he', and the all-knowing omniscient narrator.

The elites' literary translations played a major role in simplifying the Arabic language. Daniel Newman recognises the simplistic but necessary approach that places translations and new literary genres like the novel and drama midway between 'conservative', 'high literature, including religious output (Quran and hadith exegesis)' and 'creative' or 'liberal' journalistic writing.[140] The 'modernisation' of the language was the domain of the elite's translations, and while they impact the people's relationship to Arabic, they remain the prerogative of the educated, both the Christian Syrian emigrés and the Muslim translators who were more hesitant to renovate the language (see Chapter One). Thus, the 'profanation' of the Arabic language (à la Agamben) through translation as adaptation, appropriation, and commentary reconfigures both the elites' and the masses' languages.[141] I discuss in every chapter the inclusion, exclusion, and imagination of the masses in this aesthetic project both to recognise how differences in political languages get established and to unsettle the originals' universal claims through close reading.[142]

What becomes of the translator's prophetic aspiration in this complicated 'conceptual economy'? *Nahḍawī* intellectuals have retrospectively been attacked for their chosen depoliticisation. Under the obligation of *iltizām* or commitment, later intellectuals denigrated the earlier preoccupation with aesthetics over politics. But what if aesthetics in translation suggest a different politics of liberation from a master/text?[143] If translation reproduces the original's failure to produce a coherent meaning, and the translator still exercises some form of choice, how do we read the impact of prophetic translation? Although censorship relaxed in the nineteenth century and early twentieth, al-Ṭahṭāwi was exiled because of his translation of François Fénélon's *Télémaque*, and Ḥusayn was put on trial for his claims in *Fī al-shiᶜr al-jāhilī*. The depolicitisation of the translator's role arguably compelled him to seek authority in the master text. Stephen Sheehi describes this dynamic in the work of Syro-Lebanese Buṭrus al-Bustānī to conclude that 'only the supplemental mediation of the European Self can bestow knowledge, and thereby mastery and subjective presence, to the modern Arab'.[144] Similarly Tageldin finds that Orientalist discourse seduced Egyptians under French and British rule because it seemed to cast both Europeans and Egyptians as equals.[145] Seduction enables a forgetting of power difference and makes it possible for the 'colonised [to] lose themselves in the coloniser in order to regain their "sovereign" selves'.[146] The prophetic specifically as manipulative translation, however, hinders these absolute equivalences.

The complex identification and seduction between coloniser and colonised plays out in Niranjani's 'conceptual economy', wherein the colonised is made to fall in love with the European text. However, through literary translation as manipulation, this conceptual economy also critiques colonial power. I focus on the literary encounter between two politically inequivalent languages in translation to rethink the political; in my analysis, the political transcends pronounced commitment into a counter-discourse of aesthetic criticism that disables authorial intention. For instance, I emphasise the adaptations of the Arabic language to accommodate the European text, which translate the foreign while maintaining its foreignness from both source and destination.[147] These adaptations, I argue, are a product of the prophetic narrative voice that legitimates them not necessarily as conscious rewritings or imitations of an original, but more importantly as inevitable products of the slippages between an authoritative, originary text and its derivative, secondary translation and not only in the political opposition established between the two. As such, they echo Gayatri Chakravorty Spivak's task of the translator as 'surrender to the text', listening to the silences and gaps, making translation 'the most intimate act of reading'.[148] The prophetic narrative voice treats the original with an intimacy that rewrites colonial supremacy and translation pays its debt to the original in its afterlife by revealing its inevitable failure of signification as just that – inevitable. I have divided the book into chapters that focus on specific translation styles that show us how narrative self-constitution undid voiced political positions and how translation unmade the object it meant to construct – namely, modern Arabic literature.

## Notes

1. In 'A Defence of Poetry' (1821) published in 1849 in Percy Bysshe Shelley, John E. Jordan (John Emory), and Thomas Peacock, *Love, Four Ages of Poetry: A Defence of Poetry* (Indianapolis: Bobbs-Merrill Co., Library of Liberal Arts, 1965), pp. 1–51, p. 34.
2. In *Fajr al-Qiṣṣa al-Miṣriyya* [The Dawn of Egyptian Fiction] (1960) (Cairo: al-Hayʾa al-Miṣrīya al-ʿĀmma li-l-Kitāb, 1987), pp. 23–4. I owe this reference to Muhammad Siddiq, *Arab Novel*, pp. 28–9.
3. [Dedication], in *Al-Shāʿir* (Beirut: Dār al-Thaqāfa, 1983), p. 7.
4. For my own purposes, I am not looking at poetry, although it is undeniable that poetry, literary history, and criticism are interrelated in the history of Arabic literature. I am rather interested in prose as a space of negotiation of genres.
5. Siddiq, *Arab Novel*, p. 16.
6. Benedict Anderson describes Islamic Arabic, Christian Latin, and imperial Chinese as 'truth-languages', being languages of revelation (*Imagined Communities*, p. 25).
7. In *Lan Tatakallama Lughatī* (2002), Abdelfattah Kilito, *Thou Shalt Not Speak My Language*, Wail Hassan (trans.) (New York: Syracuse University Press, 2008).
8. See, for example, Shaden Tageldin (*Disarming Words*, 2011) and Mehmet Akif Kirecci who defines *self-Orientalism* 'not [as] acceptance of the West in its own right, but rather a wilful locating of the self (and, by extension, all aspects of one's native region) below the dominating Other'. See 'Invasive Translations: Violence and Mediation of the False-Colonial, France and Ottoman Egypt (1780–1840)' (2008), Dissertations available from ProQuest, AAI3309438. http://repository.upenn.edu/dissertations/AAI3309438, p. 26.
9. These efforts, especially in Ḥusayn's work, sought to reconcile modernist elements with the Arab critical heritage and involved adjusting existing rules to accommodate the new elements.

10. *Translingual*, p. 16.
11. I do not mean to treat the novel only through narrative voice; rather this voice becomes the site of confluence of languages, styles, and other devices, some traditional and some adapted in translation. This voice sometimes echoes Qurʾānic style, for example, to establish its authority or claim cultural authenticity. I argue that the complexities of this voice make it difficult to frame it in a nationalist paradigm, as has often been done, or subdue it to a 'secular' instance of colonial modernity.
12. Those include biographies of Muḥammad and other prophets, moral treatises based on Qurʾānic stories, and textual appropriations of Qurʾānic *sūras* and discourse.
13. In *Al-Nabī al-insān wa-maqālāt ukhrā* [The Human Prophet and other Essays] (Cairo: Maktabat al-Ādāb, 1900), pp. 11–13. I owe this quotation to M. M. Badawi, *Modern*, p. 158.
14. Examples include Michael Allan, Jeffrey Sacks, Rebecca Johnson, and Samah Selim.
15. Michael Allan locates *adab*'s transformation from habitus to 'modern literature' in Ḥusayn al-Marṣafī's 1876 lectures on literary criticism (*In the Shadow*, pp. 81–2). Nadia al-Bagdadi describes how the multilayered term *adab* before modernity is so encompassing that it resists translation ('Registers of Arabic Literary History', p. 439).
16. Cachia, 'Translations and Adaptations', p. 30.
17. Selim, 'The People's Entertainment', p. 37.
18. Ibid., p. 38.
19. Allan, *In the Shadows*, p. 195.
20. See Allen, 'Literary History and the Arabic Novel'.
21. See *The Future of Culture in Egypt* (1944) (Washington, DC: American Council of Learned Societies, 1954), p. 86.
22. Mitchell, *Colonising Egypt*, p. 141.
23. Sacks, *Iterations of Loss*, pp. 7, 149.
24. Badr, *Taṭawwur al-riwāya*, p. 13.
25. He would reproduce ideas in the *Dīwān* and other places without citing the original.
26. Al-ʿAqqād, *ʿAbqarīyat*, p. 3.
27. Badawi, 'Islam in Modern Egyptian Literature', p. 166.
28. The translation is quoted in ʿAbdul-Hai, *Tradition*, pp. 60–1.
29. Ibid., p. 61.

30. See *Al-Abṭāl, ta'līf al-faylasūf al-akbar Tūmās Kārlayl* (1930 [1911]).
31. ʿAbdul-Hai, *Tradition*, p. 20.
32. Ibid., p. 69.
33. Cachia, *Ṭāhā Ḥusayn*, p. 183.
34. Haykal, *Tarājim*, pp. 256–61.
35. ʿAbdul-Hai, *Tradition*, p. 21.
36. ʿAbdul-Hai, *Tradition*, p. 64.
37. Gibran modelled his *Prophet* formally on Nietzsche's *Thus Spoke Zarathustra* in the way the prophet addresses the community, but the messages of Gibran's prophet differ radically from Nietzsche's philosophical speculations. (See Waterfield, *Prophet*, p. 258.)
38. Jayyusi, *Trends*, pp. 91–2.
39. Another Lebanese poet whose work dealt with prophecy was Mikhāʾīl Nuʿayma (1889–1988). He translated Gebran's *The Prophet* into Arabic in 1956, prefacing his translation with a confirmation of his loyal adherence to the original. (See *Jubrān Khalīl Jubrān: Al-Nabī*, tarjamat Mikhāʾīl Nuʿayma [Beirut: Dār Nawfal, 2015] p. 34.) Despite Nuʿayma's popularity in Egypt, his poetry also did not impact the translators under study.
40. In the 1930s, the resurgence of Islamic sentiment was spurred by the rise of the Muslim Brotherhood, al-Azhar's reforming efforts, and the Islamic writings of prominent, previously considered 'secular' intellectuals. While scholarship (Nadav Safran, H. A. R. Gibb, and Von Grunebaum) has mostly read this turn as failure of reconciliation with Western thought, Charles D. Smith finds it to be an existential crisis definitive of the period.
41. I owe this reference to Smith, *Islam and the Search*, p. 16.
42. Cohn, *Colonialism and its Forms of Knowledge*, p. 4.
43. *Islamic Reform and Conservatism*, p. 7. In fact, al-Azhar in the early twentieth century had its own reform movement that generally falls out of the modernists' accounts. For more, see Gesink, *Islamic Reform and Conservatism*, pp. 195–7.
44. Carlyle, *On Heroes*, pp. 53, 90.
45. H. A. R. Gibb, *Arabic Literature*, 2nd edition (Oxford: Oxford University Press, 1963), p. 159.
46. 'Back to Napoleon?', p. 82.
47. See Laroui, *The Crisis of the Arab Intellectual*, pp. 1–10.
48. For a recent discussion of the *nahḍa*, see *Arabic History Beyond the Liberal Age: Towards an intellectual History of the Nahda*, edited by Jens Hanssen and Max Weiss (Cambridge: Cambridge University Press, 2016), especially their intro-

duction, 'Language, Mind, Freedom and Time: The Modern Arab Intellectual Tradition in Four Words', pp. 1 – 38.

49. Abdel-Aziz Abdel-Meguid's *The Modern Arabic Short Story: its Emergence, Development, and Form* (late 1950s) describes three stages of progress as embryonic, trial, and formative, culminating with the birth of the short-story child who still needs to grow (Cairo: al-Maᶜārif Press, 1956?), esp. pp. 77, 102, 109, and 132. Roger Allen's *The Arabic Novel: An Historical and Critical Introduction* (1995 [1982]) also describes a period of maturity, p. 3. For Matti Moosa, 'Arabic Fiction Comes of Age' (Matti Moosa, *The Origins of Modern Arabic Fiction* (1983) [Boulder: Three Continents, 1997], p. vii). Hafez's *The Genesis of Arabic Narrative Discourse* describes early Arabic narrative as an embryo, followed by the 'birth' of new genres and a final 'maturation', pp. 7–8. Peter Gran sums up the traditional view of this period: 'a very stagnant and very "Turkish" eighteenth century was replaced by a very progressive and increasingly Arab and European nineteenth century following the "Coming of the West," or Napoleon, in 1798' (Peter Gran, *Islamic Roots of Capitalism: Egypt, 1760–1840* [Syracuse: Syracuse University Press, 1998]), p. xiv.

50. George Antonius in *The Arab Awakening: The Story of the Arab National Movement* (New York: Capricorn Books, 1946) and Hourani in *Arabic Thought in the Liberal Age* relate the *nahḍa* to changes in literary sensibilities, especially in the fiction of Salīm al-Bustānī, Rifāᶜa Rāfiᶜ al-Ṭahṭāwī, Jurjī Zaydān, and Faraḥ Antūn. Abdulrazzak Patel adds the important contributions of Muslim reformers (*The Arab Nahḍah*, pp. 20–31).

51. For a historical and economic perspective, see, for example, Kenneth M. Cuno's *The Pasha's Peasants: Land, Society, and Economy in Lower Egypt, 1740–1858* (Cambridge: Cambridge University Press, 1992).

52. 'The post-classical period' in *Arabic Literature in the Post-classical Period*, p. 2. Other efforts include Joseph E. Lowry and Devin J. Stewart's refusal of M. M. Badawi's 1992 representation of Arab literary decline as of the sixteenth century ('Introduction: The Background', in *Modern Arabic Literature*, edited by M. M. Badawi [Cambridge: Cambridge University Press, 1992, 1997], pp. 1–22). See their introduction to *Essays in Arabic Literary Biography, 1350–1850* (Wiesbaden: Harrassowitz Verlag, 2009).

53. For example, the Syrian critic ᶜAlī Aḥmad Saᶜīd Isbar (b.1930), known as Adonis, cites the Mongol, Crusader, and European colonial invasions as three historical moments that instigated modernisation efforts in Arabic cultural

production. See Adonis, *Introduction to Arab Poetics* (French 1985), Catherine Cobham (trans.) (London: Saqi, 2003), esp. pp. 75–81; 98–102.

54. For more on this critique, see Thomas Bauer, 'In Search of "Post-Classical Literature": A Review Article', *Mamlūk Studies Review* 11.2 (2007): 137–67.
55. Ze'evi, 'Back to Napoleon?', p. 85.
56. Ibid., p. 86.
57. See 'Alternative Modernities: Globalization and the Post-Colonial', *Ariel* 40.1 (2009): 81–105.
58. Ze'evi, 'Back to Napoleon?', pp. 89–90.
59. Sheehi, 'Towards a Critical', p. 298.
60. Gayatri Chakravorty Spivak, 'Can the Subaltern Speak,' in Cary Nelson and Lawrence Grossberg (eds), *Marxism and the Interpretation of Culture* (London: Macmillan, 1988), pp. 271 – 313, esp. p. 281.
61. Venuti, 'Translation as Cultural Politics', p. 75.
62. Venuti, *The Translator's Invisibility*, p. 20.
63. Benjamin's task of the translator has informed my own: my translations are almost literal rendering of the original syntax, in an honest effort to maintain the original mode of signification.
64. 'The Task of the Translator', p. 79.
65. De Man, 'Conclusions', p. 35.
66. Ibid., p. 44.
67. Ibid., p. 41.
68. Ibid., pp. 36, 44.
69. Derrida, 'Des Tours of Babel', p. 122.
70. Derrida, 'What is a "Relevant" Translation?', pp. 178–9.
71. Gesink, *Islamic Reform and Conservatism*, p. 5.
72. André Lefevere made this argument in his classic, *Translation, Rewriting, and the Manipulation of Literary Fame* (London: Routledge, 1985).
73. Some examples include Ṭāhā Badr (1963), Matti Moosa (1997 [1983]), and Muḥammad Muṣṭafā Badawī (1992).
74. Venuti, *The Translator's Invisibility*, p. 20.
75. Niranjana, *Siting Translation*, pp. 48–9.
76. Venuti, *The Translator's Invisibility*, p. 19. Translation studies has also long made a case for the complex place of translated literature within national canons. Itamar Even-Zohar, for example, describes translated literature as a 'stratified system' in and of itself that paradoxically introduces new ideas and

forms while also 'becom[ing] a means to preserve traditional taste' (Even-Zohar, 'The Position of Translated Literature', p. 49).

77. Venuti, 'Local Contingencies', p. 180.
78. 'Translation and Political Engagement: Activism, Social Change and the Role of Translation in Geopolitical Shifts' *The Translator* (6)1 (2000): 23–47.
79. In discussing the untranslatability of poetry, Roman Jakobson finds semantic equivalence impossible and thus all translations to be creative acts. See 'On Linguistic Aspects of Translation' (1959) in Lawrence Venuti (ed.), *The Translation Studies Reader* (London: Routledge, 2000), pp. 232–9.
80. Venuti, 'Local Contingency', p. 180.
81. Venuti relates '[n]ationalist agendas in translation' to the institution of the nation because national unity emerges as a fiction and represses 'the differences among the heterogeneous groupings and interests that comprise any social collective' ('Local Contingency', p. 189). Through these translations selected by an elite class of intellectuals, the translating culture adopts an imagined homogeneous identity.
82. *Translingual*, p. xvii.
83. Translations of Plato during the Abbasid age framed the distinction between anti-Muslim and Muslim poets as that between inspired and non-inspired poetry; however, Plato makes philosophy superior to poetry, while in the Islamic tradition religion comes before poetry. Literary representations of the Prophet's birth and life proliferated in oral accounts throughout the Muslim world, and so these translators did not initiate something new (for more on this subject, see Annemarie Schimmel's *And Muhammad is His Messenger: The Veneration of the Prophet in Islamic Piety* [Chapel Hill: University of North Carolina Press, 1985]). However, their accounts were importantly influenced by the translation of Western literature.
84. Derrida, 'Des Tours de Babel', p. 115.
85. Derrida, 'The Eyes of Language', p. 193.
86. Ibid., p. 199.
87. Viswanathan, *Masks of Conquest*, p. 97.
88. Ibid., p. 97.
89. Ibid., p. 112.
90. Al-Musawi, *Islam on the Street*, p. 30.
91. Tomoko Masuzawa examines the orientalist construction of Islam as a particularly national religion, inferior precisely in not having the same claims to universality that the prophetic origin of both Christianity and Judaism are

given. (See Tomoko Masuzawa, *The Invention of World Religions: Or, How European Universalism Was Preserved in the Language of Pluralism* (Chicago: University of Chicago Press, 2005), pp. 194–5).

92. Roberto Schwarz, *Misplaced Ideas: Essays on Brazilian Culture* (London: Verso, 1992), p. 25. For similar accounts on the travels of the novel, see Christopher Hill, 'The Travels of Naturalism and the Challenges of a World Literary History', *Literature Compass* 6 (2009): 1198–210, and Mary Layoun, *Travels of a Genre: The Modern Novel and Ideology* (Princeton: Princeton University Press, 1990).
93. Agamben, *Profanations*, p. 73.
94. Ibid., p. 77. On the other hand, Talal Asad finds the 'profane' to be an Enlightenment product that legitimates universal reason. Profanation does not move us from the 'transcendental to the mundane', but simply readjusts the 'barriers between the illusory and the actual' (*Genealogies*, 1993). Asad isolates a modern experience of reading imaginative literature (specifically nineteenth-century romantic literature) that promises 'direct access to reality' by making the 'pre-modern past' seem enchanted and removing the sacred (pp. 13–14). I am suggesting, however, that instead of approaching this secularising reading practice as absolute, reading translations shifts the focus to *how* these processes became established ways of perceiving the world.
95. In advanced capitalist societies, the profane loses its power because 'in its extreme form, the capitalist religion realises the pure form of separation, to the point that there is nothing left to separate' (Agamben, *Profanations*, p. 81).
96. Al-Azhar's curriculum changes in the nineteenth century, especially with Muḥammad Ali's establishment of military schools and the creation of a class of technocrats as the new educators. For more on this, see Indira Falk Gesink's *Islamic Reform and Conservatism*, esp. pp. 16–23.
97. Blanchot, *The Infinite Conversation*, p. 380.
98. Ibid., p. 384.
99. Ibid., p. 462.
100. Ibid., p. 385.
101. Blanchot, *The Book to Come*, p. 79.
102. Ibid.
103. Cited in Ian Balfour's *Romantic Prophecy*, p. 7
104. Ibid., p. 8.
105. Although the translators are writing from within an Islamic education, their readings of Western literature influence their approach to literary prophecy,

and the poetic word's creative power comes from translation, not from the translator. Jan Wojcik and Raymond-Jean Frontain describe the prophetic in British literature as an imperative to 'see', 'reveal', and 'uncover' a world beyond this one that in fact 'determines the moral and spiritual significance of the quotidian'. This imperative, both the poet's prerogative and a legacy of 'the visionary tradition . . . the greatest one in English Literature' (*Poetic Prophecy in Western Literature* [New Jersey: Fairleigh Dickinson University Press, 1984], pp. 21–22), is bound to the prophet's eloquence. As John Leavitt puts it, 'Both poetry and prophecy are culturally marked forms of speech, and one criterion, at least, of the marking of both of them is power' (*Poetry and Prophecy: The Anthropology of Inspiration* [Michigan: Michigan University Press, 1998], p. 3).

106. For more on the rise of Islamist literature post the 1960s and its struggle for literary legitimation, see Reuven Snir's *Religion, Mysticism and Modern Arabic Literature* (Wiesbaden: Otto Harrassowitz Verlag, 2006), esp. Chapter One.
107. Said, *Beginnings*, p. 81.
108. This is not to conflate Arabic pre-modern prose and Islam but simply to reiterate that fictional Arabic prose before the translation of the novel did not offer a complete narrative world or teleology.
109. M. M. Badawi reiterates the centrality of the Prophet Muḥammad to *nahḍawī* Egyptian poetry, giving the example of neoclassical poets who exploited 'the traditional view with all the popular supernatural accretions' (Badawi, 'Islam in Modern Egyptian Literature', p. 157). Trevor Le Gassick finds Haykal's interest in Islam a direct outcome of reading 'Washington Irving's enthusiastic romantic portrayals of the rise and progression of the faith and culture of Islam' (Le Gassick, 'The Faith of Islam', p. 99) while al-Manfalūṭī was the only one producing Islamic writing from 1911 to 1930 (p. 100). Muhsin al-Musawi (*Islam on the Street*) finds a new literary discourse on religion in post-1967 Arabic literature that engages the masses but confirms that the Islamic writings of the intellectuals of the 1930s like Ḥusayn only solidified the state's secular language.
110. The translations do not use Qurʾānic discourse (either as citations or commentaries) as intertext. In discussing the intersection of Greek tragedy, French literature, and the Qurʾān in the works of Tunisian Maḥmūd al-Masʿadī, Mohamed-Salah Omri uses the term 'confluence' to avoid reinforcing discursive hierarchies, especially when 'the intertext (the word of another) is the word of God, the Qurʾān' (*Nationalism, Islam and World Literature*, p. 73). Omri includes a conversation between Ṭāhā Ḥusayn and al-Masʿadī that is very

telling in this context: in a review of the latter's play *al-Sudd* (The Dam) (1938), Ḥusayn likens it to Camus's 'Myth of Sisyphus' (1942), while acknowledging an important difference between the two: while the Arab hero desires to create change and achieve an objective, the Greek hero is fated to fail. However, both heroes accomplish nothing, and the Arab hero's imagination builds no dam (pp. 98–9). Al-Mas<sup>c</sup>adī defends his text, which was written before Camus's.

111. Liu, *Translingual*, p. 40.
112. See Derek Attridge's 'Literary Form and the Demands of Politics: Otherness in J. M. Coetzee's Age of Iron', in George Levine (ed.), *Aesthetics and Ideology* (New Brunswick, NJ: Rutgers University Press, 1994), p. 248.
113. Tageldin, *Disarming Words*.
114. Al-Shayyāl, *Ḥarakat*, p. 35.
115. Hourani, *Arabic Thought in the Liberal Age*, p. 49.
116. Napoleon had claimed his conversion to Islam and found his Deism to be compatible with such a claim. In ᶜAbd al-Raḥman al-Jabartī's account of the first encounter with the French expedition (1st edition, written in 1798 as *Tarīkh muddat al-Faransīs bi-Miṣr*), he meticulously deconstructs Napoleon's failed translation. See ᶜAbd al-Raḥman Jabartī and Shmuel Moreh (trans.), *Napoleon in Egypt: Al-Jabarti's Chronicle of the French occupation, 1798* (Princeton: M. Wiener, 1993).
117. Pierre Cachia emphasises the lasting 'association of Western ways with power and success first demonstrated by Bonaparte's forces' (*An Overview*, p. 29). Until 1882, the Syrian immigrants concentrated on translating French fiction but the translation of British fiction increased after 1882 and came from two sources: 'the Syrian immigrants who had been trained at the American University in Beirut, and the Egyptian students who had graduated from schools under British control' (Moosa, *Origins*, pp. 98–9).
118. See Tājir, *Ḥarakat*, p. 8.
119. Al-Shayyāl, *Ḥarakat*, p. 46.
120. Ibid., p. 70.
121. Badr considers al-Ṭahṭāwī's translation of Fénélon's *Les Aventures de Télémaque* (written in Sudan in 1851, published in Beirut in 1867) to be the first novelistic activity in Egypt in the nineteenth century (*Taṭawwur*, p. 57).
122. Allen finds Muḥammad ᶜUthmān Jalāl's (1829–98) translations, not al-Ṭahṭāwī's, more impactful, for Jalāl 'egyptianised' the originals, inviting imitation in Arabic translations of the European novel (Allen, *The Arabic Novel*, p. 21).

123. For example, Sabry Hafez identifies two phases of translation: the last decades of the nineteenth century with free appropriations to domesticate the form for an Egyptian readership, and the early twentieth century with more literal translation and less stylistic interference in the text, because the translators were not trained in classical Arabic literature (Hafez, *Genesis*, p. 90.). Pierre Cachia partially agrees that nineteenth-century translations kept the story line but used *saj*ᶜ (rhyming prose) and rhyming titles to 'bear witness to the persistence of the stylistic preferences of previous centuries', but there were also complete adaptations that made writers '*creators when translating, and translators when creating*' ('Translations and Adaptations', p. 31). Richard Jacquemond finds that these early *creative* translations of French fiction liberated the translators from the colonial master-text (Jacquemond, 'Translation and Cultural Hegemony', p. 142).
124. Matti Moosa, Pierre Cachia, and Ṭāhā Badr contend that the novel came into Arabic mainly through the translation of Western fiction. Mohammed-Salah Omri, Sabry Hafez, Roger Allen, Maḥmūd Taymūr, and Saad Elkhadem describe the Arabic novel as an integration of traditional narratives into the *new* form coming in translation.
125. Franco Moretti first coined the term 'distant reading' in his 2000 essay 'Conjectures on World Literature' (*New Left Review* 1 [2000]: 54–68), proposing a study of literary history based on second-hand research and reception instead of textual analysis.
126. Selim, 'Nation and Translation', p. 9.
127. See *The Novel*, esp. pp. 70 – 73.
128. Tageldin, *Disarming Words*, p. 5; emphasis in the original.
129. Badr, *Taṭawwur*, p. 129.
130. Jad B. Ali disagrees with Badr's correlation between the 1919 Egyptian Revolution, the rise of the bourgeoisie, and the Arabic novel: 'The fact that 1919 coincided with the growth (not the rise) of the short story rather than the novel itself shows that the novel needed more than optimism and (rightful) pride in political consciousness and national solidarity to rise, grow and flourish' (*Form and Technique in the Egyptian novel: 1912–1971* (Oxford: Ithaca Press, 1983), p. 16).
131. Badr, *Taṭawwur*, p. 220.
132. Moosa, *Origins*, pp. 116–17.
133. Cachia, 'Translations and Adaptations', p. 107.
134. On the oral legacy of the *Arabian Nights*, see Peter D. Molan's '*The Arabian Nights*: The Oral Connection', *Edebiyat* nos. 2. 1–2 (1988): 193–4; Rebecca

Carol Johnson, Richard Maxwell, and Katie Trumpener, 'The Arabian Nights, Arab-European Literary Influence, and the Lineages of the Novel', *Modern Language Quarterly* (2007) 68.2: 243–79; and Srinivas Aravamudan, *Enlightenment Orientalism: Resisting the Rise of the Novel* (Chicago: University of Chicago Press, 2012), esp. pp. 57–69.

135. Niranjana, *Siting Translation*, p. 13.
136. Fanon describes three phases of colonial and postcolonial writing in 'On National Culture' (1961) (*The Wretched of the Earth* [London: Penguin Classics, 1990], pp. 166–89). Fanon's national culture is not the domain of the elite, but 'the whole body of efforts made by the people in the sphere of thought' – in a sense it is the narrative that people create for themselves and sustain through resistant culture (p. 233). At this point in Egyptian cultural history, national culture was not established yet and definitely not the domain of the entire people, but significantly it starts to involve the people through cultural appropriations of religious stories.
137. Ḥusayn, *Khiṣām wa-naqd* (1955) (Beirut: Dār al-ᶜilm li-l-malāyīn, 1978), pp. 44–5.
138. Selim, 'The People's Entertainment', p. 45.
139. Ibid., p. 53.
140. Newman, 'The Arabic Literary Language', pp. 483–4.
141. Benedict Anderson's idea in *Imagined Communities* that serialised fiction created the imagined community is challenged by questions of readership, illiteracy, and circulation of translations that imagined *other* places and not native ones. If Anderson's imagined nation develops over time, then it must be constantly interrupted in the reading of serialised and other translations so that the national narrative remains incomplete.
142. The translators were working within a polemic that had started much earlier in the nineteenth century on reforming and simplifying the Arabic language. For more on the subject, see Adrian Gully, 'Arabic Linguistic Issues and Controversies of the Late Nineteenth and Early Twentieth Centuries', *Journal of Semitic Studies* XLII.1 (1997): 75–120.
143. Zeina G. Halabi has recently explored the legacy of the intellectual-prophet in post-1990s Arab intellectuals' works to counter a depoliticisation of contemporary Arabic literature and locate residuals of the earlier legacy. See her book *The Unmaking of the Arab Intellectual: Prophecy, Exile and the Nation* (Edinburgh: Edinburgh University Press, 2017).
144. Sheehi, *Foundations*, p. 35.

145. Tageldin, *Disarming Words*, p. 9.
146. Ibid., pp. 14, 26.
147. Homi Bhabha describes the excess 'produced by the ambivalence of mimicry (almost the same, but not quite)' as an 'uncertainty' that makes the colonial subject into 'a 'partial' presence' until she resists (*The Location of Culture* [London and New York: Routledge, 1995, p. 85). However, I insist that focusing on the linguistic encounter in colonial translation in relation to the traditional body of Arabic narrative and romantic aspirations complicates distinctions between the resisting colonised and the subservient one, the mimicking and the faithful translation.
148. Spivak, 'The Politics of Translation', p. 398.

# 1

# Translation in Motion: A Survey of Literary Translation in Lebanon and Egypt during the *Nahḍa*

> We blame translators, and particularly those who translate romances, for suppressing the names of authors. What is the wisdom of doing so? If these translators claim these works to be their own, we could then say that they want to ascribe these works to themselves. But when they admit that they have only translated these works, would it not be better if they affixed the name of the author, who has consumed his brain and spent nights in research and exposed himself to bitter criticism and reproach to write a romance? . . . Should not his right in writing his work be preserved as we preserve our right of publishing these works?
>
> Editor of *al-Hilāl*.[1]

In his momentous dictionary *Muḥīṭ al-muḥīṭ: qāmūs muṭawwal li-l-lugha al-ᶜarabiyya* (1870) [The All-encompassing Comprehensive: An Extended Dictionary of the Arabic Language], under the entry *rawā* (to narrate or tell a story), Buṭrus al-Bustānī surprisingly includes no reference to the neologism *riwāya* (novel) and its novel generic connotations, but adheres to the word's older references (basing his dictionary on Majd al-Dīn al-Fayrūzᵓābādī's *al-Qāmūs al-Muḥīṭ*). This seems surprising given al-Bustānī and his son Salīm's direct role in introducing and propagating the novel and story forms in Lebanon. Al-Bustānī translated *The Pilgrim's Progress* (1678; Arabic 1844) and *Robinson Crusoe* (1719; Arabic 1861),[2] while Salīm took over the cultural journal *al-Jinān* (Gardens/Paradise) in Beirut, which published translations and original fiction, such as his *al-Hiyām fī futūḥ al-shām* (1870) (Love during the Conquest of Syria), considered a pioneering Arabic novel. Yet, under the entry *rawā* in al-Bustānī senior's *Muḥīṭ,* we find: 'rawā al-ḥadīth yarwīhi riwāyatan . . . ḥamaluhu wa naqaluhu . . . al-rāwī . . . ᶜind al-muḥaddithīn nāqil al-ḥadīth bi-l-isnād . . . wa alladhī yarwī al-ḥadīth aw al-shiᶜr yuqāl huwa riwāyat fulān' (to narrate a story by telling it . . . carry it and copy/transmit it . . . for the tradition transmitters the narrator is the one who copies/transmits the story through reference . . . and the narrative produced is the account of the one who told the story or poetry).[3] In line with the tradition of 'transferring' stories in Arabic literature, al-Bustānī retains the original act of *naql* – to copy and transmit – significantly another name for translation.

Buṭrus al-Bustānī, born in 1819 in the Chouf region of Mount Lebanon, moved to Beirut in the 1840s where he studied English with the American missionaries and translated the Bible with the Reverend Eli Smith (1848–56), before embarking on his translation of *Robinson Crusoe.* He was also simultaneously publishing a political journal, *Nafīr Sūriyya* (Trumpet of Syria), which included his *waṭaniyyāt*: *waṭan* is translated as nation or homeland, and the suffix *-iyyāt* describes these entries as musings on the nation. Every *waṭaniyya* addressed the 'sons of the nation', the people of Mount Lebanon. His most known literary translation is also one of the earliest translations from the region, *Riḥlat Rūbinṣun Kurūzī (or Kitāb al-Tuḥfa al-Bustāniyya fī al-Asfār al-Krūsuwiyya: al-qism al-awwal wa al-thānī maᶜan)* (The Bustānīan Masterpiece Concerning Crusoeian Travels: Parts One and Two Together) (1861). It compares interestingly with Egyptian al-Ṭahṭāwī's *Mawāqiᶜ al-Aflāk fī waqāʾiᶜ Talīmāk* (The Positions of the Planets in the Events Concerning Télémaque), the translation of François Fénélon's *Les Aventures de Télémaque* completed in Sudan in 1851 (published in Beirut in 1867). Sasson Somekh pioneered this comparison when he argued that al-Bustānī's translation of *Robinson Crusoe* had a determining impact on modern Arabic literary style because it modernises the Arabic language in ways that al-Ṭahṭāwī's translation could not. Al-Ṭahṭāwī's 'strictly rhyming prose', he argues, makes his style 'elevated' and 'neo-classical', whereas al-Bustānī's style is 'non-classical' because it uses the colloquial. Al-Ṭahṭāwī's translation, unlike al-Bustānī's, fails to affect Arabic literary standards because his reliance on 'basic norms of late classical Arabic prose results in a text which is in the nature of a paraphrase'.[4]

For Somekh, al-Bustānī's simpler (and by deduction more modern) prose is shaped by the 1865 Eli Smith and Cornelius van Dyck Bible translation, and the spoken dialect, 'the first attempt to introduce these elements into a literary text proper', since only Christian and Jewish writers had used the colloquial in 'canonical or high-brow literature'.[5] Al-Bustānī's translation also sets the tone for the translation movement that follows; after him, Syro-Lebanese translators of fiction increase exponentially, and relocate to Egypt to escape Ottoman censorship, where they publish their highly influential 'non-classical stylistic predilections'.[6] There are many problems with Somekh's conclusions. Firstly, the style of al-Ṭahṭāwī's *saj*ᶜ (rhyming prose) oscillates throughout between extremely elegant and plain, and he occasionally uses colloquialisms and abandons the rhyme. Second, these general distinctions between the 'conservative' and thus more classical Egyptian Muslim translators and the more 'modern' Christian Syro-Lebanese translators recall many problematic accounts of the *nahḍa* that attribute its modernisation to the Christian intellectuals who found more 'natural' affinities with the West, thus homogenising the Christian thinkers and dismissing the role of Muslim writers.

Historians of the Middle East have disagreed over the Christian versus Muslim intellectual roles in the renaissance. Traditional accounts such as George Antonius's *The Arab Awakening* (1938), Albert Hourani's *Arab Thought in the Liberal Age* (1962), and Hisham Sharabi's *Arab Intellectuals and the West* (1970) have argued that the more Western-oriented Christian intellectuals, freed from the restraints of Islamic thought, are largely responsible for the 'renaissance'.[7] However, such accounts are inaccurate: for one, the Christian intellectuals were not a monolithic group, but had various political and religious affiliations and diverse relationships to Islam, and the Arabic heritage or *turāth*. And although there are differences in the choices and styles of translation between Egypt and Syria during the nineteenth and twentieth centuries, those cannot be divided absolutely given the geographical mobility between the two places. When Ottoman censorship increased in Mount Lebanon and Beirut, many Syro-Lebanese writers moved their journals to Cairo (the famous examples include *al-Hilāl* established by Jurjī Zaydān and *al-Muqtaṭaf*, co-established by Yaᶜqūb Ṣarrūf and Fāris Nimr).

There are many challenges to establishing differences in the styles and choice of translations and breadth of impact between Greater Syria and

Egypt in the nineteenth century and early twentieth. The first challenge is due to the lack of accurate bibliographical information: many of these translations were 'plagiarised' adaptations that often did not mention the originals. The second challenge relates to the translators' movement between Greater Syria and Egypt to escape censorship laws and find more conducive intellectual environments. What we can surmise is that the Syro-Lebanese literary translators were more prolific in the second half of the nineteenth century in Beirut and Cairo. In Beirut, al-Bustānī's translation efforts aimed at establishing a common sense of national identity in the aftermath of the 1860 civil war in Mount Lebanon.[8] His son Salīm invested in fiction as social critique to create a reading culture – what Elizabeth M. Holt describes as the 'newly emerging bourgeois audience'.[9] Many nineteenth-century translations by Syro-Lebanese translators in Beirut and Cairo focused on romantic fiction of social critique, mostly in adaptations that did not adhere to the originals. Unlike Holt who focuses on the readership of translated fiction in Beirut, Matti Moosa finds that early translation choices depended on the translators' tastes and not the 'desires of their readers' for 'the shallowest of European fiction: not until the first quarter of this century did translators begin to deal seriously and systematically with the more profound works of Western literature' (103).[10] Questions of readership and value also depend on the differences between the Syro-Lebanese and Egyptian translators and the changing landscape of literary translation during the *nahḍa*.

## The Translation Movement in Greater Syria[11]

The translation movement in Syria started earlier, with the missionaries, who translated the Bible and works by Daniel Defoe and established schools that used these translations as foundational textbooks.[12] As early as the sixteenth century, religious texts were translated into Arabic and then distributed in Greater Syria.[13] The eighteenth century saw more translation of religious texts, followed by literary and political translations, all generally weak in form as ᵓUsāma ᶜĀnūtī argues, but religious translation shifted from Latin to Greek sources in the feud between the Catholic and Greek Orthodox churches to consolidate their authorities.[14] Towards the end of the eighteenth century, under the oppressive rule of Aḥmad Bāshā al-Jazzār, the *Wālī* of Akkā, and the *Shihābī* princes in Lebanon (especially Bashīr al-Thānī, 1789–1840), many

Syrian litterateurs escaped to Egypt and served as translators for the French. These early translations were mostly of military and technical documents: one notable figure is Rāfāyīl Anṭūn Zakhūr (d. 1831), a Roman Catholic priest of Syrian origin who remained in Egypt and became the only Arab member of Napoleon's Egyptian Academy of Science (Institut d'Égypte). When Zakhūr returned to Egypt from Paris, Muḥammad ᶜAlī hired him to translate textbooks and serve as classroom interpreter.

Although the translation movement in Greater Syria slowed down in the first half of the nineteenth century, it regained momentum in the second half, especially due to the efforts of journals and schools. For example, Khalīl al-Khūrī's *Ḥadīqat al-akhbār* (Garden of News) (1858–1911) published mostly scientific and some literary translations, but then offset a series of journals that published literary translations.[15] The Jesuit University and Syrian Protestant College (now the American University of Beirut) contributed to this surge through the translation of textbooks for their growing numbers of students. The Al-Bustānīs' *Al-Jinān* (Gardens), founded in January of 1870, published mostly Italian and French fiction from 1870 to 1871, French and English adaptations from 1875 to 1878, some by al-Bustānī senior, generally focused on themes of love and social mobility, espousing realist literary techniques and often disowning their original sources. From 1884 until 1894, French literature predominated.[16] Qayṣar Zayniyya translated *Les deux Dianes: le Comte de Montgomery* by Alexandre Dumas in *al-Ahrām* in 1881, and Najīb Ḥaddād published a translation of *Les Trois Mousquetaires* in Cairo in 1888.[17] In Lebanon, translations of French fiction remained popular through Milḥim Karam Milḥim's periodical *Alf layla wa layla* (Thousand and One Nights) (established in 1928) and ᵓImīl Ḥabash al-Ashqar's *al-Layālī* (The Nights) (established in 1929) that published translations and historical novels.

Given the increasing religious censorship laws in Lebanon in the second half of the nineteenth century, and encouraged by the British law of 1882 that protected writers, Syro-Lebanese translators moved to Cairo and established many daily newspapers, such as *al-Ahrām* (1876) and *al-Muqaṭṭam* (1889), or weekly magazines and monthly periodicals, such as *al-Muqtaṭaf* (transferred from Beirut to Cairo in 1884), *al-Hilāl* (1892), and *al-Jāmiᶜa* (1899).[18] In Cairo, Syro-Lebanese immigrants published their popular adventure stories and romantic tales. The most popular translators were Faraḥ Anṭūn,

Muḥammad Kurd Alī, Asᶜad Dāghir, Ṭanyūs Abduh, Niqūlā Haddād, Salīm Naqqāsh, and Yaᶜqūb Ṣarrūf. The literary adaptations of the Syro-Lebanese translators found a larger audience than republished Egyptian classical works. Critics have generally condemned these adaptations as weak and mass-driven.[19] Louis Cheikho, for instance, wished that there were fewer of those bad translations, whose little literary value was further underlined by their immoral love stories,[20] but Laṭīfa al-Zayyāt disagreed, giving the example of 'good' detective fiction, historical and picaresque novels.[21] However, this translated body of work was in no way homogenous, even though it dominated the market. For example, Milḥim critiques Ṭanyūs Abduh's loose translations comparing them to Muṣṭafā Luṭfī al-Manfalūṭī's adaptations.[22] Moosa further divides Syro-Lebanese and Egyptian journals between those like *al-Ahrām*, which published translations, and others like *Rawḍat al-akhbār*, *al-Manār*, and *al-Jarīda* that paid more attention to reform – although they included some fiction.

The nineteenth-century literary translation movement in Greater Syria took on various forms of adaptation and appropriation, as demonstrated by the frequent publication of one translated novel in several parts. Laṭīf Zaytūnī isolates four trends of translation: the first is the didactic and entertainment approach, represented by Qayṣar Zaynīyya whose free adaptations aimed to deliver *al-ifāda al-adabiyya maᶜ al-fukāha* (literary/moral benefit with humour). The second trend is of popular stories (*al-qiṣaṣ al-shaᶜbiyya*) with Ṭanyūs ᶜAbduh – in this second phase, the story form was still not taken seriously.[23] For example, in his translation of Michel Zévaco's *Les Pardaillan* (1900), ᶜAbduh caters to the audience's sensibility and adapts the text under the influence of older Arab storytelling forms, adding Qurᵓanic references for further instruction.[24] The third trend is more serious and didactic, as, for example, Faraḥ Anṭūn's translation of *al-Kūkh al-hindī* (The Indian Cottage) (1906), originally by François-René de Chateaubriand,[25] and finally there is the religious trend. Lebanon preceded other Arab countries with its interest in the story form due to the earlier presence of missionary schools and fictional translations, such as Salīm Ṣaᶜab's adaptation of Bernardin de Saint Pierre's *Paul et Virginie* (1787) as *Būlus wa Virgīnī* (1864).[26] Basiliyus Bawardi gives Salīm Nawfal's introduction to his translation *al-Mārkīz dī fūntānj* (*Ḥadiqat al-akhbār*, Issue 50, 1858) as a pivotal example of translation in Bilād al-Shām. 'We liked to translate . . . an example . . . which describes the social picture in a way that attracts the reader and affects his emotions', writes Nawfal. Apologising to the reader if the translation disrupts his 'habits', Nawfal asks her to excuse the translator's weakness and 'the difficulty of translation, remembering the words of . . . Voltaire . . . that "translation in comparison with the original text is like the back of the cloth to its face"'.[27]

## Translation in Egypt

When translation slowed down in Greater Syria under the oppressive regime of Prince Bashīr al-Thānī, it assumed full force in Egypt under the reign of Muḥammad ᶜAlī. Most translations of the first half of the nineteenth century served scholastic, military, and pedagogic purposes, intended to be taught at schools, and, in 1835, Muḥammad ᶜAlī established the famous School of Languages (Madrasat al-alsun) for the sole purpose of teaching foreign languages. Rifāᶜa Rāfiᶜ al-Ṭahṭāwī (1801–73) headed the school until his banishment in 1850. Jāk Tājir divides translation under Muḥammad ᶜAlī into three periods: the first began with what he calls the new age, presumably 1811 until 1830, when translation involved mostly interpretation used to establish schools with foreign textbooks and graduate fully trained translators.[28] What he terms the second phase, from 1831 to 1835, involved the dispatching of education missions to Paris under the obligation to translate. Muḥammad ᶜAlī considered translation an actual debt; he would send students on these missions on the condition that they would translate whatever they were reading. Back in Egypt, Egyptians started replacing foreign teachers and the year 1835, which marks the opening of the School of Languages, also marks the beginning of Tājir's third phase.[29] Ibrahim Abu-Lughod divides the translation movement of the nineteenth century into five phases: focused on interpretation up until 1826, random from 1826 to 1835, organised from 1835 to 1848, declining from 1848 to 1863, and resuscitated after 1863.[30] When the Khedive ᶜAbbās came into power after Muḥammad ᶜAlī and his son, he exiled al-Ṭahṭāwī and restricted translation.[31] While in exile in Sudan in 1851, al-Ṭahṭāwī translated François Fénélon's *Les Aventures de Télémaque* (1699), giving his translation a traditional title of two rhyming parts, *Mawāqiᶜ al-aflāk fi Waqāʾiᶜ Talīmāk*, and rendering the whole text in *sajᶜ* or rhyming prose. The translation was published in Beirut in 1867. With the coming of Ismāᶜīl into power, the translation movement resumed intensely, with the years 1880 to 1899 marking the most prolific movement of translation yet.[32] Abu-Lughod counts more than 2,000 books translated in Cairo under the School of Languages when translation was centralised.[33]

In *Taṭawwur al-riwāya al-ᶜarabiyya al-ḥadītha fī Miṣr (1870–1938)* (The Development of the Modern Arabic Novel in Egypt (1870–1938)), ᶜAbd al-Muḥsin Ṭāhā Badr designates al-Ṭahṭāwī's translation of Fénélon's *Télémaque* the first novelistic activity in Egypt in the nineteenth century although it was more preoccupied with symbolism and autobiography than with the novel form.[34] Roger Allen finds al-Ṭahṭāwī's translation less influential in the history of the Arabic novel than his work in translation and with the press.[35] Although mostly officially commissioned, al-Ṭahṭāwī, both as translator and teacher, initiated a shift in the focus and practice of translation in Egypt in the second half of the nineteenth century. He also made significant contributions to the Arabic language, introducing new single and compound words (some as combinations of French and Arabic), and neologisms such as *jurnāl* and *karantīnā*.[36] He lays out his translation theory most clearly in *Takhlīṣ al-Ibrīz fī talkhīṣ Bārīz* (The Purification of Gold in the Summary of Paris) (1834): the translator must know the other language fully and be familiar with the subject, so that the Arabic language could adapt to the subject's novelty despite its superiority to other languages. Al-Ṭahṭāwī argues that since all languages have systems, immersing oneself in one system could guarantee the acquisition of another. Although this process seems simple, in fact he makes several distinctions between languages, especially when it comes to the translation of rhetoric, since Arabic poetry loses its beauty in translation.[37] He describes his own translation practice of French poetry as an art, *fann al-tarjama* (the art of translation), and his translations are of course far from accurate. In the introduction to *Mawāqiᶜ*, he describes his faithful act of translation as one that opts for simplicity to deliver the closest original meaning – as per 'usual styles' (*ᵓasālīb muᶜtāda*) of translation – ironically in *sajᶜ* forcing him to add words to maintain the rhythm and rhyme.[38]

Due in part to Muḥammad ᶜAlī's and al-Ṭahṭāwī's efforts, by the turn of the century, Egyptian translations rivalled Syrian ones and more journals published fiction.[39] The journals, literary magazines, and political newspapers played a decisive role in the dissemination of translated fiction and the modernisation of the language. Ṭāhā Badr, Saad Elkhadem, and Henri Pérès name the most notable journals that published serialised fiction, translated and otherwise, such as *Silsilat al-fukāhāt* (Humour Series) (Beirut, 1884), *Muntakhabāt al-riwāyāt* (Selected Novels) (1894), *Silsilat al- riwāyāt* (Novel Series) (Cairo, 1899), *al-Riwāyāt al-shahīra* (Famous Novels) (Cairo, 1901), *Musāmarāt al-sha*ᶜ*b* (People's Entertainment) (Cairo, 1904–11), *al-Fukahāt al-*ᶜ*aṣriyya* (Contemporary Humour) (1908), *al-Musāmarāt al-Usbu*ᶜ*iyya* (Weekly Entertainment) (Cairo, 1909), *Musāmarāt al-mulūk* (Kings' Entertainment) (Cairo, 1912), *al-Musāmarāt* (Entertainment) (Cairo, 1921), *al-Nadīm al-riwā*ᶜ*ī* (The Narrative Confidant) (Cairo, 1922), and *al-Riwāya* (The Novel) (Cairo, 1937).[40] Saad Elkhadem lists Walter Scott, Alexandre Dumas, père, Victor Hugo, W. M. Thakeray, and Charles Dickens as some of the most popular authors in translation in Egypt at the turn of the century.[41] Pérès in *Le Roman, le Conte et La Nouvelle dans la Littérature Arabe moderne* (1937) adds Bernardin de Saint-Pierre, Chateaubriand, Paul Bourget, Henri Bordeaux, Benjamin Constant, François Coppée, Alphonse Daudet, Alexandre Dumas fils, Jean-Baptiste Alphonse Karr, Alphonse de Lamartine, and Guy de Maupassant, although he makes no reference to the earlier translations in *Ḥadīqat al-akhbār*. All these authors were translated at about the same time with little or no attention given to the literary distinctions in style and language, and in most cases, the translations' titles were completely different from the originals. Pérès also includes a list of adaptations that do not reference originals, such as al-Manfalūṭī's adaptations of Chateaubriand. The 1930s saw mass translations of popular detective fiction – which Moosa describes as mostly 'superficial and erratic'.[42] Many translations of the same texts were also done in Beirut and Cairo, or by immigrants in Cairo, as, for example, Chateaubriand's *Atala* and *René* translated at least three times before al-Manfalūṭī's adaptation: the first in 1882 by Jamīl Nakhle al-Mudawwar in Beirut; the second of *Atala* by Faraḥ Antūn; and the last of both *Atala* and *René* by the Lebanese novelist Marūn Abbūd in 1919 in Lebanon.[43]

Literary translations increased drastically towards the end of the nineteenth century in Cairo to the extent that Muḥammad ᶜAlī published a letter declaring the most read literature at the end of the nineteenth century to be the *maqāmāt* and the translations.[44] Recording the frequency of publication and circulation of books in the nineteenth century, ᶜĀyda Ibrāhīm Naṣīr confirms that literary translations were more popular than traditional narratives.[45] Pierre Cachia finds the French influence to hold 'sway' over Egyptian literary sensibilities, correlating the impact with the political power and superiority that Napoleon's campaign established.[46] Moosa agrees that until 1882, the Syrian immigrants in Cairo concentrated on translating French fiction 'because of their long-standing cultural relationship with France', but that the translation of British fiction increased after 1882 and came from two sources: 'the Syrian immigrants who had been trained at the American University in Beirut, and the Egyptian students who had graduated from schools under British control'.[47] Sir Evelyn Baring, Lord Cromer (1841–1917) – the British colonial administrator who ruled Egypt for twenty-four years (1883–1907) – introduced the study of English into Egyptian public schools in 1889. Together with Cromer's more lenient censorship policy, the increased study of English encouraged the establishment of more journals with translations of British fiction, creating what Moosa describes as a 'Europeanised' middle-class reading public.[48] Popular in circulation were Yaᶜqūb Ṣarrūf's translation of Sir Walter Scott's *Talisman* and al-Bustānī's *al-Tuḥfa*.[49] In early-twentieth-century Cairo, the translation of English fiction won the market over, especially with translated works of Walter Scott, Wilkie Collins, and Charles Dickens by Muḥammad al-Sibāᶜī (1912). Moosa makes a value judgement, describing al-Sibāᶜī's Dickens translations as 'good literature' and other translations as 'popular' literature.[50] Moosa's judgement, of course, relies on a view of translation as accurate transfer of equivalences across languages. This was the general view of the *nahḍawī* intellectuals themselves: accurate translation would guarantee correct modernisation, and in this trajectory, there was also 'good' and valuable literature and bad, 'useless' literature. I will return to the repercussions of this value system in every chapter.

## Approaches to the Literary History of the Translation Movement

There are several approaches to the literary history of the *nahḍa*'s translation movement: some chronologically examine the phases with their changing trends from translation choice to problems of fidelity. Another approach focuses on the stylistics of translation in each phase. Few have considered the readership in relation to the emergence of new literacies. Pierre Cachia complicates the issue of fidelity to the original among texts that do not mention the original author and those of 'budding writers [who] found it easier to break into print if they presented their effusions under such a vague label as "freely translated"' – emphasising instead the texts' popularity and circulation as testament to a desire for Western fiction.[51] Anwar al-Jundī in *Taṭawwur al-tarjama fī al-adab al-ᶜarabī al-muᶜāṣir* (The Development of Translation in Modern Arabic Literature) (1959) distinguishes three phases of translation: the first phase was scholarly and 'dignified'; the second phase, catering to the audience's taste, was 'perverted' with 'a distinct deterioration in the quality of translation'; and the final phase returns to the seriousness of the first phase.[52] Both Hafez and Cachia find that in the last decades of the nineteenth century, translations of European literary works tended to Egyptianise or Levantise the originals.[53]

Muḥammad ᶜAbd al-Ghanī Ḥasan's *Fann al-tarjama fī al-adab al-ᶜarabī* (The Art of Translation in Arabic Literature) (1966) explains the 'distortions' of original texts as considerations of local, national, religious, and moral sensitivities.[54] For Sabry Hafez, domesticating the foreign was done for two reasons: the first falls in line with the European pedagogical programme in the Levant, which aimed at transmitting and establishing European culture within (if not in place of) the local; and the second caters to the general attitudes of the reading public, thought to be 'unprepared' for the complexities of the originals. These 'inferior' translations became 'the battleground for subjugating the language and techniques of traditional narrative to the dictates of the new narrative discourse'.[55] With the turn of the century translations became more faithful, because these were performed by translators who were not trained in Classical Arabic literature and their styles were 'far removed from conservatism' and thus more in tune with the 'dictates of modern narrative discourse'.[56] Moreover, in their literality, these translations transformed narrative in the Arab world into a particular discourse with a set of distinctive elements. The translated text was a 'new' form through which the equally 'new' (read: modern) experience of space and time could be articulated in ways that did not run against established literary norms.[57] Hafez's chapter titles bear witness to the newness of this labour, with words such as 'embryonic' and 'maturation'. And in this account, the 'better' translations are the desired offspring that made writing the modern experience of time and space possible.[58]

In the late nineteenth century and early twentieth, translations of detective and romantic fiction (such as Victor Hugo, Sir Walter Scott, and W. M. Thackeray) dominated the market.[59] These translations did away with the original author and 'unfamiliar' details like dialogue. The romantic translations in the period between the two wars, such as Aḥmad Ḥasan al-Zayyāt's 1925 translation of Alphonse de Lamartine's *Raphaël*, pointed to the gap between aesthetics and politics in the Arab novel, but these translations had no real influence on the development of the novel in Egypt and the Arab world, Badr continues, since they failed to address the Egyptian sociopolitical milieu.[60] Richard Jacquemond agrees that the first phase of translation had no real impact on Arabic narrative at the time because translation 'consisted most frequently in a very free transposition of the French narrative and actually was not called "translation" [*tarjama*], but "adaptation" [*iqtibās*], "arabization" [*ta*ᶜ*rīb*], or even "egyptianization" [*tamṣīr*]'.[61] He gives the example of al-Manfalūṭī's famous adaptations, whose original authors only a few scholars remember today. Until the 1910s, the openness towards the West was regulated by the local culture's value system.[62] However, soon afterwards, more accurate translations appeared, such as Ṭāhā Ḥusayn's adaptations of Racine's *Andromaque* in 1935, Sophocles' *Antigone* in 1938, and Voltaire's *Zadig* in 1947. Throughout these various accounts, the triumphant translation – the one that would leave its mark – is the faithful one, as it attests to the 'maturation' of both the translator and the receiving culture. Similar to the 'new' promise of Hafez's translated text, these accounts consider the realist novel the fully developed form that modern Arabic narrative was striving towards, and thus the 'bad translations' are abortive efforts, inconsequential drafts on the way to the mature form. However, these translation styles often overlapped, and the translators studied in this book both theorised and practised translation towards a different articulation of literary language and form. Thus, the concurrent periods of literary translation and the Arabic novel's development are not as clear-cut as most critics have read them to be.

## Literary Language and Purpose

Although far from definitive, some differences between the translation movements in Egypt and Lebanon relate to the attitude towards the Arabic language, choice of texts, and different approaches to literature's didactic role. Even though both Egyptian and Syro-Lebanese writers advocated language reform under the influence of translation, Syro-Lebanese translators were more radical in their approach to 'modernising' literary Arabic, opening it up to the influences of foreign languages and literatures. For example, despite his insistence on saving classical Arabic, Aḥmad Fāris al-Shidyāq supported the creation of neologisms when the Arabic language did not provide an equivalent for the foreign term in *Sirr al-layāl*.[63] In *Kanz al-Raghāʾib fī muntakhabāt al-Jawāʾib* al-Shidyāq describes the labour of translation: 'Whoever missed out on the work of translation (Arabisation), does not know what it is to be cursed', for the translator is a 'warrior [who] has been touched by fire', because he finds 'a thousand meanings that have synonyms . . . so I wish my people would know that I am seriously headed towards the pain of translation'.[64] Buṭrus al-Bustānī responds to the criticism of his weak linguistic structures that the Arabic language needs to change so it can accommodate the new material in translation, and eventually caves to the readers' preferences, saying he will return to the classical uses of the language to avoid their hostility.[65] Ibrāhīm al-Yāzijī is equally anxious about the language's inflexibility.[66] Perhaps the journal *al-Muqtaṭaf* was the most vocal when it called for the replacement of classical Arabic by the colloquial in its sixth volume (1881–2).[67] Yaᶜqūb Ṣarrūf in '*Uslūbuna fī al-taᶜrīb*' (Our Style in Translation/Arabisation) (1908) shows a gradual inclination towards *taᶜrīb*.[68] In part 4, volume 73 of *al-Muqtaṭaf* (1 December 1928), '*al-Tarjama wa maqāmahā*' (Translation and its Place), Ṣarrūf writes that Arabs never in fact overcame imitation (*al-taqlīd*) and paraphrase (*al-iqtibās*) but excelled in *naql* or translation of Greek philosophy and sciences.[69] In his narrative of modernity, Jurjī Zaydān finds the real literary renaissance to coincide with the massacres of 1860 in Mount Lebanon when many Lebanese villagers were forced to move to Cairo. Zaydān pushed for translation but also insisted on a common Arabic language that would be grounded in Islamic discourse. In '*al-Tarjama wa-l-taᶜrīb*' (Translation and Arabisation), Zaydān proposes two words: *tarjama* as interpretation and *taᶜrīb* as keeping the foreign word in the Arabic.[70] Zaytūnī gives the example of the word 'philosophy' translated as the love of wisdom and transliterated as *falsafa*. Zaydān was an enthusiastic advocator of *muṣṭalaḥāt* (nomenclature), especially in comparison with their historical presence in foreign languages.[71] But, as Thomas Philipp has argued, Zaydān also replaces Islamic Arabic with a secular Arabic bound to nationalist aspirations, such that even the changes in religious worldview become a matter of 'historical analysis'. The 'secularised interpretation of Arab history', Philipp continues, was based on a consistent use of 'evolutionary theory . . . Central to this application was his concept of the community of benefit and usefulness'.[72]

However, al-Ṭahṭāwī had already brought up the idea of benefits (*manāfi*ᶜ) in *Manāhij al-albāb al-Miṣriyya fī mabāhij al-ᵓĀdāb al-ᶜaṣriyya* (1869) (The Methodology of Egyptian Minds with Regard to the Marvels of Modern Literature), introducing social material benefits and spiritual benefits within *al-tamaddun al-ma*ᶜ*nawī* and *al-tamaddun al-māddī* (spiritual and material civilisation) as distinct entities.[73] Even earlier in his 1834 travel narrative *Takhlīṣ al-ibrīz*, he used *waṭan* – substituted throughout with *milla* and ᵓ*umma* – in describing the laws of the French state.[74] Although *Takhlīṣ* is not a translation, it includes translations and neologisms that mark a significant shift in language use in Egypt in the nineteenth century. Linguistic 'reform', therefore, was also a preoccupation of Egyptian translators, the difference being that the latter struggled with the use of vernaculars and colloquialisms in literature more so than the Syro-Lebanese writers. Ibrahim Abu-Lughod agrees with Laṭīf Zaytūnī on translation's radical impact on the modernisation of Arabic literature, since it invited the foregoing of *saj*ᶜ and poetic flights, and introduced quotations, new prose, history, law, and the sciences.[75] Zaytūnī specifically attributes this radical reform to the Lebanese writers since they had been exposed to translation earlier and were thus more prepared. During the second phase of translation in Greater Syria, translations become more literal, importing foreign styles and structures that inevitably transform composition (*al-inshā*ᵓ) to resemble Western models.[76] Again, it is difficult to generalise this conclusion, since, for example, Marūn ᶜAbbūd argues in *Ruwwād al-nahḍa al-ḥadītha* (Pioneers of the Modern Renaissance) (1952) that the Christian role in Arabic literature should be confined to translation until their Arabic tongue *yastaqīm* (straightens).[77]

Late nineteenth-century political journalism especially encouraged simplifying the Arabic language and was not the exclusive domain of Syro-Lebanese writers as per many accounts.[78] However, in Cairo, the more openly political journals thrived in the early twentieth century, such as *al-Siyāsa*'s supplement *al-Siyāsa al-usbū*ᶜ*īyya* (The Weekly Political) (established on 19 March 1926) followed by *al-Balāgh*'s *al-balāgh al-usbūᶜī* (Weekly Bulletin) (established on 26 November 1926). Both Haykal and Ḥusayn published their critical articles in *al-Siyāsa al-ʾusbūᶜiyya*, al-Aqqād in *al-Balāgh al-usbūᶜī*, and al-Sibāᶜī in *al-Bayān* (Eloquence) and others. Al-Manfalūṭī published mostly in *al-Muʾayyad* (The Advocate). Journals soon became more specialised, such as *al-Risāla*, partially edited by Ḥusayn, and *al-Kātib al-Miṣrī* (1945–8), fully edited by Ḥusayn.[79]

## Didacticism and the Moral Function of Literature

In addition to occasionally incorporating some traditional narrative forms, what persists from the tradition of *adab* in the translated novels is the moralising function of literature. In this sense, the distinctions between the Syrian and Egyptian translation efforts matter less than the residual in each case – especially in how the different translators imagined the new role of translated fiction in the making of the nation or *waṭan*. The translators became an integral part of producing, authorising, and circulating *nahḍa* nationalist narratives, but with different approaches to the novel's role in these narratives. Some Muslim writers were more hesitant about the corrupting influence of novels than the Syro-Lebanese Christian translators. Muḥammad ᶜAbduh, for example, dreaded the potentially corrupting impact of translated novels on the Arabic language and correlative corruption in morals through what he called *khurāfāt* or superstitions.[80] However, he recommended some translations published in *al-Ahrām* and al-Ṭahṭāwī's *Mawāqiᶜ*. Moosa represents the previous position well when he writes: 'unlike the conservative Egyptians, the Syrians were not hindered by any belief that fiction was immoral and worthless'.[81] But at least one editorial introduction to an 1882 issue of *al-Muqtaṭaf* – edited by Ṣarrūf – (established in Beirut in 1876 and relocated to Cairo in 1884) resists this previous conclusion:

> If we were to examine the anxiety of the young, we would find that the root of the problem is the kind of love relationships young people commit themselves to at an early age. Novels and poetry dealing with love themes and the like can only make matters worse. This kind of writing is addictive: one thing leads to another and the end result would be a waste of time and a lowering of standards. These desires must be curbed.[82]

The edifying function of literature remained a primary promise for major Syrian and Egyptian writers. Faraḥ Anṭūn, for example, prefaced his translation of Chateaubriand's *Atala*, *al-Kūkh al-Hindī* (The Indian Cottage) (1906), with a moral call for the reader to use literature as a means of returning to the 'righteous' path described by men of religion.[83]

Due to the different colonial situations in Egypt and Lebanon, Egyptian writers were more drawn to English literature in the early twentieth century while Syro-Lebanese writers remained devoted to French literature. But, of course, these lines cannot be established absolutely: al-Manfalūṭī was adapting French literature in the 1920s and Ṭāhā Ḥusayn was translating André Gide and Voltaire in the 1940s. Moreover, in the twentieth century, Egyptian translators struggled more with the division between classical Arabic and the colloquial, while Lebanese translators embraced and developed what would become modern standard Arabic.

A final difference relates to the specific religious and educational backgrounds of the translators considered in this book: both al-Manfalūṭī and Ḥusayn studied at al-Azhar, Ḥusayn then joined the Egyptian university, and he and Haykal went to the Sorbonne while Muḥammad al-Sibāᶜī attended Madrasat al-Muᶜallimīn with its British colonial curriculum. All four translators remained attuned to the confrontation between Islam and European literature in translation and consciously addressed it in their translations. In negotiating the terms of this confrontation, they also articulated a novel understanding of the literary object in the early twentieth century. Even though some Syro-Lebanese translators and writers approached modern poetry as a prophetic force of change, they found formal liberation from classical constraints to be necessary for poetic inspiration. For example, in his 200-page introduction to the translation of Homer's *Iliad*, Sulaymān al-Bustānī confirms that liberation from classic constraints is the condition of modern poetry,[84] for even though both historian and poet record events (*waqāʾiᶜ*),[85] the poet is superior – and Homer is the ideal example here – because he is free to use the imagination and inspiration to communicate truth.[86] In that sense, a poet is like a prophet, but the former can never reach perfection.[87] In al-Bustānī's account, however, this continuous striving makes the poet superior, as he draws on other disciplines like science and history to help the nation progress.[88]

The equivalence between science, history, and literature presupposes the Western text to posit 'evidentiary' truth. Sulaymān al-Bustānī and Jurjī Zaydān, as Philipp would have it, secularised the Arabic language by subjugating the tradition to historical analysis. The translations of the Muslim writers studied in this book, however, approach translation as a space of profanation of the original, keeping the sacred and secular in constant tension and documenting this changing worldview in the overt and subtle changes they make in their adaptations. Thus, the 'value' of their translations – from absolute appropriation to literal rendition to auto/biographical presentation – matters less in relation to fidelity to the original, a popular concern of translation theory – and more in relation to the literary function they assigned their new works from within the tension between tradition and translation. This function materialised in the confrontation between the unattainable ideal of the human Prophet Muḥammad, transgressive appropriation and imitation of the original text, and the resultant profane literary voice. Chapter Two explores precisely this profanity in the prophetic translation theory of Muṣṭafā Luṭfī al-Manfalūṭī.

## Notes

1. Cited in Moosa, *Origins*, p. 107. See also Yūsuf Ilyān Sarkīs, *Maᶜjam al-maṭbūᶜāt al-ᶜarabiyya wa-l-muᶜarraba* (Cairo: Maṭbaᶜat Sarkīs, 1928).
2. The 'Damietta School' of Alexandria had already completed a translation of *The Pilgrim's Progress* in the 1810s and missionaries in Malta published a translation of *Robinson Crusoe* in 1835. For more on these earlier translations, see Peter Hill, 'Early Translations of English Fiction into Arabic: *The Pilgrim's Progress* and *Robinson Crusoe*', *Journal of Semitic Studies* 60(1) (2015): 177–212.
3. *Muḥīṭ al-muḥīṭ taʾlīf al-muᶜallim Buṭrus al-Bustānī* (Beirut: Maktabat Lubnān, 1870), p. 361.
4. Somekh, 'The Emergence of Two Stylistic Norms', p. 197.
5. Ibid., pp. 197–9. There are other models for al-Bustānī's 'simple' style, such as Mount Lebanon's history-writing tradition from the seventeenth century exemplified by Tannūs al-Shidyāq's *Akhbār al-aᶜyān fī jabal Lubnān*, which was being edited by al-Bustānī shortly before the appearance of his translation of *Robinson Crusoe*.
6. Somekh, 'The Emergence of Two Stylistic Norms', p. 199. Ottoman censor-

ship laws in Greater Syria were also not as absolute. See Donald J. Cioeta's 'Censorship in Lebanon and Syria, 1876–1908', *International Journal of Middle East Studies* 10(2) (May 1979): 167–86.

7. Ibrahim Abu-Lughod also confirms the superiority of the missionary translators to the Egyptian translators in the nineteenth century, both motivated by the same drive for modernisation (pp. 70–1).
8. After the 1860 civil war, Lebanon was separated from Syria under the rule of a non-Lebanese Christian governor and divided under confessional affiliations. The history of such religious identification is irreducible to a simple politics of tribal antagonism. For the most part, and before the invasion of Muḥammad ᶜAlī and the consequent intervention of European forces, the Maronites and Druze of Mount Lebanon did not follow religious affiliations. Rather, distinctions were based solely on rank, but al-Bustānī called for a 'nationalist' sentiment not based on a claim to a bordered land but on an abstract 'nation' that transcends religious and class identifications. For more on how al-Bustānī's translation of Defoe spoke to these issues, see my article 'Stranded in Arabic: *Robinson Crusoe* in Beirut', *Comparative Literature Studies* 52(2) (2015): 289–317. For more on the emergence of sectarianism in the Middle East, see Ussama Makdisi's *The Culture of Sectarianism: Community, History, and Violence in Nineteenth-Century Ottoman Lebanon* (Berkeley: University of California Press, 2000).
9. See Holt, 'Narrative and the Reading Public in 1870s Beirut', p. 39, and *Fictitious Capital: Silk, Cotton, and the Rise of the Arabic Novel* (New York: Fordham University Press, 2017), pp. 18–39. Rebecca Johnson has recently described the impact of journals 'on creating a global culture of readership' (Johnson, 'Foreword', p. xxv). For more on Salīm's social concern in fiction, see Moosa, *Origins*, pp. 125–46.
10. Moosa, *Origins*, p. 103. In *Composing Egypt*, Hoda A. Yousef traces the emergence of overlapping literacy publics in Egypt, providing much needed research on the reception and literacy rates of Egyptian readership at the turn of the twentieth century. In the least, her meticulous exploration of these multiple publics with various literacy levels complicates the assumed 'desires' of the reading public that has been the assumption of many popular accounts of the translation movement. For more on readership, see Ami Ayalon, *The Arabic Print Revolution: Cultural Production and Mass Readership* (Cambridge: Cambridge University Press, 2016), pp. 154–93.
11. In Palestine, because of the Greek Orthodox presence, Russian literature held

sway and the most popular translator was Khalīl Baydas. For more on the translation movement in Palestine, see Ḥusām al-Khaṭīb *Ḥarakat al-tarjama al-Filisṭīniyya min al-nahḍa ḥatta awākhir al-qarn al-ᶜishrīn* [The Palestinian translation movement from the *nahḍa* until the end of the twentieth century] (Beirut: al-Muᵓassasa al-Arabiyya li-l-dirāsāt wa-l-nashr, 1995).

12. For more on the translation of poetry, see Muhammad ᶜAbdul-Hai's 'A Bibliography of Arabic Translations of English and American Poetry (1830–1970)' in *Journal of Arabic Literature* 7 (1976): 120–50 and Zaytūnī, *Ḥarakat*, pp. 57–84.
13. The Psalms were the first publication in Lebanon in 1610 (see Zaytūnī, *Ḥarakat*, p. 15). Zaytūnī names three presses in Greater Syria in the seventeenth and eighteenth centuries: Dayr Mār Qazḥyā, Maṭbaᶜat al-Shūwayr, and Maṭbaᶜat al-Qiddīs Jarjiīūs for the Roman Orthodox denomination (pp. 14–16). For more on the history of publication in Greater Syria, see ᶜĀnūtī, *al-Ḥaraka*, pp. 45–50.
14. ᶜĀnūti, *Al-Ḥaraka*, p. 105. ᶜĀnūti relates this shift to the impact of different narrative forms in eighteenth-century Syria on polarising differences among religious confessions.
15. Rebecca Johnson reads Khalīl al-Khūrī's original novel *Wayy, idhan lastu bi-ifranjī* (Alas, I Am Not a Foreigner [1859]) as consciously participating in 'an already existing transnational circuit of literary representation' (Johnson, 'Importing the Novel', p. 250), suggesting that the novel could have emerged from other geographical intersections beyond the nation. Basilius Bawardi finds that the translations in *Ḥadīqat* that preceded al-Ṭahṭāwī's *Mawāqiᶜ al-aflāk* were more literal, such as Salīm Nawfal's *al-Mārkīz dī fūntānj* (Issue 52, 1858) (See 'First Steps in Writing Arabic Narrative Fiction: The Case of "Ḥadīqat al-Akhbār"', *Die Welt des Islams* 48(2) (2008): 170–95, p. 179).
16. Between 1884 and 1885, the journal published a serialised translation of Alain-René Lesage's *Gil Blas* (1715–35) by Jamīl Mikhāīl Mudawwar. From 1875 to 1894, there are many translations of Jules Verne, Chateaubriand, Eugène Sue; some popular translations included Yūsuf Sarkīs's rendition of Jules Verne's *Voyage en Ballon* as *al-Riḥla al-jawwiya fī al-markaba al-hawāᵓiyya* (1875). Most popular was Salīm Ṣaᶜb's serialised translation of Alexandre Dumas, Père's *The Count of Monte Cristo*, serialised in the periodical *al-Sharika al-shahriyya* (Monthly Enterprise) and then again in 1871 by Bishāra Shadīd (see Moosa, *Origins*, pp. 97–8 and note 49, p. 103).
17. Many translations of similar texts recurred in different parts of the Arab world

such as Chateaubriand's *Les Aventures du dernier Abencerage*, translated by Aḥmad al-Faghūn as *al-Jawhar al-wahhāj al-manfūsī fī Gharā*ᶜ*ib ibn sirāj al-Andalūsī* (Algiers, 1864), and then by Muḥammad al-Musayrīqī, *Khatam* ᶜ*iqd banī sirāj* (Tunis, 1909), and also by Al-Amīr Shakīb Arslān, who appended to it a short history of *Banū Sirāj*, published as *Riwāyāt ākhir banī sirāj* (Cairo, 1918) and then *al-Dhikrā* by al-Manfalūṭī (Moosa, *Origins*, p.104). Many similar translated novels were also circulating across the Ottoman Empire (see Johann Strauss, 'Who Read What in the Ottoman Empire (Nineteenth-Twentieth Centuries)?', *Arabic Middle Eastern Literatures* 6(1) (2003): 39–76).

18. Allen, *The Arabic Novel*, pp. 21, 24.
19. Elkhadem, 'Early Precursors', pp. 26–7.
20. See *Tārīkh al-*ᵓ*ādāb al-* ᶜ*Arabiyya fī al-rubū*ᶜ *al-awwal min al-qarn al-*ᶜ*ishrīn* [The History of Arab Literature in the first decades of the twentieth century] 3rd edition (Beirut: Dār al-Mashriq, 1991), p. 105.
21. Al-Zayyāt divides the topics of translation into Orientalist, historical, love, social, adventure, and detective stories. Historical novels distorted historical facts, while social stories did not really expose social problems but intended mainly to entertain, catering to the reader's tastes (see Laṭīfa al-Zayyāt, *Ḥarakat al-tarjama al-Adabiyya min al-Inglīziyya ila al-Arabiyya fī Miṣr fī al-fatra ma bayn 1882 wa 1952 wa mada* ᵓ*irtibāṭuhā bī-ṣiḥāfat hadhihi al-fatra*, [unpublished dissertation, Cairo University, 1957] pp. 80–120.) I owe the reference to Haykal in *Taṭawwur al-Adab al-ḥadīth fī Miṣr*, pp. 131–7. For a recent teleological account that also dismisses the translations, see Muḥammad Sayyid ᶜAbd al-Tawwāb's *Bawākīr al-riwāya: dirāsāt fī tashakkul al-riwāyāt al-*ᶜ*arabiyya* (Cairo: al-Hayᵓa al-Miṣriyya al-ᶜāmma li-l-kitāb, 2007), esp. pp. 78–9.
22. Zaytūnī, *Ḥarakat*, p. 125.
23. Ibid., p. 124.
24. Ibid., pp. 135–7.
25. Ibid., p. 126.
26. Ibid., pp. 120–1.
27. Cf. Bawardi, 'First Steps', p. 182.
28. Tājir, *Ḥarakat*, p. 25.
29. For more on the curriculum at the School of Languages, see John Heyworth-Dunne, *An Introduction to the History of Education in Modern Egypt* (London: Frank-Cass Publishers, 1968), pp. 220–1, Tājir, *Ḥarakat al-tarjama*, pp. 29–39, and Aḥmad al-Rāfiᶜī, *Aṣr Muḥammad* ᶜ*Alī*, 5th edition (Cairo: Dār al-Maᶜārif, 1989), pp. 394–5.

30. Abu-Lughod, *Arab Rediscovery*, p. 45.
31. Ibid., p. 72.
32. Tājir, *Ḥarakat al-tarjama*, pp. 84, 113.
33. Abu-Lughod, *Arab Rediscovery*, p. 55.
34. Ibid., p. 57.
35. Allen, *The Arabic Novel*, pp. 20–v c 1.
36. See Daniel Newman, 'The Arabic Literary Language'.
37. *Takhlīṣ*, pp. 159–60. Shaden Tageldin has argued that al-Ṭahṭāwī renders Arabic subservient to French, acceding to an inherent superiority of the French language because of its flexibility (Tageldin, *Disarming Words*, p. 134). However, I would argue that al-Ṭahṭāwī was more interested in the complex dynamics of borrowing across languages and genres than in reducing one signification system to the other.
38. See al-Ṭahṭāwī's introduction 'Muqaddimat al-mutarjim' to his book *Mawāqiᶜ al-aflāk fī waqāʾiᶜ Talīmāk*, in *al-Aᶜmāl al-kāmila li-Rifāᶜa Rāfiᶜ al-Ṭahṭāwī*, Muḥammad ʾAmāra (ed.), Volume 5 (Cairo: Dār al-shrūq, 2011), pp. 449–76, esp. pp. 453–54.
39. Moosa, *Origins*, p. 104.
40. See Moosa, *Origins*, note 56, p. 105.
41. Elkhadem, 'Early Precursors', p. 27.
42. *Origins*, p. 105. Samah Selim considers the popular translations of entertainment literature as another *nahḍa*, suggesting 'two intertwined literary *nahḍahs*' (see 'The Nahdah: Popular Fiction and the Politics of Translation', p. 71). In another text, she relates the popular translations of Arsène Lupin to the production of legal subjects in Cairo. See Samah Selim, 'Fiction and Colonial Identities: Arsène Lupin in Arabic', *Middle Eastern Literatures* 13(2) (2010): 191–210.
43. For another extensive list of popular translations, see Muḥammad Yūsuf Najm, *al-Qiṣṣa fī-l-adab al-Arabī al-ḥadīth (1870–1914)* [The Story in Modern Arabic Literature (1870–1914)], pp. 7–21.
44. See also al-Shayyāl, *Tārīkh al-tarjama*, p. 46.
45. For a more general record of the publications of the nineteenth century in Cairo, see ᶜĀyda Ibrāhīm Nāṣir's *Ḥarakat nashr al-kutub*.
46. Cachia, *An Overview*, p. 29.
47. Moosa, *Origins*, pp. 98–9.
48. Lajnat al-taʾlīf wa-l-tarjama wa-l-nashr (Committee of Writing, Translation, and Publishing), instituted in 1914, came together in Madrasat al-Muᶜallimīn

and established its own library, press, school, and magazine. The Committee promoted translations of literature and philosophy such as Aḥmad Luṭfī al-Sayyīd's translations of Aristotle's *Ethics* and *Politics*. Important publishing houses that specialised almost exclusively in literary translation in the early twentieth century included Dār al-kātib al-Miṣrī, Dār al-maᶜārif, and Dār al-hilāl.

49. Moosa, *Origins*, pp. 99–100.
50. Ibid., p. 100.
51. Cachia, 'Translations and Adaptations', p. 29.
52. Cairo: Maṭbaᶜat al-risāla.
53. Pierre Cachia notes, for example, the rhyming titles that recall 'the stylistic preferences of previous centuries', such as ᶜUthmān Jalāl's (1829–98) rhymed translation of *Pierre et Virginie* as *al-Amānī wa al-minna fī ḥadīth Qabūl wa Ward Janna*, '*Longings and Bestowal* or, more freely: Hope and Fulfillment in the Story of Qabul and Ward Jannah' (see Cachia, 'Translations and Adaptations', p. 36). For more on the Egyptianising influence of Jalāl's translations, see Carol Bardenstein's *Translation and Transformation in Modern Arabic Literature: The Indigenous Assertions of Muḥammad ᶜŪthmān Jalāl* (Wiesbaden: Harrassowitz Verlag, 2005).
54. p. 135.
55. Hafez, *Genesis*, pp. 85–8, 89.
56. Ibid., p. 90.
57. Ibid., p. 108.
58. Fayṣal Darrāj also describes the early Arabic novel as a 'half-bred' form (*hujīn*), another incomplete version of an anticipated mature form (see *Nazariyyat al-riwāya wa-l-riwāya al-ᶜArabiyya* [Theory of the Novel and the Arabic Novel], p. 144).
59. Badr, *Taṭawwur*, p. 129.
60. Ibid., p. 220.
61. Jacquemond, 'Translation and Cultural Hegemony', p. 141.
62. In fact, the first proposal for replacing *fuṣḥā* with *ᶜammiya* was by two British colonialists in Egypt, and it was received as a colonial ploy by the Egyptian literati. Cromer refused to extend the teaching of foreign languages to the kuttāb and village schools, and even though Saᶜd Zaghlūl changed the language of teaching to Arabic when he became minister of education in 1906, the masses still did not have enough influence on language change. Renovating the language, in other words, did not consider ways of making education more accessible to the masses. See Yousef, *Composing Egypt*, pp. 140–3.

63. Zaytūnī, *Ḥarakat*, p. 41.
64. Cf. Zaytūnī, *Ḥarakat*, p. 25.
65. Cf. Zaytūnī, *Ḥarakat*, p. 25. See *al-Jinān*, 1871, p. 177.
66. Cf. Zaytūnī, *Ḥarakat*, p. 26. See especially *'Al-lugha wa-l-ᶜaṣr'* [Language and the Times] (1897).
67. Zaytūnī, *Ḥarakat*, p. 27.
68. Cf. Zaytūnī, *Ḥarakat*, p. 28. See *Al-Muqtaṭaf*, 1908, Volume 33, p. 595.
69. Cf. Zaytūnī, *Ḥarakat*, p. 28. See Ṣarrūf, 'Al-Tarjama', p. 361.
70. Cf. Zaytūnī, *Ḥarakat*, p. 29.
71. Zaytūnī, *Ḥarakat*, p. 48.
72. Thomas Philipp, *Foundations of Arab Nationalism*, p. 79.
73. Al-Ṭahṭāwī, *Manāhij*, pp. 12–13, 21–2.
74. For more on al-Ṭahṭāwī's contribution to linguistic reform, see Mohammed Sawaie, 'Rifaᶜa Rafiᶜ al-Tahtawi and His Contribution to the Lexical Development of Modern Literary Arabic', *International Journal of Middle East Studies*, 32(3) (2000): 395–410.
75. Abu-Lughod, *Arab Rediscovery*, pp. 76–7.
76. Ibid., pp. 152–4.
77. Beirut: Dār al-thaqāfa wa-l-nashr wa-l-tawzīᶜ, 1977, p. 28.
78. Some important Egyptian papers include ᶜAbd Allāh Abu al-Suᶜūd's *Wādī al-nīl* (the Nile Valley) (established 1867) and Ibrāhīm al-Muwaylīḥī's *Nuzhat al-afkār* (promenade of thoughts) (established 1869) (see Elisabeth Kendall, 'Between Politics and Literature: Journals in Alexandria and Istanbul at the End of the Nineteenth Century', in Leila Tarazi Fawaz and C. A. Bayly with the collaboration of Robert Ilbert (eds) *Modernity and Culture: From the Mediterranean to the Indian Ocean* (New York: Columbia University, 2002), pp. 330–42, p. 335). Perhaps the most important figure here is the Egyptian ᶜAbd Allāh al-Nadīm whose popular journalism radically changed the Arabic language (for more, see Hafez, *Genesis*, pp. 113–29).
79. For more on the journals, see John Heyworth-Dunne 'Printing and Translations', *Journal of the Royal Asiatic Society* (1940): 325–49, p. 332), and Stephen Sheehi, 'Arabic Literary-Scientific Journals: Precedence for Globalization and the Creation of Modernity', *Comparative Studies of South Asia, Africa and the Middle East*, 25(2) (2005): 438–48.
80. See 'al-Riwāyāt al-mutarjama', pp. 53–5.
81. Moosa, *Origins*, p. 98.
82. Cited in Selim, 'The People's Entertainment', p. 69.

83. Literature written in *fuṣḥā* by both groups maintained a sense of its locality. See, for example, Sasson Somekh, 'Biblical Echoes in Modern Arabic Literature', *Journal of Arabic Literature* 25(1–2) (March–June 1995): 186–200.
84. *Ilyādhat Hūmirūs – muᶜarraba naẓman wa-ᶜalayhā sharḥ tarīkhī adabī* (Cairo: Maṭbaᶜat al-hilāl 1904), p. 101.
85. *Ilyādhat Hūmirūs*, p. 166.
86. Ibid., p. 176.
87. Ibid., p. 144.
88. Ibid., p. 158. In this case, Sulaymān al-Bustānī articulates an important attitude towards literature: namely, that it could be history and truth. Such truth, though, is found in the Western canon that he and others imitate. The Western classic becomes the truth-text, while we find more resistance to this equivalence with the Muslim translators considered in this book.

# 2

# Plagiarised Prophecy in the Romantic Works of al-Manfalūṭī, al-ᶜAqqād and al-Māzinī

> If the prophetic word . . . makes of the prophet a historical character burdened with heavy temporal weight, it seems nonetheless tied essentially to a momentary interruption of history, to a history having become for a moment the impossibility of history.
>
> Maurice Blanchot, *The Book to Come*

> We know of no orations [*khutba*] except by the Arabs and Persians. . . . The Greeks have philosophy and the craft of logic, but the author of the Logic [Aristotle] himself . . . was not described as eloquent . . . [As for] the [speech] of the Arabs it is all extemporaneity and spontaneity, as though it is [simply] inspiration.
>
> Al-Jāḥiẓ (d. 868/9), *al-Bayān wa-l-tabyīn*

In the introduction to *Fī Sabīl al-tāj* (1920) (For the Sake of the Crown), an adaptation of François Coppée's 1895 play *Pour la Couronne,* dedicated to Saᶜd Zaghlūl (1859–1927) – leader of the nationalist Wafd party – Muṣṭafā Luṭfī al-Manfalūṭī (1876–1924) describes art's 'didactic' mission to explain his choice of translation. He relies on the promising analogy between the Balkan people's resistance to Ottoman invasion and Egypt's 1919 Revolution. Al-Manfalūṭī uses the play to model historical resistance and draws a parallel between the Balkan king and Zaghlūl in their quest to unite the people under *kalimat al-umma* (the nation's word).[1] However, in his contemporaries' view, al-Manfalūṭī's work was too detached from political reality. He was both a bad romantic and a bad translator. The realists found his writing irrelevant and the romantics deemed it not 'subjective' enough to modernise Arabic literature.

In the introduction to *al-Dīwān fī al-naqd wa-l-adab* (1921) (A Book on Criticism and Literature), which he co-wrote with Ibrāhīm ᶜAbd al-Qādir al-Māzinī (1890–1949), ᶜAbbās Maḥmūd al-ᶜAqqād (1889–1964) muses that 'a true poet does not need to show what objects look like but to express his peculiar mode of perception',[2] a view distinctly opposed to al-Manfalūṭī's neoclassical, ornate style. The two poets make a claim to an earlier modernity. Much like the later Syrian poet Adonis,[3] they recall classical Arabic literature's elasticity and openness to foreign influence in pushing their modernist agenda: namely, the free adaptation of European literature to expand the Arabic language, literary themes, and generic forms.[4] Al-ᶜAqqād, as founding member of the Dīwān group and a poet well versed in English literature, commends the romantic ideal of the poet as prophet with a vision, an eye to what cannot be seen by others, coincident with the pre-Islamic idea of poet as seer.[5] His portrayal of the poet-prophet appears in essays in *Saᶜāt bayn al-kutub* (1914) (Hours Spent among Books) and *Murājaᶜāt fī al-ᵓādāb wa-l-funūn* (1966) [Thoughts on Literature and the Arts]. Al-Māzinī corroborates al-ᶜAqqād's view of the poet's prophetic mission, translating Percy Shelley's famous dictum on the poet as prophet and legislator (in 'A Defence of Poetry') in his book *al-Shiᶜr: wasāᵓituhu wa ghāyātuhu* (Poetry: Its Means and Ends) (1915).[6] For both romantics, the poet legislates the new in Arabic poetry as self-expression in a simple language that rejects imitation (*taqlīd*) of classical Arabic verse.[7] In the heated debates between neo-classical poets like Aḥmad Shawqī and modernisers like Khalīl Muṭrān and the Dīwan group, romanticism mobilised the quest for the poet-prophet destined to lead Egypt out of its poetic slumber and into a *modern* literary aesthetic. In the introduction to the *Dīwān*, al-ᶜAqqād attacks 'imitators' like Shawqī who are still rehearsing the classical style and have yet to transition to the new style of *transparent* expression, whereby language succumbs to the immediacy of feeling. However, much like al-Manfalūṭī's adaptations, al-ᶜAqqād's and al-Māzinī's 'peculiar mode of perception' develops through plagiaristic translation. Al-ᶜAqqād translated British and American literature, notably the poetry of Thomas Hardy, Shakespeare, Edward Burns, and William Blake, and al-Māzinī translated Charles Dickens, Percy Shelley, and others. Both adapted the originals freely, claiming parts to be their own, and defended themselves by dismissing the seriousness of the crime given the urgent task of *liberating* Arabic literature.[8]

Adapting previous texts to new contexts is an established Arabic literary tradition; after all, pre-Islamic poetry became primary material for later Abbasid studies of literary figures, to establish a grammar for poetic (and occasionally Qurʾānic) interpretation. Distinct from a Western priveleging of originality, Arabic literature continued to derive authority from a recognised model: it began as repetition, and rewriting was testament to the author's skill.[9] If in the Western tradition, translation was derivative and secondary within an Abrahamic fall from grace, for Muslim scholars, the Qurʾān is a miraculous text that is impossible to translate perfectly but that provides the rules of *bayān* (form) and good writing. The measure of 'good' literature is the creative appropriation of those rules. Rewriting is thus constitutive of the tradition, and this iterability persists in translation with the Dīwān poets and al-Manfalūṭī as plagiaristic adaptation.[10]

Al-ᶜAqqād's and al-Māzinī's translations are interesting models in that they claim to be rewriting tradition while engraining themselves fully in the very logic of this tradition. The Dīwān poets' agenda recalls the attempts of Abbasid poets Abī Tammām and Ibn al-Rumī to correlate poetic vision with meaning. It further recalls classical Arabic criticism that also emphasised poetic unity, essence as opposed to rhetorical exaggeration, and poetic theft.[11] Thus, their 'modernist' aspirations were not as cut off from the tradition as they had once hoped, and their emphasis on subjective representation is *not* solipsistic but closer to imitation than modernisation, for they also criticised and praised others in their poetry.[12] Even their plagiarised translations pretend to a recognisable cultural model while translating romantic ideas into their new context. Ironically, however, the polemical al-ᶜAqqād would attack other writers for 'stealing' from Western literature and not recognise his own theft.[13] The Dīwān group's use of translation works against the discontinuity that they longed for between classical and modern Arabic literature. Rather, their plagiarised adaptations, meant to mediate Arabic poetry's radical rebirth, return to the classical tradition to make a case for the poet's subjectivity as organising principle of the literary work. The two poets' attacks on al-Manfalūṭī are telling: although they reject his style as exaggerated and artificial, they are still drawn to how his work stages the poet's feelings and invites the readers' *emotional* response. Al-Manfalūṭī's style is iconic, for no other writer stirred as much emotion in the reader. Moreover, all three authors indulge in plagiarism, advertising translated works as their original creations.

At the age of twelve, Al-Manfalūṭī was sent to study at al-Azhar for ten years. In 1897, the khedive ᶜAbbās II imprisoned him for one of his poems: he supported Muḥammad ᶜAbduh's reformist ideas and took his side against the Egyptian government. In 1907, he began publishing articles in the newspaper *al-Muᵓayyad* (The Advocate), later collected in *al-Usbūᶜiyyāt* (The Weeklies) and finally as *al-Naẓarāt* (Contemplations) in three volumes, published in 1910, 1912, and 1920. He was known as Imām al-bayān (Leader of Eloquence) and the press named him Amīr al-bayān (Prince of Eloquence).[14] His other collection *al-ᶜAbarāt* (1915) (The Tears) has four 'translations' of longer French novels and four of his original short stories.[15] Aḥmad Haykal describes his unique style as '*ṭariqat al-Manfalūṭī fi-l-kitāba*' (Al-Manfalūṭī's way of writing).[16] Al-Manfalūṭī's 'translations' of French literature should more appropriately be called adaptations, since he did not know any French and freely adapted the original. He describes his translation method best when he explains how his friend Muḥammad Fuᵓād Bek Kamāl read him an Arabic rendition of Jean-Baptiste Alphonse Karr's *Sous les Tilleuls* as *Majdūlīn, taḥt Ẓilāl al-Zayrafūn* (Magdeleine, Under the Zizyphus Tree) (1912). Al-Manfalūṭī rewrote the novel from memory and made changes according to *potential* coincidences between the two narratives.[17] It may seem completely inappropriate to call his adaptations translations, but in this context, they rest midway between 'domesticating translation', which compulsively removes any trace of foreignness, and 'foreignising translation', which celebrates the original's foreignness in the target language. Al-Manfalūṭī's adaptations are simultaneously domesticating and foreignising: they address the Egyptian readership with alien themes. They still maintain a relationship – albeit a very tenuous one – to the original as they are clearly not native expressions, but they change its references and form to produce their own. These interventions into the original produce al-Manfalūṭī's idiomatic translations, texts that translate a foreign idiomatic structure into Arabic and remain neither fully foreign nor fully Arabic texts.[18]

Although al-ᶜAqqād was more acquainted with European languages than al-Manfalūṭī, he was a self-taught writer who went to the village *kuttāb* at the age of six, and then elementary school, ending his formal education in 1903. Al-ᶜAqqād was a Wafdist member of the Chamber of Deputies in 1930 and was imprisoned once by Ismāᶜīl Ṣidqī's dictatorial government for his threats to King Fuᵓād and allegiance to the 1923 constitution. In jail for nine months, he taught himself French and joined the Saᶜdist party, becoming senator in 1944. Two years earlier in 1942, al-ᶜAqqād had begun writing his fourteen-volume *ᶜAbqariyyāt* (Accounts of Genius) series on historical religious figures, including Christ, Abraham, and Muḥammad. He wrote only one novel, *Sāra* (1938), but it was not a success. In 1954, al-Aqqād published a two-volume collection of translations of world literature (*Jawāᵓiz al-adab al-ᶜālamiyya*). In 1958, he published two books of literary criticism, *al-Taᶜrīf bi-Shaksbīr* (An Introduction to Shakespeare) and *al-Lugha al-shāᶜira* (Poetic Language). Al-ᶜAqqād died on 12 March 1964 in Cairo after earning himself the title of cultural icon of modern Egypt. Al-Māzinī was more formally educated than al-ᶜAqqād and also a more prolific translator, although his references to Western literature were mostly adapted and uncited. He was editor of *al-Siyāsa* from 1926 to 1930, *al-Ittiḥād* from 1932 to 1934, and *al-Balāgh* (The Report) for the last fifteen years of his life. Although he opposed the Wafd and was once tried for attacking the late Saᶜd Zaghlūl, he never developed a clear political stand. He gave up writing poetry in 1917, turned exclusively to prose, and became known for his novel *Ibrāhīm al-kātib* (1931), a pseudo-autobiographical fictional account of his life as a writer.

Al-ᶜAqqād and al-Māzinī's approach to romanticism differs radically from al-Manfalūṭī's, most significantly when it comes to the choice of genre. Boutros Hallaq identifies a *gibrāno-manfalūṭien* current of Arab romanticism, which came out of both Gibran's and al-Manfalūṭī's writing and echoed the German group Iéna's (1799–1802) romantic thought. For one, the Arab romantic current with Gibran and al-Manfalūṭī approached literature as essentially prophetic, not in the religious sense, but in the sense of being capable of 'making and recreating another world'.[19] Second, they reject the division between poetry and prose and consider all literature poetic (*la poésie*). If Iéna was an attempt to surpass and recreate Greek antiquity, so this Arab romantic current wants to measure up to Semitic antiquity as represented by the Old and New Testaments and the Qurᵓān, to create its own modernity.[20]

Oscillating between the essay, short fiction, and poetry, al-Manfalūṭī's work was the most resonant with the reading public.[21] His remarkable popularity invited hostility across the literary spectrum from the realists, traditionalists, and modernist romantics.[22] Ṭāhā Ḥusayn detailed his admiration for and repulsion from al-Manfalūṭī's style in six articles from April to May of 1910, accusing him of superficial expression and theft from other Arab writers.[23] In '*Adab al-Manfalūṭī*' (Al-Manfalūṭī's Literature) included in *Murājᶜāt fī al-Ādāb* (1966), al-ᶜAqqād praises al-Manfalūṭī for being closer to the 'modern free style of writing' and liberating Arabic writing from its traditional rhetorical constraints.[24] But he considers him a skilled composer (*muʾallif*) not a writer (*kātib*), because a writer's words are organic, an extension of his being, so that 'in every writer there is something of the nature of prophecy because he carries a "special" message'.[25] Al-Manfalūṭī is not a prophet with a message, but a craftsman of an ornament that is inevitably lost in translation. But since all language promises loss in translation when it intends to communicate, as Walter Banjamin tells us, al-ᶜAqqād's attack loses ground. Al-ᶜAqqād concedes, however, al-Manfalūṭī's influence: despite his affected sentiment and typical characters who model absolute virtue or vice, he was an instrumental transitional figure, providing readers with the poetic resonance they longed for.[26]

In volume two of *al-Dīwān* (1921), in '*Uslūb al-Manfalūṭī*' (Al-Manfalūṭī's Style), al-Māzinī dismisses al-Manfalūṭī's short stories as generically troubled, simultaneously autobiographical, mimetic, and incredible, and thus impossible material for *correct* literary criticism.[27] Al-Māzinī's critique of al-Manfalūṭī's style hinges on two important points: the need to keep genres uncontaminated in producing sound literary criticism and the impact of al-Manfalūṭī's style on its readers. Al-Māzinī scathingly criticises *Al-ᶜAbarāt*'s 'feminine' style, the worst that could happen to *adab* as it fakes the feeling and its expression.[28] Advocating for verisimilitude in modern literature, al-Māzinī conflates al-Manfalūṭī's person with his narrator. Both become unreliable because the sentiment does not suit the incident (*al-ḥāditha*) nor the person her environment. Al-Māzinī's aesthetic measure is the coincidence between the stories and the author's real life. As Mattityahu Peled has noted, he could not accept 'that in a literary narrative absolute validity must be attributed to the narrator's mimetic discourse'.[29] Referring to al-Manfalūṭī's original story 'The Orphan' (*al-Yatīm*), al-Māzinī faults the former for being too particular in his descriptions, making the story unbelievable.[30] Al-Manfalūṭī's verbosity, his 'effeminate' style, is just empty repetition.[31] Al-Māzinī berates al-Manfalūṭī's lack of verisimilitude for its unforgivable disconnection from the context. Significantly, the realists will hurl the same accusation at al-Manfalūṭī.

However, al-Manfalūṭī presents his translations as originals, making it difficult to make a claim to his verisimilitude in style and content. His work's popularity celebrates an accessible language that speaks directly to the average reader. Gibb finds *al-Naẓarāt* 'down to the present the most widely read book in modern Arabic literature',[32] and Roger Allen describes al-Manfalūṭī's 'curious blend of Islamic modernism, an awareness of the classical heritage and anti-western sentiments' significant only as a milestone on the way to the novel's simpler diction.[33] Set in remote places, al-Manfalūṭī's fictions were a great source of identification for Egyptian readers in the early twentieth century, and his position in this polemic is noteworthy inasmuch as what the romantics and the New-School realists dismissed as 'unrealistic' is nonetheless what the readership found the most relevant. Al-Manfalūṭī's 'cult of emotionalism'[34] appealed to the masses, the majority that was still immersed in the 'reality of unyielding taboos, especially in the most sensitive areas of human existence'.[35] Translation is the missing link in the study of this polemic, since all three writers engaged in thieving when rendering foreign texts in Arabic. The word *mutarjam* (translated) appears repeatedly in their works but never denotes intralinguistic translation. For al-Manfalūṭī, *mutarjam* implies bad expression (and bad translation) while for al-ᶜAqqād and al-Māzinī it is a derogatory reference to *taqlīd* or imitation as derivative. Never associated with translation, the adjective *mutarjam* nonetheless organises the discussion on verisimilitude in representational narrative.

## In Context: al-Manfalūṭī's Successful Failures

In *al-Risāla* (1937) (The Message), Aḥmad Ḥasan al-Zayyāt describes al-Manfalūṭī's style as a necessary transition and a *corrective* to the Mahjar writers' 'awkwardly constructed . . . distorted forms'. Al-Manfalūṭī's style resonated with the literati, al-Zayyāt continues, for through him, all readers 'saw the writers of this *new* art in a way they had never seen them before . . . So they craved it, just as homeless wanderers crave the only sweet source they find.'[36] Al-Zayyāt conveniently forgets al-Manfalūṭī's plagiaristic translations and presents the latter as a prophetic figure, heralding a new Egyptian art that reconciles East and West.[37] Al-Zayyāt is almost alone in his judgement, for many of al-Manfalūṭī's contemporaries perceived him as a 'bad' translator, because he chose to translate sentimental, escapist French fiction and not because he could not read French. Even his critics did not address his stories as translations; they read them as his original works and found them alarmingly disengaged from Egyptian reality after the 1919 Revolution. Al-Manfalūṭī's popularity polarised the literary debate between the self-proclaimed realists such as ᶜĪsā ᶜUbayd and self-declared romantics like al-ᶜAqqād and al-Māzinī. His romantic style domesticated the imported aesthetics of European romanticism through popular didacticism.[38] This general assessment of al-Manfalūṭī's work leaves out questions of genre, readership, and the expectation of literary verisimilitude.

Just like al-Manfalūṭī, al-Māzinī produced 'free translations of English romantic poetry . . . attributing them to himself'.[39] When ᶜAbd al-Raḥmān Shukrī (1886–1958) – the third member of the Dīwān group – accused al-Māzinī of plagiarism, al-Māzinī retorted that due to his weak memory, even in adopting William Wordsworth's and Matthew Arnold's poetic projects as his own, he failed to give readers 'understanding and illumination of their own lives and the lives of others'.[40] Al-Māzinī's poetic agenda unfolded in plagiarism: in *al-Shiᶜr*, he includes an uncited translation of the Shelleyian description of poet as legislator and prophet. The poet can see the future 'from behind the present' (*min warāᵓ al-ḥāḍir*); he is the messenger of revolution in thought, 'the priest of divine descent and apostle of holy inspiration [*waḥy*] . . . the mirror in which are reflected the . . . thick shadows of the future projected onto the present'.[41] Removing some lines, he disagrees with Karl Wilhelm Friedrich Schlegel's view of poetry as mirror of eternal thoughts, since poetry can only be the mirror of contemporary realities, expressing the poet's unique historical moment. The only semblance of an eternal or universal truth that a poet can have derives from his sincerity of emotion. Al-Māzinī and al-ᶜAqqād both find a sincerity of feeling in Shelley that lends itself to their modernising projects while recalling the pre-Islamic poet-seer. Al-Māzinī now insists on an aesthetic of feeling rather than form; the poetic voice rises above the collective in its search for words adequate to the sentiment.[42] Citing Edmund Burke, he likens the poet's access to truth to God's ability because the purpose of religion is the same as the task of poetry, to elevate people to the appropriate moral standards.[43] Al-Māzinī uses the adjective *mutarjam* (translated) pejoratively to describe the 'imitators' who resort to other poets' words to communicate their own feelings. Denying his own complicity in translation as theft, he also denies his debt to the tradition.

Al-ᶜAqqād also articulates the modern poet's prophetic role in relation to both translation and tradition, in an entry on Muṣṭafā Ṣādiq al-Rāfiᶜī's *ᵓIᶜjāz al-Qurᵓān* (1928) (The Miracle of the Qurᵓan) in *Sāᶜāt bayn al-kutub*. Al-ᶜAqqād distinguishes between impossible and miraculous, and relates genius and prophecy (here in a secular sense) to the aptitude of poets, specifically to Shakespeare, who is capable of producing poetic prophecy precisely because he is inimitable.[44] For al-ᶜAqqād, the status of genius is tied to emulation. In *ᶜAbqariyyat Muḥammad*, the prophet of Islam is also presented as a genius to be emulated through embodying the word he left behind. However, Shakespeare is substitutable but Muḥammad is only imitable.[45] This new poetic function must undo the natural inclination towards rhetorical mastery, and move naturally towards a national style, for in this age of 'humanity', all styles should seem natural and not sound '*mutarjama*', like translations of foreign thoughts or sentiments.[46] But such universal humanism is precisely poetic. Generally averse to the novel, al-ᶜAqqād's prophetic writer is a struggling poet because his 'metres and rhymes are too narrow to comprise the aims of a poet the locks of whose soul have opened, and who has read Western poetry'. Western poetic metres are 'so flexible that they are able to enclose within them what the Arab poet is able to phrase only in prose'.[47] Al-ᶜAqqād accused al-Manfalūṭī's style of being too ornate and disconnected from reality, but finds that his sentimentality could empower poetic subjectivity in modern Arabic poetry. Al-Māzinī, on the other hand, finds no measure of truth in al-Manfalūṭī's work. Al-ᶜAqqād's and al-Māzinī's poetry, however, also remains disconnected from Egyptian reality.[48] In their critique, prose emerges as a conflictual site of representation while poetry is beyond the immediate context, its subject emanating from the poetic self.

The other group who attacked al-Manfalūṭī's lack of verisimilitude was the self-appointed realists who professed Luṭfī Jumᶜa's *madhhab al-ḥaqīqa* (the way of truth). They went the way of prose but encountered the problem of language: good *adab* used classical Arabic, emulating the Qurᵓān. However, representation of the real required new words and potentially the colloquial dialect. Some writers, trying to compensate for the lack of correspondence between classical Arabic and modern reality, used moral didacticism.[49] The point was to bind art to life, the main project of the New School Group (Jamāᶜat al-madrasa al-ḥadītha), which came together in 1917 in Cairo as a reading group.[50] One of its major figures, ᶜĪsā ᶜUbayd, was also its least typical member: the only one to insist on using *fuṣḥā* and adopting the mimetic methods of French realism.[51] Nonetheless, ᶜUbayd's articulate theory on narrative realism, form, and function is symptomatic of the realist agenda at the time, and he develops it polemically in yet another attack on al-Manfalūṭī's sentimentality and its disconnection from reality. ᶜUbayd prescribes psychological analysis as the proper antidote, and translates Arab literary realism as *madhhab al-ḥaqāᵓiq* (the way of truths),[52] in the introduction to his short stories collection, *Iḥsān Hānim* (1923) (Mrs Ihsan):

> The purpose of fiction must be the investigation of life and its sincere portrayal as it appears to us. [The writer must collect] the greatest number of observations and documents so that the story becomes a kind of 'dossier' in which the reader can peruse the history of an individual's life or a page from that history. The writer uses this individual history as a means of studying the secrets of human nature and the hidden recesses of the obscure human heart . . . the function of the writer is to dissect the human soul and to record his discoveries.[53]

Realism assumes no mediation, echoing al-Māzinī's critique of the lack of verisimilitude in al-Manfalūṭī's short story '*al-Yatīm*'. Because al-Manfalūṭī is not trained (by his Azharite education) for literary observation of detail and psychological probing of characters, ᶜUbayd continues, he fails to distinguish any of them with a unique self. In his translation of Bernardin de Saint-Pierre's *Paul et Virginie* (1923), al-Manfalūṭī privileges the setting of the lovers' encounter to its intimate details, so he has to exaggerate the natural scene because he is not concerned with presenting universal human ideals.[54] For ᶜUbayd, literary representation expresses ideals when it meticulously addresses all the details that define any situation. ᶜUbayd's intellectual revolution would also destroy the canon and repeat 'the revolution of Victor

Hugo against institutional literature, and the one Zola called for against idealism and in favor of adopting realism as the literature of tomorrow'.[55] In ᶜUbayd's literary history, al-Manfalūṭī becomes a *translated* romantic symbol, a necessary milestone to be remembered and quickly forgotten.

But ᶜUbayd also fails to address the Egyptian milieu when in his sample short story '*Iḥsān Hānim*', a nine-page demonstration of 'dossier' realism, the main character, Iḥsān, writes a letter to her friend Dawlat explaining her ailing marriage: 'For you to know the reasons, you should know the old and modern influences that make up my personality.'[56] Iḥsān and Dawlat had learned love from reading existential novels, but alas, their 'fathers do not know pure love' or modern psychology, and so Iḥsān longs for the coming revolution that will liberate Egyptian women from Eastern traditions.[57] Ironically, Iḥsān's imported (translated) ideals keep her with her husband, despite her unhappiness and his abuse. Existential ideals are both radical in their novelty and certain in their unattainability, and they end up keeping Iḥsān in place, not *liberating* her. What kind of Egyptian woman would Iḥsān Hānim represent? Samah Selim finds the New School's narrator standing outside the collective, critiquing it from that comfortable (permissible) distance.[58] ᶜUbayd's abstracted social collective is more 'escapist' than the islands of al-Manfalūṭī's translations: while he mimics the form of Western realism, he fails to produce its content in a way that resonates with the Egyptian milieu he wanted to represent.

Between popular[59] and 'socially-engaged' literature was the reforming intellectuals' moral agenda. While popular narratives played on 'the formal act of deception' to seduce the masses, Samah Selim notes, the new realist fiction promised social and individual truth.[60] Genealogical accounts have taken the realists at their word, dismissing the popular fiction of al-Manfalūṭī and others as sentimental escapism following the failure of the ᶜUrābī Revolution (1879–82), as opposed to the more 'artistic' works of ᶜUbayd and Muḥammad Ḥusayn Haykal.[61] Popular fiction's powerful appeal is inconsequential because it was based on a 'bad' form of translation from Western literature. Translated entertainment fiction typically does not mention the original author, removes unfamiliar details like dialogue and introduces a significant number of foreign words that quickly become popular currency. These insertions produce what Ṭāhā Badr calls a 'crisis in expression' that threatened the precise reference (*dalāla*) of a word to a thing. At al-Azhar, language study was restricted to Qurʾānic interpretation and not extended to artistic expression, leaving writers with a paralysed diction.[62] The masses, not privileged enough to receive an Azharite education, turned away from the Arabic canon to popular literature. But Badr is only able to dismiss the entertainment novel if he accepts the New School's realism, and 'the ontology produced by nationalism', as Selim describes it, that forces individual reality into the discursively imagined nation.[63] For it is only in the artistic novel, Badr writes, that the individual finally develops a relationship to place, because the writer stops relying on inspiration (*ilhām*).[64] But *nahḍawī* realism replicated colonial nationalism's dominant attitudes towards class, gender, and culture in mimicking the nineteenth-century European novel's language.[65] This early failure of realism is not due only to the ingress of a ready-made, foreign modernity into colonial Egypt; it also points to the perils of importing a form that is a specific product of a European historical moment. Even if realist techniques of representation can be replicated in Arabic prose, the original context that produced these techniques cannot be reproduced in translation.

In choosing remote settings, al-Manfalūṭī's adaptations of Chateaubriand and Saint-Pierre do not fall into the pitfalls of realism in translation. While Badr pits *ilhām* against *nahḍawī* realist ethos in the history of the Arabic novel, al-Manfalūṭī's recreational literature uses *khayāl* or imagination to produce a kind of literature that begins from translation as appropriation but returns to address the Egyptian milieu. His translation aesthetic also engages the untranslatable, when it acknowledges that there are aspects of the original that cannot be rendered in Arabic. If we disregard the untranslatable in al-Manfalūṭī's writing, we misread the significance of his translations. Al-Manfalūṭī may have 'misread' French romanticism and diluted its professed commitment to the Revolution, but such misreading is far from a failure. Rather, translation confronts us with the fact that even if the content can be translated fully and transmitted as is, the context is impossible to transfer. Would better translations have led to a better literary revolution? This correlation can only work if we believe context is in fact transferable, in a historical account that purposefully ignores 'bad' translations. Al-Manfalūṭī's translations expose precisely this untranslatability of context and end up rewriting the original rather than reproducing it in the receiving culture.

Al-Manfalūṭī's translation theory recognises its own impossibility, while simultaneously confronting its necessity. In bearing witness to the originals, al-Manfalūṭī's translations overcome the paradoxes of an imported realism that assumes we can conveniently reproduce European realist aesthetics in Arabic literature. His appropriation of a prophetic authorial position through *khayāl* turns untranslatability into his own political project.

## Prophetic *Khayāl* and Idiomatic Translation in *al-Naẓarāt*

Right before naming untranslatability 'the defining characteristic of [Arabic] poetry' through the examples of al-Ḥarīrī's and al-Hamadhānī's *maqāmāt*, Abdelfattah Kilito opens his book *Lan Tatakallama Lughatī* (Thou Shalt Not Speak My Language) with al-Manfalūṭī, who tried but failed to mask his illicit affair with European literature. Kilito names al-Manfalūṭī the poet of sadness, an origin to be emulated and then rejected by modern Arab writers; moreover, in forgetting the original authors, al-Manfalūṭī becomes 'Edmond Rostand, Bernardin de Saint-Pierre . . . and Chateaubriand'.[66] Stephen Sheehi is right to critique Kilito's orientalist reading of al-Manfalūṭī and other *nahḍawī* writers as the romantic bearers of novelty.[67] However, Kilito's reading of al-Manfalūṭī points to a more complex relationship to translation in the *nahḍa*: al-Manfalūṭī's translations *celebrate* the Arab translator's simultaneous identification with and alienation from the European master text.

Translation as appropriation becomes a sophisticated theory of literary expression in al-Manfalūṭī's introduction to the first volume of *al-Naẓarāt*, which begins by addressing his potential emulators: since his originality comes from resisting slavish imitation, he cannot be an example to be emulated. He establishes himself in the line of prophets, advising the reader not to succumb to imitation and claiming, like al-Māzinī in defending his plagiarism, that what has enabled his originality is his weak memory and 'its inability to retain but little of the things [he] read that passed [him] by', for he would read 'whatever God willed [him] to read. Then [he] would quickly forget it and all that would be left in [his] memory was the beauty of its traces . . . and its musicality.'[68] In 'La Littérature selon Manfalūṭī' (2003), Boutros Hallaq explains how al-Manfalūṭī's weak memory, in a text full of literary clichés, confirms his surpassing of the ancients, as the narrator receives his vision '*de plus loin, ressortant au divin*' (from further away, emerging from the divine).[69]

In my analysis, translation, rather than the divine, becomes this '*loin*' from which al-Manfalūṭī derives his prophetic vocation. His task of translation is not derivative or secondary but original in its permissible theft: what remain with him from the original text are only traces that are then rewritten to replace the original. Instead of *ilhām* or inspiration, which the New School writers found deceptive, al-Manfalūṭī invokes *khayāl* or imagination.

*Khayāl* establishes al-Manfalūṭī's claim to prophecy as it allows him to transcend the given text and present something coming to him from an *other* origin. Throughout the introduction, it becomes more and more difficult to distinguish between imagination and translation, which intersect in the term *khayāl*. His Azharite education confirms the haunting presence of the sacred text. However, in replacing the divine with the translated text as displaced origin, al-Manfalūṭī translates the sacred into Agamben's profane – in other words, he replaces the divine as source with the unnamed original text, thus profaning the origin of the prophetic word. This new form of prophecy is not divine. Rather, it usurps the prophet's position for its own political ends: rewriting the received original texts and transmitting them to a receiving community. His translations are profane in that they empty the sacred forms of prophetic writing and re-inscribe them within a *contingent* prophetic mission – the situated act of literary reading and not of religious interpretation. For *khayāl* is an aesthetic experience that enables a departure from the self: 'I felt as though I had exchanged myself for another . . . so I started to see things in a different way.'[70] He continues, 'it seemed to me [*khuyyila ilayya*] that I had moved from this world that I was in to another one of history's transient worlds, and so I witness [*ashhadu*] with my own eyes those beautiful epochs'.[71] '*Khuyyila*' is the passive form of the verb '*khayyala*' or 'to make believe'. He is made to believe that he is being transported into another time – his particular experience becomes de-individualised into a general one and his utterances gain credibility in supplying truth. The verb '*ashhadu*' comes from the verb '*shahada*', meaning to witness: not only does this transportation come to him (from the outside and not necessarily from the divine), but he is also a direct witness to it.[72] The author is now both prophet and visionary, witnessing different epochs and recording his visions in prose.[73] The translated text figures as the impression's displaced source.[74]

Significantly, what most advocates of realism failed to see is that al-Manfalūṭī uses his new definition of author as visionary to rewrite the education he received at al-Azhar. The Azharites intervene between him and his love of literature as a father intervenes to control his son's appetites, treating his love affair with literature as an illicit sexual relationship.[75] After all, the Azharites could not read the Qur'ān without the literary inheritance that provided them with the terms for religious interpretation. For al-Manfalūṭī, literature precedes the real world, and religious interpretation is made possible through literary aesthetics.[76] The Azharites' rejection of this debt leads them to frantic interpretation (*ta'wīl*), for when the tight bond (or knot) between words and their meanings loosened, 'every word had possibly infinite meanings in their [the Azharites'] opinion, so that not one of them negated the other's interpretation' and the 'boundary between truth and metaphor, and truth and the imagination [*khayāl*] dissolved'.[77]

How is al-Manfalūṭī's prophetic imagination as truth different from the Azharites' equally tenuous claim to truth? The answer is his *khayāl*: imagination only makes the message more transmittable, but *khayāl* ensures that the message is truth itself. *Khayāl* 'has the greatest influence on the make-up of human society and makes it possible for society to conform to the image the imagination produces of it'.[78] This is not, however, a predetermined poetic design; rather, it guards against al-Manfalūṭī's main fear that in times of war and occupation, literary language would lose all practical and political significance. Under Ottoman imperialism and British colonial rule and with the residual legacy of the French occupation, how does an author write when language betrays her at every step? When meaning can so easily be influenced by the language of an occupying presence, how does one ensure that the language she speaks is hers? For al-Manfalūṭī, once words lose immediate reference, the social landscape is completely unsettled, and human relations become dysfunctional.[79]

To guard against chaos, al-Manfalūṭī substitutes translation for expression, so that a bad translation becomes synonymous with weak literary expression. He understood the colonial tongue's threat, even though he did not speak it. An advocate of translation and imposter in the foreign tongue, he nonetheless insists that the Arabic language should not succumb to the former's demands; as a result, he warns against literal translation subduing the native tongue. Literal translation inserts a foreign, alien body into the translated text and compromises the unmediated relationship between word and meaning. He uses '*mutarjim*' in both senses of translator and interpreter. Al-Manfalūṭī has a radical view of literal translation, as potentially bringing about the nation's doom (*halāk*). As the anointed one, the prophet of this new literature, al-Manfalūṭī gives his thanks to God first and to *adab* second for saving him from this doom. Where Benjamin wants translation to forgo communication, al-Manfalūṭī presents his language as an invisible vessel that transmits the truth of his imagination, the moral destined for the reader. Just as language is meant to be a transparent representation of the idea, the original is incidental. The translation thus becomes the primary text, such that the original, like the linguistic vehicle, is an empty shape that finds its actual form in the translation. He compares convoluted and complex forms of expression to literal translations that favour content to rhetoric, damaging the Arabic language in the process. The bad writer dresses up his inadequate thoughts in complicated structures, just like 'a foreigner who thinks that the Arabic language is . . . letters and words, . . . so his speech sounds like literal [*ḥarfiyya*] translations in Arabic'.[80]

The bad translator blames the untranslatability of modern imaginings or spectres (*al-khayālāt al-ḥadītha*) on the lack of appropriate Arabic words:

> As though he [the translator] thinks that meanings and thoughts are plans and sections . . . this is for the East and that for the West . . . [and] finds these meanings in his foreign language attached to their original garments [*athwābihā al-ᵓaṣlīya*]. When he wants to relate these meanings to his Arab readers. . . he is unable to remove the garments [*athwābahā al-lāṣiqa*] attached to the original expression. Instead he copied it as it is, except for exchanging one letter for another and one meaning for another.[81]

Bad translations into Arabic remain too close to the originals and polarise the duality of East and West. Literality (read fidelity) in translation disables the process of finding the right Arabic idiom that could reproduce the original in Arabic. Al-Manfalūṭī puts forth his version of idiomatic translation as the good kind of translation that will ensure that the target text is not just a vessel carrying the original's ideas. Idiomatic translation, an extreme form of 'domesticating translation', licenses al-Manfalūṭī's free adaptation of the source text. What I am calling idiomatic translation also guarantees that the translation can be read as an original product of the target language; ironically, al-Manfalūṭī's translations take idiomatic translation so far that the original author's name slips out of the text.

Although al-Manfalūṭī wants to maintain the solid relationship between word and meaning, his idiomatic, non-literal translation demands no reciprocity between translation and original. He also transforms unfaithful translation into a sophisticated theory of writing as unmediated correspondence between sound and meaning:

> And here I am in the hands of this dark, creepy world, the world of truth and pain, so I look at it with the air of a confused stranger to a country [from *ʿālam* or world to *balad* or country] he has nothing to do with and no home in, so I see its shame and its evils . . . the disconnection of names from what they name and the ensuing confusion between them, the bewilderment of borders . . . places and positions *until something invades that world that was not there before, and something leaves it that was not meant to leave.*[82]

'Good' translation is the domain of the *kātib*, who leaves his self behind to float across different historical epochs. The *kātib* is also a translator who intentionally breaches the contract of fidelity. Under the burden of prophecy, the *kātib* becomes a stranger to the homeland with access to the world's evils, the worst being the dissolved relationship between word and reference.

Al-Manfalūṭī's word is a prophetic word, which, like Blanchot's word, wanders and then returns to the context of its utterance, bringing a promise of deliverance from error. Literal translation, in subduing the Arabic language to the source language, threatens the relationship between symbol and meaning. For one, copying European ideas in the original sentence structure into Arabic does not engage the receiving context or the Arabic language. The *nahḍawī* authors misread al-Manfalūṭī's sentimentalism as disengagement, for his vision needs a communal setting that can receive it. Arabic prophetic literature depends on a deep-seated rootedness in a certain culture – a 'real experience of place' – indispensable to the one called on to be the mouthpiece of the prophetic.[83] If al-Manfalūṭī's truth that is part of a divine design loses its real correspondence, there will be what Hallaq describes as an inversion of value. Al-Manfalūṭī gives the example of *al-taʾwil* or multiple interpretations of the Qurʾān as a symptom of this inversion because religion can no longer be serving its natural end of unmediated communication. Literal translation invites infinite interpretation, but *khayāl* guarantees the *kātib*'s safe distance from such chaos:

> It occurred [*khuyyila*] to me – because of the proximity of my age to what I was seeing – that I was seeing something bizarre . . . as if . . . the world of the imagination [*khayāl*] that I was in was a true picture of the world of truth and of the reality into which I was being transported, so I was troubled by the great difference between the two worlds. I sent out one word followed by another . . . Some people read what I had written and called it writing [*kalāman*] . . . they named me *kātib* [writer].[84]

*Khayāl* grants the *kātib* access to truth, which coexists with the real world outside of the literary vision. As *kalām*, the description and its object coincide, such that there is no delay between vision and narration. There is the illusion of transparent representation because al-Manfalūṭī, the *kātib,* has simultaneous access to truth and reality. Al-Manfalūṭī represents narration as *īfḍāʾ*, communicating a secret rather than expressing a thought, and implicates the reader in interpreting his work as *vraie parole* or *kalām*. So '*l'adab produit l'adab*', Hallaq writes, in '*un univers autonome qui ne renvoie qu'à lui-même*' (literature produces literature in an autonomous world that refers only to itself), affirming itself by overcoming the external world.[85] Hallaq finds that literature as prophetic separates the individual 'me' from the authorial 'I', and so al-Manfalūṭī's vision of a literature of individuation constitutes a complete rupture with *nahḍawī* social realism.

But this is not a European subjective 'I', as becomes more evident in his actual translations, for *adab* is the *ethical* obligation to expose the evils of borrowing from Western civilisation. When al-Manfalūṭī suffers the judgement of his time, he finds himself compelled 'to become either an atheist in my religion or hateful of my homeland, so I managed – and people had already embraced all they could of this Western civilisation [*madaniyya*] – to sit on one side of it'.[86] The duality of worlds translates into a duality of choice for the prophetic author. Confronted with Western modernity, he strives for that delicate position between preserving his religion and language while maintaining contact with Western thought. In the article '*al-Madaniyya al-gharbiyya*' (Western civilisation), he warns against imitating only the forms of nationalist and scientific thought in the desire for a fast-track modernisation. Critiquing the logic of colonial universalism, al-Manfalūṭī lobbies for the replacement of the Western canon with the Eastern one, because it is a shame to know Shakespeare and not al-Maᶜarrī, and for reading translations critically without surrendering to the original.[87]

If the acquisition of a foreign tongue serves only to communicate with the masters, then 'the writer becomes a mere maker not a writer . . . a translator not a speaker [*qāᶜil*]'.[88] The *qāᶜil* (writer as speaker) avoids this pitfall of translation only in finding the perfect form of original expression, even when the idea comes in translation. Kāmil Muḥammad ᶜUwayḍa describes how al-Manfalūṭī's obsession with finding the perfect form results in an externalisation of emotion so that the subjective becomes a shared objective reality.[89] Al-Manfalūṭī uses the classical style to subdue the emotion's intensity in a recognisable form that binds a community of readers over a shared tradition. That tradition is a rhetorical (not a historical or national) one that al-Manfalūṭī locates in the *bayān*, the classical form of Arabic writing of which Qurʾānic discourse is the model (*mubīn*). *Bayān* mimics the soul's natural movement, and is 'not a commodity that gets passed around by traders from one market to the next', and it emerges 'spontaneously without any . . . artificiality, like the rising of the sun and the echo of a voice'.[90] He describes the *bayān* and translation in the same language: 'And the *bayān* is not the insertion and removal of words, and not the entrance of one letter and the exit of another, but it is in composition, harmony and unison [*insijām*].'[91] Like a good translation, the perfect *bayān* is not in the re-arrangement of words but in harmonious piecing, so that words surrender to meaning.[92] As such, *bayān* can escape the use value of colonial economy. In the article '*al-Bayān*', he defines *bayān* as a reader-oriented form of self-expression in his critique of contemporary political writing as too solipsistic. The journalistic style – also used in translations – is devoid of an Arab '*ruḥ*' (soul) – because it forgets that the Arabic language can grow through *ishtiqāq* (derivation) and does not have to steal from the classics.[93]

Perfect *bayān* is described as speech, *ḥadīth*, but speech and writing, just like *kalām* and writing, coincide in al-Manfalūṭī's vision of prophetic narration. There are three kinds of speech: the speech of the tongue, mind, and heart.[94] The lowest form is speech of the tongue, meaningless rhetorical display, followed by the speech of the mind, which is figurative and philosophical, but alienated from the reader. For al-Manfalūṭī, the real is not in the decorative details, but in the precise linguistic form that corresponds fully to its object and avoids superfluous expression. The prophetic author produces *adab* that precludes such confusion, for *khayāl* makes 'the veil of words . . . become so thin in your hands in light of the meaning that it dies out', just like 'the surface of a mirror dissolves . . . or disappears in the hands of the one who is looking into it. All he sees is his picture tilted in his hands, with . . . no glass there.'[95] Al-Manfalūṭī's theory of expression proposes a different verisimilitude to that of the realists. The medium of veiling words is likened to the reflecting surface of a mirror and just like the words disappear in relation to meaning, the reflecting surface disappears in relation to the object, so that the reflected image coincides with the thing through *khayāl*.

This theory of expression is also a theory of imitation; bad or literal translation would trap the original in its own language – bad imitation – while idiomatic translation would liberate both. When the word and thing coincide in the *kātib*'s prophetic vision, the copy becomes the original. Imitation becomes identity. Mimetic realism may reproduce the coloniser's language unscathed in Arabic, al-Manfalūṭī warns; however, *khayāl* affords the *kātib* a position outside the immediate context but within real time, and mobilises his task of translation as an imperative to rewrite the original so that the translation can usurp its position, not necessarily in an act of subversion.[96] This is not to suggest that al-Manfalūṭī escapes colonial discourse; rather, al-Manfalūṭī's theory of translation exposes the representational logic that privileges realism as truth. In remaining faithful to prophetic *khayāl*, this form of translation is politically motivated to the extent that it disables easy appropriation, which qualifies ᶜUbayd's realism. Al-Manfalūṭī recognises both the untranslatability of context and the specific communal setting he is addressing: hence in his translations he renders the subjective as a shared objective reality.

## Al-Manfalūṭī's Literary Adaptations

In 1915, al-Manfalūṭī rewrote François René de Chateaubriand's *Atala* (with traces of *René*), into a twenty-four-page short story entitled '*al-Shuhadā*''

(The Martyrs) (1915), included in the collection *al-ᶜAbarāt*.[97] In 1923, he translated Bernardin de Saint-Pierre's *Paul et Virginie* as *Al-Faḍīla, aw Paul wa Vīrgīnī* (Virtue; Or Paul and Virginie). While the first translation completely forgets Chateaubriand, the second names Saint-Pierre. The adaptation of *Paul et Virginie* remains close to the original's plot, but rearranges scenes, changes pronouns, and adds moralistic commentaries as extended dialogue or narratorial introspection to critique Western modernity and colonialism. Al-Manfalūṭī also changes the novel's ending, and the storyteller figure emerges as an inverted Scheherazade, who tells his story to die, under the same burden of prophecy that Haykal finds in Shakespeare. The prophetic *kātib* of *al-Naẓarāt* emerges in the translations' narrative voice, which profanes both the original text and traditional Arabic narrative through 'good' or idiomatic translation.

'*Al-Shuhadā*ᵓ' opens with a realistic description of a poor French widow who remains, along with the other characters, unnamed in the story; the only character who is named is her brother Raphael, who had left France for America twenty years before the story begins. As in *René*, a sister is looking for her brother and pining for him in his absence, but the missing brother in '*al-Shuhadā*ᵓ' resembles the Spaniard Lopez in *Atala*. The widow cries over her brother in the dark every day, until, one day, her son discovers her crying and decides to go to Washington to participate in a painting contest and find his uncle. In Washington, he wins the award for best painting, a rendering of the farewell scene between him and his mother, and decides to go looking for his uncle. At this point, the story is interrupted by the first aphoristic insertion, relayed by an omniscient narrator: 'Oh, how time lures man with false hope back into its vicious cycle, like a prey led to the slaughterhouse.' Soon after, the hero falls prey to a tribe and is imprisoned in an underground dungeon for a year,

> wandering aimlessly like a confused soul in the darkness of the graves. As soon as he figured out his place in the darkness, he walked in the raging battlefield [*muᶜtarak*] searching for his self and feeling for it with his hand until he heard the rattling of the chain [*samiᶜa ṣalṣalat al-silsila*] wrapped around his feet . . . exhausted from the walk and the search . . . he fell on himself weeping.[98]

In the Arabic translation, the repetition of the 's' sound in '*samiᶜa ṣalṣalat al-silsila*' exemplifies al-Manfalūṭī's 'classical' inclinations. The subjective experience of the trapped character is both formalised and externalised as the translation adapts Chateaubriand's '*vague des passions*' to an Arab audience.[99] Al-Manfalūṭī uses his translation of romantic tropes to put forth a more severe criticism of oblique signification. For instance, he transforms the figure of the all-consuming grave into two literal burial sites (the dungeon and the widow's self-dug grave), and the character literally searches for his 'self', an objectified other presence in the darkness of the tomb where 'there was no connection or link anymore between himself and himself'. The *literal* versions of these figures translate the '*vague des passions*' into a critique of tradition that dictates life's path from the darkness of the womb to the tomb. The omniscient narrator asks: 'since when was the dumb animal and inanimate matter [*al-jamād*], you cruel dictators, of more importance than the speaking human being and more deserving than he of the grace of love and life?!'[100] Organised religion, an implicit reference to the Azhar, denaturalises love into a prohibition and silences individual stories. Literature can crack *al-jamād*. Although al-Manfalūṭī was known for his 'Islamic articles', and his stories were typically received as *maqālāt* or *risālāt adabiyya* (essays or literary letters) and not proper *qiṣaṣ* (stories), his fiction was appealing precisely because it returned religion as *practice* to the domain of everyday life. While creed remained the domain of al-Azhar, al-Manfalūṭī suggests, lived Islam could become the realm of literature.[101] His literature profanes the colonial separation between morality and religion specifically through its generic hybridity: it points to a nuanced understanding of the real as a product of overlapping discursive modalities and situates the literary within that nexus as a contingent act of reading.

## *Paul et Virginie* on Egyptian Shores

The contingency of the literary becomes more deliberate in *al-Faḍīla*. In 1923, four years after the 1919 Revolution in Egypt, al-Manfalūṭī translates Bernardin de Saint-Pierre's 1789 novel *Paul et Virginie*.[102] A novel of sentimental escapism published in the year of the French Revolution, al-Manfalūṭī's choice gives credence to his critics' accusations that he wrote stories set in far-away places with no immediate bearing on the Egyptian situation. The translation's dedication commends 'courage and daring' in the young man, and 'good manners and shyness' in the young woman. As per his commitment to all readers, he dedicates the story to the 'young boys and girls of Egypt, so that they may . . . base their future lives on the foundation of virtue as did Paul and Virginia'.[103] Al-Manfalūṭī doesn't translate the original '*Préambule*', which Saint-Pierre added to the 1806 edition (*l'édition de luxe*).[104] Saint-Pierre explains that he deliberately set the novel on an island, l'île de France, away from Paris's political present, so that he could write the modern epic and show that '*il y a une Providence qui se manifeste aussi bien au milieu du désordre de nos sociétés, que dans l'ordre de la nature*' (there is a Providence that manifests itself as much in midst of the disorder of our societies as in the order of nature).[105] If in the years after the 1789 Revolution, Bonaparte unsettled the natural and social orders, *Paul et Virginie* would reinstitute natural order through its characters who are '*ramené à ses lois éternelles, par des révolutions*' (returned to its eternal laws, through revolutions).[106] The novel does not call for communal understanding through resemblance on this utopian island; rather, the dream of absolute identity overwrites difference and presents this fictional world as a paradise where all things coincide. Its imaginary world resonated well with readers and inaugurated a cult of sentimentalism that al-Manfalūṭī found appealing. For instance, in his earlier article '*Madīnat al-sa$^{c}$āda*' (The City of Happiness) – a curious socialist manifesto – he opposes the animal's natural freedom to man's social imprisonment, and reflects his preference for 'beauty in imagination more than in reality'. Describing the garden, al-Manfalūṭī confesses, 'gives [him] more pleasure than to view it'. He prefers to read about cities than see them, so he would not be spoiling 'this imaginative delight . . . afraid that the reality would rob [him] of it'.[107]

However, despite his utopian literary ideals, in translating the original, al-Manfalūṭī adapts the storyteller figure to testify to the persistent threat of difference that the original wants to silence, here between self and other, East and West, the European novel and the Arabic tale. Al-Manfalūṭī's intention may be purely didactic, but his translation tells another story, especially when it brings the old (traditional narrative) and new (translated text) into confrontation. He divides the novel into chapters and names the first chapter 'The Island of Maurice' (Mauritius), beginning with a description (and naming) of the island, while the original begins with a reference to the women's two cabins. The translation then refers to the small number of black people dispersed on the island's mountains as slaves to the European colonialists before describing the cabins.

The original novel opens with the narratorial '*je*', and its frame tale has the narrator and old man exchanging a story about the two abandoned cabins, first placed in quotations but then the story is relayed without any identifiable markers. The original also opens with multiple doubles set up symmetrically (the two cabins; the two women; Dominique and Marie; Paul and Virginie drinking the same milk).[108] The symmetry creates a sense of wholeness, paradise on earth, an Adam and Eve with two of everything; for example, the old man admires Paul's arrangement of trees in his garden such that the whole can be seen at a single glance.[109] Bernardin de Saint-Pierre had said his novel would *perform* Providence and posit a 'natural' order, much as in Benjamin the act of naming *posits* the thing it names, for we are told that Paul's amphitheatre of green does not deviate from nature's design, but confirms that all is in its proper place.[110]

However, in the self-referential space of the novel, there is colonial exploitation (both in the original and in exaggerated form in the translation). The narrator is lost near the mountain of the Three Breasts (*Trois-Mamelles*), where there are slaves and plantations. The historical intervention of colonisation in this seemingly ahistorical space threatens the novel's fantasy of absolute identity. The translation opens with a reference to colonialism that frames the encounter between the old man and narrator. In the second chapter, '*al-Shaykh*' (The Old Man), we meet the storyteller who tells our narrator the story. The original 'I' of the listener is absent from the translation's opening pages and the old man speaks directly. The narrator appears only accidentally, through the dialogic verb '*qultu*' – the first-person active form of the verb 'to say'. The story of the two families on the island becomes subservient to the frame tale, which delivers a critique of European colonialism. For instance, when the old man is telling the narrator about the two women's happiness despite their miserable poverty, al-Manfalūṭī writes that the only stories Europeans want to hear are those that resemble the lives of 'heroes of the novels that you read'.[111] But he is not writing a European tale. In order to break the vow of verisimilitude, in line with al-Māzinī's critique of al-Manfalūṭī's questionable authorial testimony, al-Manfalūṭī adds to the narrator's speech:

> Yes sir, I confess that we Europeans do not know the meaning of happiness except in the ways you have described! . . . And we are not impressed with a story unless its heroes are those of cruel kings, and blood-shedding dictators! . . . But we cannot listen . . . with pleasure and content to the speech of the poor and the miserable! . . . No matter how cruel the human heart gets, and even if lust devours its feelings and being, a wind of divine instinct will blow its way, refresh it, and wake its feelings, so the heart could return to itself . . . and understand that there are kinds of happiness in the world that it already knows and is familiar with . . . so tell me your story sir, for I am merely a desperate poor man who was let down by happiness when he demanded it from cities/communities [*ḥawāḍir*] and present times. . . . So he placed his hands on his wrinkled forehead as though searching for old memories . . . and he began talking to me, saying.[112]

The *isnād* structure whereby the account's authority is established through a continuity – a structure found in *A Thousand and One Nights* and *ḥadīth* – frames the exchange; the story, however, can only be told, heard, and read in one way.[113] In the chapter '*al-Saᶜāda*' (Happiness), al-Manfalūṭī links happiness directly to reducing interpretation or *al-taʾwīl.* Because in the world of *Paul et Virginie*, God is everywhere, the book of nature is open and unmediated and requires no interpretation. In the original novel, religious faith is intuitive, '*car leur théologie était toute en sentiment, comme celle de la nature, et leur morale toute en action, comme celle de l'Évangile*' (for their theology was all sentimental, like that of nature, and their morality in action, like that of the Gospel).[114] This line becomes in translation: 'They did not care to understand [nature's] meanings, or penetrate its secrets, as though they felt themselves above all of that with what God had given them of an instinctual and simple faith that does not require any explanation.'[115] Al-Manfalūṭī removes the comparison to the Gospel: if God's word is clearly reflected in nature, why would one need the text?[116] If translation in *al-Naẓarāt* promises delivery from mimetic error, then *al-Faḍīla* reminds readers that religion is instinctual, and this remembering happens in the reading of the literary text.

If religious differences between East and West must be kept at a distance, spurning especially the Gospel as mediator, the reading of novels *stages* their necessary encounter. In the article '*al-Islām wa-l-masīḥiyya*' (Islam and Christianity), he critiques his contemporaries' infatuation with Lord Cromer's representation of Islam. Addressing Cromer as the historical philosopher he is, he asks him to allow freedom of faith and undo the evangelist project, for Western civilisation today is an imprint of yesterday's Islam and Islamic *inḥiṭāṭ* – referring to the politically and culturally impoverished conditions of the modern Arab world – is a consequence of Christianity's earlier blows (literally, *ḍarbāt*).[117] As opposed to abstract Christian universalism, al-Manfalūṭī continues, Islam is an equaliser and fully civilisational as it considers every aspect of life.[118] In another article, '*Siḥr al-bayān*' (The Magic of Form), al-Manfalūṭī allows for similarity between Christian and Muslim history through literature, namely the *bayān* of Shakespeare's *Julius Caesar*, including a translation of Caesar's speech and the people's response in dialogue.[119] Again, as in *al-Faḍīla*, literature stages the necessary encounter between two discourses, even when colonial power limits their exchange.[120]

Classical literature has helped Paul idealise Virginie, but novels offer him a realistic presentiment of how Paris will change her, since he knows that novels offer a sincere picture of European ethics.[121] In the translation, the seeds she sends him from Paris:

> only survived for a little while until they withered and disappeared . . . because the soil was not conducive to their growth, or because East is East . . . and West is West! . . . and it is impossible that the two should mix and mingle, and partake in the same system, and in the same life . . . And, as Rousseau says, the human spirit is a mirror which reflects different pictures and colors! . . . and one – as de Maupassant says – is the product of the environment in which he lives.[122]

The names of Rousseau and Guy de Maupassant are not found in the original and the line that divides East and West in the first part of the quotation is blurred. The 'East' in the original is really L'île de France, but in the translation, it comes to suggest Egypt, so that the combination of a Rousseauesque romanticism and Maupassantian naturalism is a symptom of untranslatability in al-Manfalūṭī's adaptation. In simple terms, the reference to de Maupassant suggests that for Western seeds to grow in Eastern soil, one would have to change the environment in the East to resemble that of the West. Rousseau suggests a spirit that can wander the world unrestricted by territorial boundaries. Both references explain why East and West shall never meet; curiously, the explanation is based in a meeting of the two. We need the references to de Maupassant and Rousseau in order to understand the East in its difference from the West. Representation is already mediated, in other words, and much like the translation, it cannot be a pure communication of an original. Al-Manfalūṭī's translation theory echoes Jacques Derrida's similar argument about the secular: since secularisation and translation need to communicate in language, their original intentions are always already compromised. Armando Salvatore explains this compromise well: 'the distinctive properties of the trans-cultural space between the "West" and "Islam" . . . are phenomena of meaning's merging between the two sides of the space, up to the point when the location of the original source of a certain signification is either no longer possible or has become irrelevant.'[123]

Al-Manfalūṭī's translation begins to speak from the East as Egypt, from his particular position as Egyptian author. What enables this spatial mobility is the temporal transportation of the prophetic *kātib* that al-Manfalūṭī develops in *al-Naẓarāt*, for the exilic author figure accesses different historical epochs from the present moment of narration. We encounter this figure in the original novel when the old man describes his inscriptions on the monuments:

> il me semble alors qu'une voix humaine sorte de la pierre, se fasse entendre a travers les siècles, et s'adressant a l'homme au milieu des déserts, lui dise qu'il n'est pas seul, et que d'autres hommes dans ces mêmes lieux ont senti, pensé, et souffert comme lui: que si cette inscription est de quelque action ancienne qui ne subsiste pas, elle étend notre âme dans les champs de l'infini, et lui donne le sentiment de son immortalité, en lui montrant qu'une pensée a survécu à la ruine même d'un empire [it seems to me then that a human voice comes out of the stone, is heard through the centuries, and addresses man in the middle of the deserts, tells him that he is not alone, and that other men in these same places have felt, thought, and suffered like him: that if this inscription is of some ancient act that has not survived, it still extends our soul into the fields of the infinite, and gives it

> the feeling of its own immortality, showing us that a thought has survived the very ruin of an empire].[124]

In the translation:

> There I felt as if I had moved from my present into my past, and that I was living in those ancient times with my fathers and grandfathers, talking and listening to them, revealing to them my self [*afḍī ilayhum bi-dhātī*], hearing them reveal themselves to me, so I spend an hour in that conversation, then I go about my business, my self overflowing with the feeling that the human self is immortal, not inferior to . . . time, the years and days unable to deface its image.[125]

The verb '*afḍī*' recalls the description of narration in *al-Naẓarāt*. While in the original text, the human voice emanates from the rock, the translation's authorial 'I', the old man's voice, replaces the inscription that connects past to present. This is not a romantic subjective 'I', however, but the storyteller's prophetic narrative voice accessing different times from within the story. Once again, the literary emerges here as a contingent act of reading through 'bad' translation.

In another metatextual moment of actual staging, al-Manfalūṭī reframes the prophetic use of *khayāl* from *al-Naẓarāt* in the family's theatrical performances.[126] For instance, Madame de La Tour's identification with the character of Ruth is rewritten in the translation to emphasise that (the good brand of) *khayāl* is none other than reality:

> As soon as she reaches with her imagination the happy ending that concludes that novel/story [*riwāya*], she calms down . . . on that day we used to enjoy all that happy people in their clubs and societies [enjoyed] . . . with no difference between us and them except that we do not decorate the stages that we move on with false, mendacious pictures of the ocean and shore and sand . . . for all that was present to us in our hands was a reality not a fantasy [*haqīqatan la khayālan*].[127]

European art relies on bad *khayāl*, the kind that needs decorating images to simulate verisimilitude. The good *khayāl* of the characters' performances merges harmoniously with the background. In other words, the frame that separates stage from performance and tale from background dissolves. This is al-Manfalūṭī's own fantasy (not far from Saint-Pierre's): the closed world of the story would offer the reader not a version of reality, but reality itself. In the process, the frame becomes the tale; form is content, and the mirror dissolves in one's hand.

While the romantics and realists dismiss al-Manfalūṭī's work as escapist, *al-Faḍīla* develops its own theory of verisimilitude. The original novel ends with the old man walking away in tears, and the narrator in no better shape after 'ce funeste récit' (this fatal narrative).[128] In the translation, al-Manfalūṭī adds a final chapter in which the narrator descends to the old man's house (another figure of the grave) to find him dead in his bed. The narrator loses himself in tears, and we read these poetic lines: 'And there is no eye but a weeping one; and no cheek but for tears' (*wa lā ᶜayn illā wa hiya ᶜayn min al-bakā; wa lā khadd illā li-l-dumūᶜ bihi khadd*).[129] In *al-Naẓarāt*, he explains that tears enable a sense of human fellowship, of feeling with others. While many readers may dismiss this last chapter as another example of al-Manfalūṭī's infatuation with tears, the old man's death (after the telling of the tale) points to a nuanced appropriation of romanticism. As we read in *al-Naẓarāt*, *khayāl* provides the author with an exteriority to the scene of narration or translation and, by extension, access to the world of the story and the world of its narration simultaneously.

The strange insertion of an omniscient narrator alerts us to the conflation of romanticism and realism in the early Arabic novel. While thematically the translation engages romanticism, formally it treats romanticism realistically by isolating elements of romantic literature and re-inscribing them within its own realist aesthetic – one located in the context of reading French sentimental fiction in early twentieth-century Cairo. In his adaptations, al-Manfalūṭī succeeds in articulating an authorial function that is both prophetic and individual, addressing the community from the contingency of literary reading.[130] His poetics of translation mobilise a subtle politics that in supposedly copying French romanticism is most successful at rewriting it. Al-Manfalūṭī reads into the escapism of *Paul et Virginie* a more faithful engagement of Paris because it allows the author enough distance from the event to see it in its entirety. With *René* and *Atala*, al-Manfalūṭī adapts the *vague des passions* to an Arab audience not familiar with this form of subjective consciousness.

His translations make the *mal de siècle* – not of his own history – speak to the colonial situation of Egypt.

## A Painted World

In the dedication of *al-Shāᶜir* – *'Ilā al-shuᶜarā'*'– to all poets for they are 'its heroes', the only reward al-Manfalūṭī asks for in return (*jazā'* with the double meaning of reward or penalty) is to 'see all of them in their social and literary life as Cyrano de Bergerac'.[131] The translator's debt to all poets is two-fold: first, to remind them of the painted picture of the world, as he renders the play in the form of narrative prose; and, second, to make it possible for them to become the other in freely appropriating her literature into Arabic. *Al-Shāᶜir* as another version of the modern-day *kātib* has an obligation to stage the literary encounter between East and West. Al-Manfalūṭī's prose becomes the site of generic struggle between classical notions of what poetry should sound like and what translation could offer, so he confronts European ideals of subjectivity with the formal externalisation of classical Arabic poetry. What he bequeaths on to the nation of poets in the previous dedication is precisely that painted picture of the world.

Echoing al-Manfalūṭī's own prophecy in *al-Faḍīla* on East and West never converging, Kilito's metaphorical use of al-Manfalūṭī's work demonstrates the paradoxical burden of translation in Arabic literary history. Kilito describes al-Manfalūṭī as obsessed with becoming European in two ways: on the one hand, he hides his Eurocentrism well since he knows no foreign languages and, on the other, he tries his best to understand European culture and be faithful to its representation.[132] This chapter has shown, however, that al-Manfalūṭī's self-orientalism is not as definitive as Kilito would have it. Under this burden of translation, he transmits the other text, but always in another tongue, constantly aware that it is a language not his own.

Al-Manfalūṭī's appeal persists today in his ability to render Western texts in a familiar style, all the while presenting both the original and its translation in such a way that one does not become subservient to the other. Perhaps this came easy to him since he knew no Western languages and received Western literature in a form of indirect translation through intermediaries. But his translations are not so naïve, especially when they actively interrupt the original. The adaptation of Chateaubriand's *Atala* rewrites Chateaubriand's metaphorical language, interrupting the latter's romanticism from an afterlife, namely, the weighty inheritance of European Enlightenment thought in Egypt. In a nation torn between Western impulses and traditional legacies, al-Manfalūṭī's work tested the promise of Enlightenment thought to legitimate the individual, both as author and reader. It provided a niche for readers who were equally drawn to Western ideas and tales written in an Arabic style, away from local themes and yet in a local idiom – thus translating romantic aspirations of subjectivity in narration to a realistic engagement with the nation. Al-Manfalūṭī's stories craft an intersubjective space of reading that heeds an invocation of personhood but not solipsistic subjectivity in literature. Al-ᶜAqqād will try to do the same thing with transposing Coleridge and Shelley onto Arab poetics, but his aspiration remains limited to the modernising poet as locus of the utterance while al-Manfalūṭī, although he will theorise a sophisticated position for the *kātib* as repository of truth, uses his translations to engage readers. Unlike al-ᶜAqqād's view of poetic language as purely subjective, al-Manfalūṭī's prophetic literary language promises to deliver its meaning absolutely with no room for deliberation or error. This ideal of pure language is possible through reader-oriented translation and in turn makes al-Manfalūṭī's romanticism more relatable than his contemporaries' realist writing. Al-Manfalūṭī gets his prophetic wish: Aḥmad Ḥasan al-Zayyāt described al-Manfalūṭī's lingering community of readers, who eagerly anticipated his Thursday articles in *al-Muᵓayyid*, 'rereading those five, six, seven times, believing that God chose al-Manfalūṭī to bring about this revival in writing style'.[133]

## Notes

1. '*Al-ᶜIhdāᵓ*' [Dedication], *Riwāyat fī sabīl al-tāj* [For the Sake of the Crown: A Dramatic Novel of this Name by the Famous French Writer François Coppée with Some Amendments].
2. Semah, *Four Egyptian Literary Critics*, p. 20.
3. See Adonis, 'al-Shiᶜr al-ᶜarabī wa-mushkilat al-tajdīd', in *Al-Fikr* Issue 6 (March 1, 1962) (Tunis), pp. 516–33, found at http://archive.sakhrit.co/newPreview.aspx?PID=2090730&ISSUEID=9826&AID=197587, p. 516.
4. Brugman, *An Introduction*, p. 96.
5. The Dīwān group was made up of al-Māzinī, al-ᶜAqqād, ᶜAbd al-Raḥmān

Shukrī, ᶜAbbās Ḥāfiẓ, and Muḥammad al-Sibāᶜī. The second romantic group Apollo – which called for imitating Hellenic culture in the literary renaissance – included Aḥmad Luṭfī al-Sayyid (realistic narrative literature), Muḥammad Ḥusayn Haykal, and Ṭāhā Husayn. (See Hafez, *Genesis*, p. 299).

6. Al-Māzinī, *Al-Shiᶜr*, p. 35.
7. In 1947 Lūwīs ᶜAwaḍ's *Brūmithiyūs Ṭalīqan* (Prometheus Unbound) returns Shelley as a model for committed literature. In *Shīlī fī al-adab al-ᶜArabī fī Miṣr* [Shelley in Arabic literature in Egypt] (Cairo: Dār al-Maᶜārif, 1982), Jīhān Ṣafwat Raᵓūf lists popular translations of Shelley's poems in *al-Sufūr* (1919), *al-Siyāsa al-Usbūᶜiyya* (1926), *al-Risāla* (1933), and *Abūlū* (1933).
8. Samir Elbarbary writes that al-ᶜAqqād's translations of Hardy's poems could be his own works ('Al-ᶜAqqād's Hardy: Essays and Translations', p. 66), while Shmuel Moreh finds the modernists' poetry to be completely severed from the classical tradition (Moreh, *Modern Arabic Poetry*, p. 1).
9. See Kilito, *The Author and his Doubles*, Wail Hassan (trans.), p. 4.
10. For more on literary theft and its place in the Arabic tradition, see Badawī Tabbāna, *Al-Sirqāt al-adabiyya: Dirāsa fī intiḥāl al-ᵓaᶜmāl al-adabiyya wa taqlīdihā* (Beirut: Dār al-thaqāfa: 1986). Tabbāna especially emphasises the tradition of memorising other poetry to become a poet (p. 4). The ancients considered theft a unique skill, measured by the poet's ability to disconnect from the original and produce something new, naming it '*ḥusn al-akhdh*' (p. 161).
11. ᶜUmar al-Dasūqī, *Fī al-adab al-ḥadīth*, 1970 (Cairo: Dār al-fikr al-ᶜArabī li-l-ṭibāᶜa wa-l-nashr, 2000), p. 271.
12. Al-Ḍayf, *al-Adab al-muᶜāṣir fī Miṣr*, pp. 134, 137.
13. Ibid., p. 143.
14. See Abū al-Anwār, *Al-Manfalūṭī*, pp. 7–8.
15. His works include: *al-Naẓarāt* (Visions), Volume One (1910), Volume Two (1912), and Volume Three (1921), collections of articles, essays, and twenty-five original and adapted short stories; *Mukhtārāt al-Manfalūṭī* (al-Manfalūṭī's Selections) (15 March 1912), his selections from classical and other literature; *Majdūlīn* (1912, appended to Volume Two of *al-Naẓarāt*), adaptation of Alfonse Karr's *Sous le Tilleul* (*Taḥt ẓilāl al-zayrafūn*, 'Under the Zizyphus Tree'); *al-ᶜAbarāt* (The Tears), 1915, four original stories and four translations; *Fī sabīl al-tāj* (For the Sake of the Crown) (1920); *al-Shāᶜir* (The Poet) (1921), adaptation of Edmond Rostand's *Cyrano de Bergerac* (1898); and *al-Faḍīla, aw Paul wa Virginie* (Virtue; Or Paul and Virginie) (1923), adaptation of Bernardin de Saint-Pierre's *Paul et Virginie* (1788).

16. Haykal, *Taṭawwur al-adab al-ḥadīth fī Miṣr*, p. 178.
17. See Abu al-Anwār, *al-Manfalūṭī*, pp. 61–2.
18. Ibtessam El Esnawi calls al-Manfalūṭī's adaptation of *Cyrano de Bergerac* in *al-Shāʿir* '*al-iqtibās al-multazim*' (committed paraphrase) as it maintains the spirit (*rūḥ*) of the original ('Rostand and al-Manfaluti', p. 111).
19. Hallaq, 'Transgénérique', p. 161. Translation mine.
20. Hallaq, 'Transgénérique', p. 162.
21. Yaḥyā Shāmī (*Muṣṭafā Luṭfī al-Manfalūṭī*, p. 23) finds that political critique unifies fiction and essay in *al-Naẓarāt*.
22. See Ḥamad Khalīl's book *ʾArāʾ al-Manfalūṭī fī shuʿarāʾ wa kuttāb ʿaṣrihi* (Al-Manfalūṭī's Opinions on the Poets and Authors of His Age) (Saudi Arabia: al-Nādī al-adabī al-thaqāfī, 2005).
23. In an article in *Miṣr al-Fatāt* on 31 August 1909, Ṭāhā Ḥusayn admits his infatuation with al-Manfalūṭī's style and simplicity of expression; however, in a series of later articles beginning with '*Al-Naẓara fī al-Naẓarāt*' (20 April 1910), and ending with '*Al-Kadhdhābūn wa-l-taghrīr fī Kitāb al-Naẓarāt*' (11 May 1910) and '*Naẓarāt fī al-Naẓarāt – al-Naẓarāt al-sabʿa*' (17 May 1910), Tāhā Husayn criticised al-Manfalūṭī for stealing from al-Rāfiʿī, fabricating *khayāl* but not needing it, and using 'wrong' and 'inappropriate' words. He later retracts his indictment: 'I feel ashamed when I have to talk about this because it was an erroneous evaluation; I was actually criticizing his use of words from a linguistic point of view . . . and I was only about eighteen years old' (quoted in al-Dasūqī, *Fī al-adab al-ḥadīth*, p. 45).
24. Al-ʿAqqād, *Murājaʿāt*, p. 559.
25. Ibid., p. 560.
26. Ibid., pp. 562, 567.
27. *Dīwān*, Volume Two, pp. 103–14.
28. Ibid., p. 89.
29. Peled, 'Did al-Manfalūṭī', p. 64.
30. *Dīwān*, Volume Two, '*Al-ʿAbarāt: Qiṣṣat al-Yatīm*', pp. 96–102 and '*ʾUslūb al-Manfalūṭī*', pp. 103–14.
31. Ibid., p. 108.
32. Cited in Peled, 'Did al-Manfalūṭī', p. 58. From Hamilton Alexander Rosskeen Gibb, *Studies in the Civilization of Islam*, S. J. Shaw and W. R. Polk (eds) (London: Beacon Press, 1962), pp. 258–68, 263.
33. Allen, *The Arabic Novel*, p. 30.
34. Salma Jayyusi, *Trends*, pp. 140–4.

35. R. C. Ostle, 'The Romantic Poets', p. 100.
36. Aḥmad Ḥasan al-Zayyāt, in '*Muṣṭafā Luṭfī al-Manfalūṭī: bi-munāsabat dhikra al-thālithat ᶜashar*', in issue 210 of *al-Risāla*, published on 12 July 1937 (its fifth year) (pp. 1,121–2), p. 1,122; emphasis added. Al-Zayyāt was also editor of *al-Riwāya* (The Novel), which published serialised translated novels from 1936 to 1937. In 1937, he started *al-Risāla*, focusing on literary criticism. The word '*al-hiyām*', which I translated as 'wandering', can also mean 'passionate love', and the 'sweet source' could either be the source of water in the desert or the loved one.
37. Al-Manfalūṭī used his writing to call for reconciliation between past and present and different political factions. He advocated the liberation from *taqlīd*, and the correct use of the Arabic language, and wrote 'for the man in the street, not for specific people, he wrote to empower the people, not to impress them'. His Islamic writings called for a pure Islam against empty religious practices, and his politics were strictly against the British occupation, invested in unifying Egypt. See Riyāḍ Qāsim, *Muṣṭafā Luṭfī al-Manfalūṭī: Fī sabīl al-tāj*, 1987 (Beirut: Muᵓassasat baḥsūn, 2001), pp. 20–1.
38. Ṭāhā Badr considers Jurjī Zaydān's (1861–1914) twenty-one historical romances to be transitional mediators between al-Manfalūṭī's entertainment novel and Muḥammad Ḥusayn Haykal's artistic novel. At this point in Arab literary history it is difficult to imagine autonomy of literature. Even though the *maqāma* as a narrative form privileged deliberate linguistic play over plot, it is not accurate to say that the *maqāma* is an autonomous Arab narrative – meaning that it engaged in a liberatory art for art's sake project. The modern *maqāma* made possible modernising the Arabic language but not liberating narrative art from reality.
39. Moreh, *Modern Arabic Poetry*, p. 3.
40. Ibid., pp. 77–8.
41. Shelley, 'A Defense of Poetry'; al-Māzinī, *al-Shiᶜr*, p. 35.
42. *Al-Shiᶜr*, p. 93.
43. Ibid., pp. 44, 96
44. '*Sāᶜāt bayn al-kutub*', p. 22.
45. Al-ᶜAqqād, *ᶜAbqariyyat*, p. 23.
46. '*Al-Ḥaqāᵓiq al-shiᶜriyya*' [Poetic Truths] (13 April 1928) in *Sāᶜāt bayn al-kutub*, pp. 512–13.
47. As cited in Moreh, *Modern Arabic Poetry*, p. 56.
48. Modern Arabic poetry knew three major schools: neo-classical, romantic, and

modern. The neo-classical style returned to familiar forms such as the *qaṣīda*. Salma Jayyusi privileges the neo-classical school because it relied on tradition to produce 'wholesome verse' (p. 36). For Robin Ostle, the romantics' isolation from political realities meant that they had no relationship to Arab nationalism (Ostle, 'The Romantic Poets', p. 94). Mounah A. Khoury finds that the modernists' emphasis on *wijdān*, being, or emotion makes their poetry 'a partial and superficial copy of its European model' (*Poetry and the Making of Modern Egypt*, pp. 134–5).

49. Jaroslav Stetkevych refers to the *nahḍa* writers' return to analogy or *al-qiyās* (the tradition of Abu ᶜAlī al-Fārisī (919–87) and ᶜUthmān Ibn Jinnī (932–1002)) 'to revive and modernise the Arabic language' through derivation from Arabic roots (*al-ishtiqāq*) and assimilation of foreign words (*al-taᶜrīb*) (Stetkevych, *The Modern Arabic Literary Language*, p. 5, pp. 6–7). For Pierre Cachia, the romantics were instrumental in the turn away from formalism towards an 'emotional' and not 'ornamental' language that would be closer to reality (Cachia, 'The Development of a Modern Prose Style', p. 71). In this sense, the European novel in translation facilitated the breaking away from Classical Arabic towards the language of fiction.
50. Maḥmūd Ṭāhir Lāshīn was the group's main figure. The group also read translations from various national traditions: from the French, Baudelaire, Flaubert, and Rimbaud; from the British, Scott, Carlyle, and Dickens; from the American, Poe and Twain; and from the Italian, Dante, Boccaccio, and Pirandello; and from the Russian, Pushkin and Dostoevsky.
51. The other members of the New School wanted to move away from the mimetic style towards a dialectic interaction between the literary work and its context (see Hafez, *Genesis*, p. 216).
52. Eventually, through the translation of Russian literature, Aḥmad Luṭfī al-Sayyid coins the term '*adab qaṣaṣī wāqiᶜī*' (realistic narrative literature).
53. ᶜUbayd, 'Muqaddima' in *Iḥsān Hānim*, p. 9.
54. ᶜUbayd, *Iḥsān Hānim*, pp. 3–5. In this context, ᶜUbayd gives the example of al-Manfalūṭī's rendition of the character of Estephan in his translation of Alfonse Carr's novel *Sous Les Tilleuls* (1912).
55. Ibid., p. 11. ᶜUbayd calls Maḥmūd Taymūr's use of the colloquial 'extremist' and 'dangerous'. He finds the middle ground in a language free of complicated linguistic structures and with some spoken expressions (p. 16). For more on the debate on using the colloquial and the 'middle language' (*al-lugha al-wusṭā*) used by Haykal, al-Māzinī, and ᶜUbayd, see Nawfal, *al-Fann al-qiṣaṣī*, pp. 250–60.

56. ᶜUbayd, '*Iḥsān Hānim*', p. 1.
57. Ibid., pp. 2–5.
58. See Selim, 'The Narrative Craft', pp. 112–13.
59. The most famous were the serialisations of the stories of Maurice Leblanc's *Arsène Lupin* and Sir Arthur Conan Doyle's *Sherlock Holmes*.
60. Selim, *The Novel*, p. 65.
61. See Badr, *Taṭawwur*, p. 86.
62. Ibid., p. 13.
63. Selim, 'The Narrative Craft', pp. 117–18.
64. Badr, *Taṭawwur*, p. 198.
65. Selim, 'The Narrative Craft', p. 123 and *The Novel*, p. 68.
66. Kilito, *Thou Shalt Not*, Wail Hassan (trans.), pp. 3–4.
67. Sheehi, 'Towards a Critical', p. 271.
68. Al-Manfalūṭī, 'Muqaddima' in *al-Naẓarāt*, p. 5.
69. Hallaq, 'La Littérature', p. 141.
70. Al-Manfalūṭī, 'Muqaddima', p. 6.
71. Ibid., p. 7. Al-Manfalūṭī's *khayāl* recalls the relationship between imagination and inspiration in the Arabic philosophical tradition of al-Farābī, Ibn Sīnā, and al-Ghazālī. Naṣr in *al-Khayāl* describes al-Farābī's Platonic use of the prophetic imagination as the maximisation of human creativity, for if the human mind reaches its full creative force it can comprehend present and future ideas in their particular manifestations as a prophecy of the divine (p. 98). Ibn Sīnā finds meaning to precede the manifested image in the prophetic mind, but *khayāl* is needed to mediate the passage of the idea. This form of inspiration requires no *taʾwīl* or mediation, much like prophecy in dreams has no expression in conscious thought. Al-Ghazālī also establishes the prophetic mind's access to the world of true ideas in a waking state through the 'glass of the imagination', and the prophet is able in the same moment to recognise the secret and symbolic significance of the image (p. 99). Maha Abdel Megeed reads the use of *khayāl* in Muḥammad al-Muwaylīḥī's *Ḥadīth ᶜĪsa ʾIbn Hishām*, as a similar differentiation between *takhyīl* as a 'particular process' and *khayāl* as 'general conceptualization', both emerging as responses to Aristotle's *Kitāb al-Shiᶜr* (Poetics) (see '*Ḥadīth ᶜĪsa ʾIbn Hishām*: *Khayāl al ᶜālām* and the Problem of Seeing World Literature', *Comparative Critical Studies*, 12 (2) (2015): 267–81).
72. The verb '*ashhadu*' is also the first word of the Muslim *shahāda*; it means 'to know and believe without suspicion, as if witnessed'. The *shahāda* is the

Muslim declaration of faith in the oneness of God and the acceptance of Muḥammad as His prophet.

73. Boutros Hallaq argues that the modern form of the symbolic vision or 'voyage', a remnant of pre-Islamic literature, came together at the end of the Abbasid period.
74. Al-Manfalūṭī describes his pleasure when transported into another world in implicitly sexual undertones (*al-Naẓarāt,* p. 9). The possible reasons behind his crying are: recognising mercy in others, life as *mawāṭin* (plural of *mawṭin* – homelands), and all the beauty of the world expressed in *Adab* (literature) as the explosion of hearts (p. 20). For Buṭrus al-Bustānī in *Udabā᾽ al-Arab* (1937) (Arab Writers), al-Manfalūṭī's sentimentalism found in European naturalism resonance with 'the spirit of the East in its lack of freedom . . . and in the dissolution of its morals and the spread of corruption in its midst so al-Manfalūṭī in his tears did not depart from the rule of his contemporaries except that he . . . exaggerated his weeping . . . till he became the messenger of death' (quoted in ᶜUwayḍa, *Muṣṭafā al-Manfalūṭī,* p. 173).
75. *al-Naẓarāt,* p. 10.
76. Hallaq, 'La Littérature', p. 161.
77. *al-Naẓarāt,* p. 12.
78. Ibid., p. 41.
79. This may seem to be an emphasis on presence and an Arabic form of logocentrism. However, al-Manfalūṭī is relying on a different tradition and linguistic model based on Islamic philosophies of language.
80. *al-Naẓarāt,* p. 13.
81. Ibid., pp. 14–15.
82. Ibid., p.22; emphasis mine.
83. Hallaq, 'La Littérature', p. 142.
84. *al-Naẓarāt,* p. 23
85. Hallaq, 'La Littérature', p. 139.
86. *al-Naẓarāt,* p. 26.
87. Al-Manfālūṭī, 'Al-Madaniyya', pp. 118–20.
88. *al-Naẓarāt,* p. 28.
89. Uwayḍa gives the example of *sajᶜ* or Qur᾽ānic rhyming prose in al-Manfalūṭī's eulogy of Jurjī Zaydān (*Muṣṭafā al-Manfalūṭī,* p. 43).
90. *al-Naẓarāt,* p. 29.
91. Ibid., p. 31.
92. Ibid., p. 33.

93. 'al-Bayān', pp. 212–14.
94. *al-Naẓarāt*, pp. 34–5.
95. Ibid., p. 40; emphasis mine.
96. The *kātib*'s position does not derive from Western notions of authority but from translation and repetition. The real here is discursive, mapping intersections of various literary, political, and social discourses, and is not 'outside' of time or the text.
97. The collection includes four originals (*mawḍuᶜa*), '*al-Yatīm*' (The Orphan), '*al-Ḥijāb*' (The Veil), '*al-Hāwīya*' (The Abyss), and '*al-ᶜIqāb*' (The Punishment) described as composed, and four mutarjama or translated stories: '*al-Shuhadā*ᵓ' (The Martyrs), '*al-Dhikrā*' (The Remembrance), '*al-Jazā*ᵓ' (The Reward), and '*al-Ḍaḥiyya*' (The Victim). '*Al-Shuhadā*ᵓ' rewrites *Atala* (1801), while '*al-Dhikrā*' is based on *Les Aventures du dernier Abencerage* (1826), set during the collapse of Islamic rule in Spain. '*Al-Ḍaḥiyya*' is based on Alexandre Dumas fils's *La dame aux camellias* (1848).
98. Al-Manfalūṭī, '*Al-Shuhadā*ᵓ', p. 35.
99. Chateaubriand uses 'vague des passions' in his *Génie du christianisme* published in 1802. His novel *René* was intended to condemn this condition.
100. Al-Manfalūṭī, '*Al-Shuhadā*ᵓ', p. 50.
101. ᶜAbbās Bayyūmī ᶜAjlān in *al-Manfalūṭī wa-atharuhu fī al-adab al-ḥadīth* (1977) (Al-Manfalūṭī and His Impact on Modern Literature) points to al-Manfalūṭī's lack of distinction between Islamic creed and Muslim practice (p. 79).
102. He based his adaptation on Muḥammad ᶜUthmān Jalāl's and Faraḥ Anṭūn's versions (Abū al-Anwār, *Al-Manfalūṭī*, p. 63).
103. Al-Manfalūṭī, 'ᵓIhdāᵓ al-riwāya', in *al-Faḍīla*, p. 5.
104. Saint-Pierre initially published *Paul et Virginie* in the fourth volume of *Études de la nature* in 1788. In 1789, contemporaneous with the Revolution, the first separate edition of *Paul et Virginie* appeared.
105. Saint-Pierre, *Paul et Virginie*, p. 103.
106. Ibid., p. 159; emphasis mine. He describes post-revolution moral law as natural law.
107. *al-Naẓarāt*, p. 355. In his ideal city, everyone is *naturally* equal, and he critiques Rousseau's need for education as a socialist equaliser.
108. Saint-Pierre, *Paul et Virginie*, pp. 212–13.
109. Ibid., p. 239.
110. Ibid., p. 240.
111. Al-Manfalūṭī, *al-Faḍīla*, p. 21.

112. Ibid., pp. 21–2.
113. Ibtessam El Esnawi also notes al-Manfalūṭī's framed dialogue in *Al-Shā*ᶜ*ir* as consistent with the *Arabian Nights* and *maqāmāt* (p. 101).
114. Saint-Pierre, *Paul et Virginie*, p. 251.
115. Al-Manfalūṭī, *al-Faḍīla*, pp. 77–8.
116. In the section on the missionary priest in the translation, there is an indictment of colonial power: 'he is one of those deceitful pretenders whom the colonial governments use to invade weak hearts and win them over without bloodshed and spending money! . . . and who are always in the surroundings of the colonial rulers to aid them in their habits of occupation and invasion' (Al-Manfalūṭī, *al-Faḍīla*, p. 102).
117. Al-Manfalūṭī, '*Al-Islām wa-l-masīḥiyya*', p. 158.
118. Ibid., p. 159.
119. Al-Manfalūṭī, '*Siḥr al-bayān*', p. 317.
120. Edward Said summarises that Cromer assumed the Oriental lived 'in a world of his own', but that only Cromer's language could render this world legible: 'the Oriental is *contained* and *represented* by dominating frameworks' (see Said, *Orientalism*, pp. 35–40). I am not suggesting that al-Manfalūṭī's view of literature undoes those frameworks, but simply that his deliberately literary critique emerges from within a sensitivity to colonial representational language.
121. Saint-Pierre, *Paul et Virginie*, pp. 299–300, 307.
122. Al-Manfalūṭī, *al-Faḍīla*, pp. 136–7.
123. See *Islam and the Political Discourse of Modernity* (New York: Ithaca Press, 1997), p. 68.
124. Saint-Pierre, *Paul et Virginie*, p. 242.
125. Al-Manfalūṭī, *al-Faḍīla*, p. 71.
126. Like the *kātib* of *al-Naẓarāt*, in *al-Faḍīla*, the characters feel 'transported into another world of the worlds of abstract souls filled with wonders and strange sights. Then we would return to ourselves . . .' (p. 83).
127. Al-Manfalūṭī, *al-Faḍīla*, p. 83.
128. Saint-Pierre, *Paul et Virginie*, p. 377.
129. Al-Manfalūṭī, *al-Faḍīla*, p. 189.
130. Most of his writing on revolution is published from 1921 to 1923. The most famous article is the '*al-Qaḍiyya al-Miṣriyya*' (Egyptian Cause) (1921), published with *al-Shā*ᶜ*ir*, and that led to his banishment. The article describes the revolution as the beginning of a storm and the *kātib* renders the storm's power when everyone else is in awe of it.

131. Al-Manfalūṭī, 'Ilā al-shuᶜarāʾ', introduction to *Al-Shāᶜir* p. 5.
132. Kilito, *Thou Shalt Not*, p. 4.
133. Aḥmad Ḥasan al-Zayyāt, in '*Muṣṭafā Luṭfī al-Manfalūṭī: bi-munāsabat dhikrā al-thālithat ᶜashara*', p. 1,122. The 3 May 1937 issue of *al-Risāla* published an advertisement for a festival to commemorate the death of al-Manfalūṭī, asking writers to prepare literary readings to celebrate '*adabihi al-khālid*' (his immortal literature) (p. 757).

# 3

# The Hero at Home: Muḥammad al-Sibāᶜī and Thomas Carlyle

> The nineteenth century was known to them [the Egyptian writers] as the school of *al-nubūᵓa* [prophecy] and *al-majāz* [metaphor or allegory] . . . [that] school counted among its leading lights such names as Carlyle, John Stuart Mill, Shelley, Byron, and Wordsworth. It was succeeded by a similar school which brought 'reality' and 'allegory' together – the school of Browning, Tennyson, Emerson, Longfellow, Poe, Whitman, Hardy, and others . . . A great deal from the spirit of these men pervaded the writings of the Egyptian poets who sprang up after Shawqī and his colleagues; but it pervaded them not because these poets were imitators or had no literary identity [of their own] but because it was a spirit common to the inclination of the whole era.
>
> Al-ᶜAqqād, *Shuᶜarāᵓ Miṣr*[1]

Unlike Muṣṭafā al-Manfalūṭī, Muḥammad al-Sibāᶜī took translation very seriously. Born in Cairo in 1881, he was one of the most dedicated students of Madrasat al-muᶜallimīn (Teachers' College), established in 1889, a landmark of the British colonial education system in Egypt, where students studied more English than Arabic literature.[2] Graduating in 1904, al-Sibāᶜī became a prolific translator of English literature and thought, his translations including Shakespeare's *Julius Caesar* (*Riwāyat Yūlyūs Qayṣar*) (n.d.), Thomas Carlyle's *On Heroes* (*al-Abṭāl*, 1911), *Macaulay's Essay on Addison* (1852) (*Maqālat Macaulay ᶜan Addison*) (1910–11), Herbert Spencer's *Education* (*al-Tarbiya*) (1908), Wilkie Collins's *The Woman in White* (*Riwāyat dhāt al-thawb al-abyaḍ*) (n.d.), and Charles Dickens's *A Tale of Two Cities* (*Qiṣṣat al-madīnatayn*) (1912).[3] The translation of Carlyle became a canonical text of the colonial school's curriculum while the translation of Dickens was made a required text in secondary school education in 1912.[4]

Al-Sibāᶜī practised faithful translation, and by supposedly adhering closely to original texts, intended translation to initiate a cultural renaissance in Egypt. In his translations and original works, al-Sibāᶜī sought the most apt Arabic expression for the English one and used classical Arabic, *taḍmīn* (inserting Arabic poetry) and *sajᶜ* (rhyming prose) to give his literature cultural legitimacy. In the introduction to al-Sibāᶜī's first 'original' book, *al-Ṣuwar* (Images), written in 1908 and published in 1909, Ibrāhīm ᶜAbd al-Qādir al-Māzinī writes that although al-Sibāᶜī was the editor of *al-Jarīda* (Newspaper) edited by Aḥmad Luṭfī al-Sayyīd, he was interested in translation and not politics. Al-Māzinī describes al-Sibāᶜī's translation as a faithful act of love, for he forgot 'himself when he was translating', overcome by the text. He would 'give it his heart and mind altogether, and then produce one of his exemplary pieces with his personal stamp of fidelity and precision'. In this scene of devotion, 'he would rarely change the original, or ignore a part of it': if he were to 'adapt the original', it would only be because 'the Arabic phrase that came to him . . . took over his core . . . for he was . . . enraptured by eloquence'.[5] Nur Sherif reiterates al-Sibāᶜī's fidelity in his translation of *A Tale of Two Cities*.[6] But al-Sibāᶜī has been accused of plagiarism, and some of his original works are creative rewritings of Western classics, such as his book *al-Ṣuwar* (1912), an appropriation of Irving Washington's *Sketchbook* that he later translates as *Kitāb al-Ṣuwar*. Al-Sibāᶜī's professed translation project, however, confirms Samah Selim's observation that *nahḍawī* intellectuals, considered 'anything less than strict equivalence in the translation process . . . to be . . . textual *mutilation*'.[7] *Nahḍawī* writers rejected the authorless, forged translation, advocating for absolute fidelity in transplanting European Enlightenment ideals in Egypt.

Al-Sibāᶜī certainly saw himself doing just that in his translation of Carlyle's *On Heroes*, and especially the lecture on Muḥammad as the prophet-hero, originally delivered on 5 May 1840. Carlyle's lecture was the first Orientalist defence of Islam and its prophet, and it influenced the representation of both in British culture.[8] His 1840 lectures on heroism focused on a historical and teleological account of heroism from gods to prophets, poets, writers, and politicians. Although a historian, Carlyle bases his account on three universal attributes of heroism: first, heroes are leaders, whose thoughts become history, for 'the soul of the whole world's history . . . [is] the history of these';[9] second, the essence of all heroes is the same, for they 'are all originally of one stuff; that only by the world's reception of them, and the shapes they assume, are they so immeasurably diverse';[10] and, finally, heroes operate according to 'that great central Law' of absolute good.[11] Choosing Muḥammad as the exemplary prophet-hero with these traits proved an easy sell to al-Sibāᶜī. The translation of Carlyle's *On Heroes* came out in instalments in the Cairo-based journal *al-Bayān* (Eloquence/ Bulletin), established in 1911 and edited by Sheikh ᶜAbd al-Raḥman al-Barqūqī, with the lecture on Muḥammad appearing first in translation while it is the second one that Carlyle gave.[12] The *Bayān* translations list the title of the original faithfully, as *al-Abṭāl wa ᶜibādat al-buṭūla* (Heroes and the Worship of Heroism). However, the complete translation, also published in 1911, changes the title to *al-Abṭāl* (Heroes), removing the reference of deifying people.[13] Al-Sibāᶜī must have translated many English texts that were published anonymously; however, his translation of Carlyle was the most influential, especially on the Dīwān School and Muḥammad Ḥusayn Haykal.[14]

After graduating from the Teacher's College, al-Sibāᶜī was granted and then denied a scholarship to attend Borough Road College near London because he refused to stand up to greet the British educational official, Douglas Dunlop.[15] His disrespect for British authority eventually resulted in a forced resignation from his position as a secondary school teacher.[16] Ironically, as Shaden Tageldin notes, al-Sibāᶜī's translation of Carlyle's *On Heroes* became a canonical text of the colonial school's curriculum. After all, due to his affiliations with Aḥmad Luṭfī al-Sayyid's political party, Ḥizb al-Umma, and Saᶜd Zaghlūl's Wafd, al-Sibāᶜī came to believe that 'the structural logic of the modern liberal nation-state required the reconstitution of the human as a subject of secular law'.[17] Carlyle's text was mostly appealing because it offered a spiritual replacement for French thought, Tageldin continues, and it *resembled* Islam,[18] but al-Sibāᶜī reproduces the original's secular representation of Islam in a Christian, English idiom. As a result, his translation perpetuates the English colonial project in Egypt.[19] Tageldin still invests too much in the translator's 'intention'. By making subtle changes to the original, *al-Abṭāl* does not simply *reproduce* English liberal thought in Egypt. In the introduction to the complete translation, al-Sibāᶜī presents *On Heroes* as a defence of man's greatness first and a defence of the prophet second, against the diatribes of Western scholars.[20] He describes Carlyle as an ultimate defender of Islam, and invites his Muslim readership to pay its respect and gratitude.[21] However, mesmerised as he was by Carlyle's defence, his translation changes the order of the narrative, deletes significant parts, changes the objects that the original pronouns refer to, and inserts Qurᵓānic language and classical Arabic poetry. As such, *al-Abṭāl* rewrites the original's narrative logic and reinscribes its secular history of great men into a contextual discourse on prophecy.

Jan Brugman questions the real impact of such translations, given that the choice was personal and eclectic, and usually of second- and third-rate literature. The popularity of al-Sibāᶜī's translation of *On Heroes* 'is without a doubt partly due, not to its literary merits but to the fact that Carlyle admired Mohammed'.[22] However, this particular translation was taught at the colonial school and had a decisive impact on al-ᶜAqqād, al-Māzinī, Ṭāhā Ḥusayn, and Muḥammad Ḥusayn Haykal, who describe its author as formative to their own education. Shaden Tageldin rightly points to a religion of literature mobilised by al-Sibāᶜī's translation, and specifically the lecture on the writer-hero: through these 'godly' writers, Carlyle's text does not 'cure' the West's 'epidemic of "atheism and unbelief" . . . since the century of Voltaire, al-Sibāᶜī suggests, but the Muslim "disease of unbelief" ["*dāᵓi al-kufri*"] in "great men"!'[23]

This religion of literature, however, born in the translation of British literature, does much more than seek a cure for Muslim unbelief. Focusing less on the translator's intention and more on the translation's influence, we find that al-Sibāᶜī's adaptation of Carlyle's text describes a deliberately *literary* critique of *doctrinal* religion. In other words, the translation does not separate religion and literature within a secular frame as much as it implicates both in revisionary reading and literary critique.[24] Al-Sibāᶜī's translation puts forth a distinction between good and bad writing and mobilises an elitist vocation for the writer, set apart from the public, in the likeness of a prophet but *not* a 'godlike' intellectual.

These aesthetic criteria also contributed to the changing readership of the

1920s and 1930s, and the increasing cultural representations of Islam. Israel Gershoni details the intellectuals' new-formed attention to the reading public in the 1930s.[25] Even though al-Sibāʿī's translation came out before this cultural shift, it anticipates it as we see in the modernists' self-presentation as cultural prophets (Chapter Four). After all, Carlyle's *On Heroes* glorifies the way in which print culture mobilises the individual reader by making it possible for him or her to become an active participant in the text's interpretation – and the hero-writer orchestrates this participation. In the fifth lecture in *On Heroes*, Carlyle enthusiastically declares printing to be equal to democracy, for the writer's speech 'becomes a power, a branch of government, with inalienable weight in law-making in all acts of authority. It matters not what rank he has.'[26] Carlyle's text does not just produce the heroic author; it also establishes his political influence on the masses.[27]

The translation also points to al-Sibāʿī's more sophisticated readership, which is no longer invested in didactic and abridged translations. However, this translated reader in al-Sibāʿī's case is both imagined and abstracted. Similar to the realists' dehumanisation of the masses, al-Sibāʿī does not think highly of the public, whom he describes as *al-dahmāʾ* (unthinking masses).[28] *Al-dahmāʾ* is meant to be an equalising term as it refers to all God's creatures from kings to slaves.[29] In fact, al-Sibāʿī emphasises the ridiculousness of the masses to offset the unique vocation of the *kātib* who gifts the reader a moral system.[30] But the writer has to distance himself from the masses to remain committed to pure philosophy and untainted by the corrupt materialism of the times.[31] This is not to say that al-Sibāʿī was *consciously* defining the individual in his translations or original works. Abdeslam M. Maghraoui explains that the masses do not fit the elites' newly imagined collective identity because the latter do not engage in any *real* deliberation on the priority of individuals. 'The masses are considered "abnormal," "socially ill," in urgent need of containment, surveillance, and medical treatment', Maghraoui continues. The 'pathological groups' of Egyptian society had to be medically cured 'to "normalise" their integration as abstract individual citizens into the newly defined political community'.[32] The liberal reformers' agenda was a response to the European gaze and not a programme of social justice.[33]

The liberal impulse that distinguished the individual writer from the masses is not a result of deliberation; rather, it is a product of the translation's reception and propagation of a religion of literature that inaugurates the writer as national prophet. In the introduction to *Khawāṭir fī al-adab wa-l-ḥayāt* (Thoughts on Literature and Life), a collection of al-Sibāᶜī's newspaper publications (1927–8), ᶜAbd al-Raḥmān Ṣidqī describes how his generation was so fed up with al-Manfalūṭī's 'romantic sadness' that it welcomed al-Sibāᶜī's works, especially the translation of Carlyle's *On Heroes*, with open arms.[34] While the reader of al-Manfalūṭī's translations was the average Egyptian, al-Sibāᶜī's reader is the intellectual drawn to Carlyle's spiritual legacy away from French atheism and Arab materialism. *Al-Abṭāl* is a successful translation because it showcases al-Sibāᶜī's skilful balance between *al-aṣāla* and *al-istiqlāl* (authenticity and independence) in mixing classical and modern styles.[35] In '*al-Adab al-ᶜaṣrī wa-l-qadīm*' (Contemporary and Traditional Literature), al-Sibāᶜī advocates for continuity between classical and modern literature as an antidote to the materialist spirit and its rejection of the past.[36] A noble word inserted within a public street style is no anomaly for al-Sibāᶜī, as the reality represented by Homer's *Iliad* and Ibn al-Rūmī's poetry is not different from today's reality, and the fall of language (*siqṭ al-kalām*) can only be remedied by bridging the old and new.[37] In the introduction to al-Sibāᶜī's *al-Faylasūf* (1957) (The Philosopher), a novel with a Socratic dialogue between a philosopher and his servant, Ṭāhā Ḥusayn acknowledges his debt to al-Sibāᶜī, who introduced thousands of men like him to British literature.[38] Ḥusayn frames al-Sibāᶜī's need for a philosopher – ancient or modern – to 'save' the useless majority within the use of *fuṣḥā* and the colloquial, defending al-Sibāᶜī's choice of *sajᶜ* and elements of 'old' literature to explain the *truths* of Western philosophy.[39] Moreover, a decade later, al-Sibāᶜī published *Abṭāl Miṣr* (The Heroes of Egypt) (1922) where he applies Carlyle's ideals of heroism to Egyptian political reality – especially Tharwat Basha's role in the Wafd's negotiations with the British – and includes several translated quotations from Carlyle's *The French Revolution*, *Past and Present*, and *Sartor Resartus*. But *Abṭāl Miṣr* is a different performance of translation: it translates the original terms of Carlylean heroism from abstract metaphor in a British context into a metonymic reality in Cairo. Cultural expression, in other words, begins to function metonymically to produce the Egyptian nation: it does not metaphorically elicit the ideals of one place against the other, but extends these ideals into the lived cultural realities of modern

Egypt.[40] Al-Sibāᶜī's conciliatory literary style that brings classical trends to bear on modern ideas, combined with his application of Carlylean heroism in *Abṭāl Miṣr,* confirms that his translation accomplished much more than reproduce Islam in a secular British idiom.[41]

After all, the secular itself is also a problem of translation. Talal Asad relates the birth of secularism in the Arab world to the influx of its terminology in translation.[42] If we were to approach these translations as critical transpositions of the terms 'modern' and 'secular' into an Egyptian colonial context, Carlyle's text, which straddles both the sacred and secular in interpreting human history, becomes a promising case study. If modernity requires transcending the sacred in the production of equal citizenship, and if, as Asad suggests, the secular cannot be conceived without the religious, then al-Sibāᶜī's translation would inevitably expose this tension by displacing it into an Egyptian milieu. We find this tension articulated most eloquently in the intellectual elite's uneasy relationship to the masses. Asad explains how under British colonialism, 'European codes arrived as *exceptions* applicable only to particular categories of subject and not as universal law applicable to everyone.'[43] Maghraoui agrees that when liberalism is exported or made to cross borders, its inherent contradictions manifest most tellingly in the exclusion of the masses since its particularistic ideology does not make room for every individual in the new nation-state.[44] For instance, Afaf Lutfi al-Sayyid-Marsot describes how Cromer's education reforms failed because he used 'Egypt's lack of education as an excuse for not extending liberal institutions'.[45] Such translated modernity ends up introducing a 'new kind of subjectivity', writes Asad, 'appropriate to ethical autonomy and aesthetic self-invention' – and these 'new' terms are annexed to familiar ones to establish the terms of recognition.[46] In this grammar of the new subject, the individual is encouraged to self-govern but these conditions are only made available to the upper classes as they are regulated by the state and the market economy.[47] Michael Ezekial Gasper locates Asad's new subject specifically in relation to the artistic representation of the peasant. The absolute translation of English and French secular, liberal thought fashioned 'individual subjectivities' as rational and industrious. Soon this new form of subjectivity 'translated into Egyptians' cultural vernacular through their extant Islamic vocabulary',[48] and nineteenth-century stories with their 'imaginary dialogues' show how the public good became moral truth.[49] With the turn of the century, after British colonialism, reform discourse begins to build on distinctions between East and West. Intellectuals borrowed European historicist ideas to criticise Europe[50] as Egypt transformed into an ideal that included the peasant as an *imagined* equal participant in the nation,[51] a 'countryside without politics'.[52]

But, I would add, the conditions of this new (literary) subjectivity are also not fully available to the intellectual elites either, placing them in a difficult position of adopting British liberal thought but realising that the abstracted ideals would ultimately fail in colonial Cairo. This delicate position explains al-Sibāᶜī's espousal of British literature but rejection of British occupation, urging us to focus less on his self-orientalising and more on his position in a society that has not reconciled liberal values with its colonial situation. Carlyle's metaphorical history, which claims universality at the expense of the particular, could not possibly be fully translated in colonial Egypt.

The role of the intellectual that emerges in *Abṭāl Miṣr* explains the simultaneous attraction to English literature and repulsion from French thought. Al-Sibāᶜī grew impatient with French thought and found English literature's pragmatic and spiritual mode more appropriate. Al-Sibāᶜī was also seduced, to use Tageldin's term, by Carlyle's belief that the poet/writer is the ultimate modern representative of his age; however, this role does not necessarily swap the Muslim prophet for the secular writer. In this chapter, I explore al-Sibāᶜī's translation as a rewriting of Carlyle's original on three levels: first, as a critique of Carlyle's politics of secular reading; second, as the romantic legacy of the poet-prophet; and, third, as the tension between 'individual' and subject in the works of Ḥusayn, al-ᶜAqqād, al-Māzinī, and Haykal.

## Politics of Reading: Sacred Undertones of Secular History

Carlyle figures as a sage in British literature,[53] and Erin M. Goss finds his turn to the past both 'an act of prophecy' and 'an act of reading' since the present is only accessible through the sage's reading of stories. Carlyle's prophetic position does not promise social cures, but intends to teach the reader specifically the skill of reading the present in order to both transcend the present predicament and transform the future.[54] Goss illustrates Carlyle's politics of reading through an example from Book III of *Past and Present* where Carlyle refers to the Qurʾānic story of 'Moses and the Dwellers by the Dead Sea' in George Sale's 1734 translation. Carlyle transforms the story's meaning, punishment for not recognising the prophet, into a 'story of the English present', abandoning both 'the sacred text' and 'sacred figure (Moses the prophet)', as per the 'revisionary reading' (read: secular) incumbent on every reader.[55] The Qurʾānic offenders lose the ability to speak, a threat to Carlyle's contemporaries who fail to recognise divine wisdom and are condemned to 'nonsense and gibberish'.[56] The exemplary tale, a secular reading of Moses's denied prophecy, demonstrates how the English people would fail to recognise the divinity of the modern-day prophet in political leaders or Carlyle himself. Only Carlyle could re-route the present time's Babelian moment: since all we are left with is 'cant' or jargon, Goss continues, the prophetic sage reminds readers of 'the metaphorical origins that have been forgotten in the language they speak'.[57] Carlyle *determines* original meaning in reducing the Qurʾānic story 'to the status of the repeated and aphoristic phrase',[58] as al-Manfalūṭī does to French stories in his adaptations. The more the aphoristic story – captured in the secular example of the prophet – is repeated, the more edifing it becomes.

In *Abṭāl Miṣr*, al-Sibāʿī adapts Carlyle's *literary* reading of the present specifically to the 1922 negotiations with the British. The book opens with severe criticism of British presence and actions in Egypt, but then takes on a *universalising* reading of Carlyle's text. In the introduction, al-Sibāʿī compares historical episodes to the *riwāya* (story), since in theatrical terms, there is always an apex after which comes a resolution,[59] even in his realistic and unmodified portrayal of events.[60] Amidst the chaos of revolution, according to divine will, the hero comes to restore order.[61] Al-Sibāʿī's retelling of great men's roles in mobilising human history also takes off from a critique of empty jargon. Al-Sibāʿī translates the following from Carlyle's *Past and Present*:

> You see if you clear your vision of this world with its words empty of meanings and its deeds empty of use, would you not find pleasure in relishing the beauty and sublimity of silence? . . . Woe to us, and shame on us if all our ammunition is speech, drone [*tanṭana*], things we just show to the vigilant eyes of others.[62]

The *ṭanṭana* is the meaningless gibberish of the masses, for, al-Sibāᶜī continues, 'Verbosity and the imagination, if not steered towards the inner truth or fact of things, are a delusion.'[63] The hero, here Tharwat Basha, is sent by nature to restore order to Egyptian life,[64] by reducing 'cant' and reintroducing a socially organic whole. In narrative terms, the hero is the end of revolution,[65] for we are born with a longing for order; the great man reinstates that order by placing people in their allotted places.[66] This restoration happens through heroic speech and not just action. Later in the book, he applies Carlyle's celebration of heroic eloquence to Tharwat Basha's speech, which combines fact with substance. He echoes Carlyle's defence of the writer in the fifth lecture, even when rejecting the atheism of Voltaire, and places Tharwat Basha – not a literary figure – among writer-heroes.[67]

The organic whole, the ultimate order of existence, materialises in al-Sibāᶜī's vision for Tharwat Basha's negotiations with the British. England used to think naively, al-Sibāᶜī tells us, that the revolutionary fever initiated by World War I would not spread to its colonies, which are governed by the same universal laws.[68] Applying Carlyle's universal doctrine against itself, al-Sibāᶜī writes that in the moment of revolt, only the human is left and labels of East and West become superfluous.[69] Egypt has proved to England what Carlyle wrote in *The French Revolution*, that the universe is one:[70] 'Egypt has cast on Britain realistically and practically in the last three years what her wise Thomas Carlyle had cast on her only *theoretically* in the previous generation.'[71] Carlyle's reading of 'secular history as prophecy', Rosemary Jann writes, coalesces in his search for regularity in historical patterns, so his approach remains metaphorical, as events are made to overlap in some greater scheme. But his literary approach to history requires 'the talents of a poet-seer to reconstitute the organic relationships' of the whole.[72] Al-Sibāᶜī selectively combines parts of the original in translation to produce his own *historicised* whole in *Abṭāl Miṣr*.

Carlyle quells his fear of the uncontrolled masses in the figure of his potential reader, using the interjectional present tense to turn readers into 'living witnesses'[73] so the narrator could coincide 'with the participants'.[74] The larger the narrative gaps become, the bigger the burden on the reader.[75] But Carlyle's reader, as Yoon Sun Lee notes, 'figures the British subject contemplating his own sublime image of the nation, forgetting his own role in the creation of that plenitude'.[76] Chris R. Vanden Bossche portrays the 'dialogue between the prophetic author and the factions dividing English society' in *Past and Present* as Carlyle's fantasy of 'the conversion of his contemporaries and the emergence of a new era'.[77] But this is an *imagined* conversion, and the reader is drawn to the sublime nation without recognising his or her involvement in its creation. The writer, moreover, has a political authority over the reader, and the task of Carlyle's text is to remind the readers of precisely this claim, for 'there is a divine right or else a diabolical wrong at the heart of every claim one man makes on another'.[78] 'All men are historians', he writes in 'On History', which appeared in *Fraser's Magazine* in 1830, for all we have is narrative: 'Cut us off from Narrative, how would the stream of conversation, even among the wisest, languish into detached handfuls, and among the foolish utterly evaporate! Thus, as we do nothing but enact History, we say little but recite it.'[79] Chaotic history is a chalkboard with layers of '[f]ormless, inextricably entangled, unknown characters', but it has at its deepest layer 'prophetic writing, still dimly legible there'.[80] Only the writer can decipher these and eventually achieve an 'Idea of the Whole'. In the lectures on heroism a decade later, Carlyle begins to approach history as biography: great men come to contain chaos in a narrative trajectory determined by the hero but guided by divine duty.

In applying Carlyle's theory of history to the Egyptian-British negotiations of 1922, al-Sibāᶜī has less faith in the reader, quoting Carlyle again on hero-worship as the necessary hierarchical structure of all social relations since the servant exists on a different plane and cannot recognise the master's heroism.[81] Perhaps that is because al-Sibāᶜī understood nationalism (through his colonial context) to be a wild instinct, one that needed to be reined in through the heroic figure's reason.[82] 'How sublime is the sound of the masses and how dangerous', he translates from Carlyle's *The French Revolution*, the 'voice of their instincts which is more truthful than their thoughts and ideas'. This voice is the 'most dangerous' one 'among all the masses of voices and ghosts that this earthly world is made of . . . whoever dares to contradict this voice and resist it has escaped the circle of time and boundaries of its prohibitions and laws'.[83] But al-Sibāᶜī does not suggest converting this mob. The paradoxes of liberal thought, which coerce the reader to imagine the nation but not his or her role in transforming it, are missing from al-Sibāᶜī's account. The religion of literature that emerges in this performance of translation is different from Carlyle's faith in metaphorical reading potentially converting the reader. The Arab masses, the majority of whom do not have access to the translation, are then further removed from the reading of history. Insofar as the reader remains unspecified, the confusion about the agent of historical interpretation is exacerbated in the Arabic translation, given that, as Tageldin notes, al-Sibāᶜī translates Carlyle's 'we' of the definitively liberal English individuals into the 'we' of the Arab readers. For Tageldin, al-Sibāᶜī's 'translated "we" . . . appropriates the touchstones of the British Empire's world-colonizing mission', making 'the colonized episteme of Islam . . . the ground of the universal itself'.[84] But even if on the surface al-Sibāᶜī's translations of Carlyle seem neatly to transpose a secular, liberal 'we' unto the Egyptian readership, his adaptations only confirm the untranslatability of context and inherent contradictions of liberal individualism.

Carlyle's literary reading of history as metaphor renders the prophet-figures of Moses and Muḥammad into demonstrations that neutralise the occasion of prophetic speech. This secularising gesture, the domain of Carlyle the sage, sits uncomfortably in al-Sibāᶜī's translation. Translation, consciously or not, interrupts this type of reading, calling attention to its stakes and conditions as a situated *act* of reading in the world. So, al-Sibāᶜī champions Carlyle's superior writer-hero, but does not reproduce the supremacy of the European poet to the Muslim prophet in the third lecture 'Hero as Poet: Shakespeare-Dante'. This lecture develops a position for the Egyptian writer that becomes formative for the romantics of the Dīwān school and modernists like Ḥusayn and Haykal. These writers cultivated the roles of poet and prophet into distinct authorial voices that derived some legitimacy from Carlyle's account in translation, but the translation itself foregrounds the boundaries between the two prophetic voices. By performing its own critical and literary reading, *al-Abṭāl* exposes how the original establishes the conditions of secular reading. It also reinstates the prophet Muḥammad as the particular universal – a divine prophet – to undo his status as mere example in Carlyle's text. In rearranging details, deleting paragraphs, and establishing a distinction between Muḥammad as *al-sirāj al-munīr* (the light-giving lamp) and Shakespeare as the *ᶜurwā al-wuthqā* (the tight bond with God) for the non-Muslim British, *al-Abṭāl* puts Carlyle's secular reading to the test.

## The Hero as Prophet

In announcing the second phase of the hero-prophet after the hero-god, Carlyle insists that 'these are all originally of one stuff', and they differ only in how the world receives them. Al-Sibāʿī renders 'stuff' as '*dhāt Allāh fahuwa jins wāḥid*', the being of God for he is one kind.[85] Al-Sibāʿī also changes the original's narrative order, beginning with the defence of Islam. His initial attraction to the text lies in its particular approach to Islam as similar to other religions. Although that is the obvious reason for the attraction to Carlyle, al-Sibāʿī was also consciously using English thought to replace French thought. The attraction to Carlyle's pragmatic thought, its resonance with the kind of spiritual rationalism that al-Sibāʿī found imperative to the nation's building, forms the stuff of *Abṭāl Miṣr*, where al-Sibāʿī applies Carlyle's precepts of heroism to particular instances of Egyptian heroes, such as Tharwat Basha. Carlyle's text becomes a manifesto of resistance to the British, and so al-Sibāʿī ignores the British context that produced the Carlylean oeuvre. One could consider this a misreading, or an inadequate reading on al-Sibāʿī's part, but intention aside, al-Sibāʿī abstracts Carlyle's work into a universal that is made to answer to the particular. In appropriating the text to his own ends, al-Sibāʿī succeeds in rupturing the original's claim to universality, its dismissal of Muḥammad's uniqueness and Egypt's right to independence.

Al-Sibāʿī had read enough English literature to understand narrative perspective, and in translating the lecture on the 'Hero as Prophet: Mahomet', he changes the original's ordering of details, beginning with a defence of Islam against those who call it full of lies. Al-Sibāʿī removes Carlyle's justification for choosing Muḥammad who is not 'the most eminent Prophet; but . . . the one we are freest to speak of' because he is not a Christian prophet. Muḥammad is also not 'the truest of Prophets' but since 'there is no danger of our becoming, any of us, Mahometans', Carlyle will represent him kindly, 'to understand what he meant with the world; what the world meant and means with him'.[86] Al-Sibāʿī removes Carlyle's non-threat of becoming Muslim and translates:

> The message delivered by that messenger has persisted over twelve centuries as the light-giving lamp [*al-sirāj al-munīr*] for about two hundred million

people like us, created by the same God as us. Could anyone think that this message by which numberless millions have lived and died is but a lie . . . I could never have that opinion.[87]

He adds '*al-sirāj al-munīr*' from the Qur'ānic sura 33:46,[88] intended to qualify the confusing original pronoun 'he' that points to all prophets, with Muḥammad as another example of the one 'kind' or '*jins*' of heroism. Tageldin reads the absent threat of becoming Muslim (a non-threat in Carlyle's text) and insertion of the Qur'ānic verse as subduing Carlyle's imperial supremacy.[89] But beyond the colonial politics of non/identification that Tageldin reads into this removal, I am interested in the translation's specifically *literary* critique of the universalising moves in Carlyle's narrative strategies.

Since it is impossible to identify with Muḥammad, despite the resonating 'like us', Carlyle applies the second universal trait to his example, access to inner truth and sincerity of voice: 'The word of such a man is a Voice direct from Nature's own Heart. Men do and must listen to that as to nothing else.'[90] The Voice's sincerity, the speaking prophet whose genuine utterances are transmitted intact, resonates well with a Muslim readership. Al-Sibāᶜī accentuates Muḥammad's genuine speech by inserting the prophet's voice in quotations[91] to replace the Carlylean quoted 'he said'.[92] He also inserts multiple poetic lines (*taḍmīn*), breaking out of the original's narrative perspective, and further distinguishing the prophet from the universalising 'he' – the original's generic hero-model.[93]

The translation responds precisely to Carlyle's *literary* critique of the Qur'ān. Carlyle describes how Mahometans ask whether it is not 'a miracle' and make it 'the light of their life'[94] – again al-Sibāᶜī uses '*al-sirāj al-munīr*'.[95] But Carlyle tells us that there must be 'discrepancies of national taste', because although George Sale's translation is 'a very fair one', the book is a 'toilsome' read, a 'wearisome confused jumble, crude, incondite; endless iterations, long-windedness, entanglement; . . . insupportable stupidity'.[96] The European reader cannot read it but 'the Arabs see more method in it than we',[97] for it is not organised teleologically into a recognisable historical narrative form:

The real beginning of it . . . lies almost at the end: for the earliest portions were the shortest. Read in its historical sequence it perhaps would not be so

> bad. Much of it, too, they say, is rhythmic; a kind of wild chanting song, in the original. This may be a great point; *much perhaps has been lost in the Translation here.* Yet with every allowance, one feels it difficult to see how any mortal ever could consider this Koran as a Book written in Heaven . . . as a well-written book, or indeed as a *book* at all; and not a bewildered rhapsody; *written,* so far as writing goes, as badly as almost any book ever was! So much for national discrepancies, and the standard of taste. Yet I should say, it was not unintelligible how the Arabs might so love it. When once you get this confused coil of a Koran fairly off your hands, and have it behind you at a distance, the *essential type of it begins to disclose itself*; and in this there is a *merit quite other than the literary one.* If a book comes from the heart, it will contrive to reach other hearts; *all art and author-craft are of small amount* . . . the primary character of the Koran is . . . its *genuineness* . . . its being a *bona-fide* book.[98]

The Qurʾān is specifically not a *literary* text, and only a book inasmuch as it promises to be the unmediated transmission of a genuine voice's revelations. Carlyle does not question the validity of the text's sources but treats it as an authentic collection of *non-literary* revelation that is most appealing in being unmediated.

The translation rearranges and condenses the entire section, beginning with the Qurʾān's '*iʿjāz*' (inimitablility) as a matter of national taste, because translation does away with the beauty of rhetoric: 'because no translation could reproduce its goodness and eloquence, the Arabs saw it as a miracle' (*wa li-anna al-tarjama dhahabat bi-ḥusnihi wa rawnaqihi fa-li-dhālika raʾāhu al-ʿArab min al-muʿjizāt*).[99] No wonder the European suffers through it because he reads it as news, but Arabs find in its verses what reflects their tastes. The particular national context – the *situated* act of reading – again here, as in *Abṭāl Miṣr*, revises the universal. As '*al-waḥy al-munzal*' (descended inspiration), the Qurʾān records a great man's true thoughts without any grandiloquence (*tanmīq al-kalām*).[100] However, the Qurʾān also includes poetry framed by the intermittent observations of a wise prophet.[101] The inadequacy of translation is offset by the sincerity of the prophet's voice that in both Carlyle's secular presentation and al-Sibāʿī's translation presents a double paradox: the Qurʾān cannot and yet must be read as a *literary* text. Rather than allow Carlyle to put down the Qurʾān's uniqueness, al-Sibāᶜī reframes the discussion within an indictment against Carlyle's, rather than his own, inferiority. After all, the Qurʾān has a Voice behind the text that Carlyle cannot understand because he does not know Arabic; perfect translation is thus impossible. The universal assumptions of Western evangelical sermons, which underlie Carlyle's lectures and reading of history, cannot be literally translated, and al-Sibāᶜī's style, inflected as it is with Qurʾānic discourse, refuses to be easily displaced by English solemnity.

*Al-Abṭāl* not only defends the prophet, but also critiques the undoing of his unique voice in imperfect translation. The translation's Qurʾānic insertions serve a double purpose: one, to replace a Christian idiom with a Muslim one; and, second, to situate the text in relation to the *adab* tradition. *Al-Abṭāl* maintains its complex position between sacred and secular, divine and literary. The Qurʾānic references and poetic insertions denote a more literary approach to translation and respond to Carlyle's critique by placing the prophet's life in an Arabic literary tradition. For instance, Carlyle sarcastically dismisses the 'wearisome Iteration' of Qurʾānic stories of the prophets, 'made up of mere tradition, and as it were vehement enthusiastic extempore preaching'.[102] For Carlyle, when the Qurʾānic tales are repeated, they do not provide any meaning, while his own 'extempore' relaying of the story of Moses in *Past and Present* repeats in order to instruct. In other words, Carlyle *still* treats the Qurʾān as a literary text, taking the sacred out of it so as to deliver his secular, prophetic message. The translation removes the original's derogatory reference to pointless iteration to undo Carlyle's monopoly over the text. Even if al-Sibāᶜī had a liberal secular agenda to propagate, his translation challenges a simple reproduction of this agenda through a deliberately *literary* critique not only of the original text but also of its simultaneous denial and assumption of perfect translation. In translating Carlyle's third and fifth lectures, al-Sibāᶜī continues to implicate religion and literature in the contingent act of reading.

## Poet-Hero and Writer-Hero

In Carlyle's lecture on the Poet-Hero, the *baṭal* (hero), *nabī* (prophet), and *shāᶜir* (poet) overlap until ultimately the *baṭal* becomes the *nabī-shāᶜir.* Carlyle reiterates the universality of his hero-model, in that the great poet is a politician, legislator, and philosopher.[103] For Carlyle, poetry and prophecy have always overlapped in being divinely inspired, and both prophet and poet have equal access to '*bāṭin al-ẓāhir*'[104] (the latent meaning) or 'open secret at the heart of all appearance'.[105] Both poet and prophet can access inner truth and tap into the original meaning of language through '*sirr Allāh al-jalīy*' (the manifest secret of God). The prophet accesses the correct moral code while the poet the aesthetic one;[106] the first tells us 'what we are to do, the other . . . what we are to love. But . . . these two provinces run into one another, and cannot be disjoined'.[107] Al-Sibāᶜī repeats Carlyle's dictum that the poet and prophet are 'inseparable' in relation to their access to God's truth,[108] but the translation soon qualifies this inseparability.

Carlyle is quick to distinguish between the Muslim prophet and universal European poet, as he does in his reading of the Qurᵓān as non-literary, for even though Muḥammad's following grew and Dante's did not, Dante's effect is 'far nobler' and 'more important'.[109] Muḥammad addresses the masses in a 'coarse dialect . . . filled with inconsistencies, crudities, follies', resonant only with great masses 'and there with good and with evil strangely blended'. Dante, however, 'speaks to the noble, the pure and great' for he 'is the possession of all the chosen of the world for uncounted time. Dante, one calculates, may long survive Mahomet. In this way the balance may be made straight again.'[110] Dante's superiority to Muḥammad is removed from the translation,[111] which treats the two as incomparable since Carlyle can never understand the Qurᵓān. After all, Dante and Shakespeare are Christian poets, and al-Sibāᶜī is just as free to evaluate their prophecy as Carlyle is to judge Muḥammad's.[112]

Al-Sibāᶜī removes the original reference to the national supremacy of England, and describes Shakespeare as *al-ᶜurwa al-wuthqā* (the tight bond) for the British who have no *kaᶜba*.[113] Shakespeare is superior because he realises through 'instinct and clairvoyance the demands of a situation [*bi-l-gharīza wa-l-fiṭra muqtaḍayāt al-ḥāl*] and the material of his poetry [*wa-l-mawād alladhī yaṣūgh minhā shiᶜrahu*]'. The 'extent of its power' is bound to 'the relationship between that material and the circumstances [*al-mawād wa-l-aḥwāl*]'.[114] Shakespeare does not receive external revelations; rather, his message is contingent. That al-Sibāᶜī places Shakespeare and Islam 'on the same metaphoric plane – the sacred', Tageldin writes, 'insinuates the exchangeability of the secular for the sacred'.[115] However, the comparison between Shakespeare's language and the Qur'ān is not viable in *al-Abṭāl* because of '*iᶜjāz al-Qur'ān*', even when prophetic inspiration remains the purview of the modern Egyptian writer. Al-Sibāᶜī's translation presents Shakespeare as the model poet-prophet, the 'untutored genius' whose work emulates Qur'ānic revelation in being inspired but does not coincide with it.[116]

In the lecture on the writer-hero, Carlyle and al-Sibāᶜī describe the 'good' writer as inspired by God. Thus, Goethe's work is prophecy in times of atheism (*kufr*).[117] Writing is 'the most miraculous art' (*min akthar al-funūn iᶜjāzan*)[118] and creates 'the state of miracles' (*dawlat al-muᶜjizāt*) in connecting past and present, East and West, Napoleon and Noah.[119] Carlyle uses the oral lecture form in a print-oriented culture, and al-Sibāᶜī uses rhyming prose (*sajᶜ*) to emphasise the writer's rhetorical eloquence and immersion in a tradition ('*yunkar*', '*tuḥqar*', '*kalām*', '*aqlām*', and so forth).[120] But the writer is specifically the new church and not the *sharīᶜa*.[121] While Tageldin reads al-Sibāᶜī's translation as a secular antidote to *kufr*,[122] al-Sibāᶜī's text recognises the Christian background of Carlyle's writer, and its dislocation in colonial Egypt. Even Carlyle admits to Muḥammad's easier task of destroying the pagans' physical statues, as compared to Samuel Johnson's battle with abstract ideology. 'Muḥammad discovered the vanities [*abāṭīl*] of his times', al-Sibāᶜī translates, in wooden forms that he could burn to empty 'his path, but the falsehoods of Johnson's time are not the kind that could be burned so they stayed in his path [*wa lākin abāṭīl zamān Jūnsūn ma kānat min mā yuḥraq bi-l-nār fa-baqiyat fī tarīqihi*]'.[123] Johnson's moment is not al-Sibāᶜī's, and the translation does not presume to equate the two, for the ideological obstacles in Johnson's path are not those of the Egyptian writer who, unlike Johnson, is an English colonial subject with access to Muḥammad's revelations. When identification with the Muslim is a structural impossibility in Carlyle's text, the reduction of Muḥammad's voice to a secular, literary example is doubly so in al-Sibāᶜī's adaptation. *Al-Abṭāl* transmits the original's tension between the sacred and secular prophet to the romantics and modernists studied in this book, and translates into a literary preoccupation with producing biographies of the prophet (al-ᶜAqqād and Haykal) and auto/biographies of the writer (al-ᶜAqqād, al-Māzinī, Haykal, and Ḥusayn).

## A Religion of Literature Caught in Translation

The Dīwān poets al-ᶜAqqād and al-Māzinī openly admit an indebtedness to al-Sibāᶜī's translations. For example, in *al-Dīwān*, they describe the poet's access to truth as an outcome of *fiṭna*, a penetrating clairvoyance, echoing Shelley and Carlyle.[124] For al-ᶜAqqād, al-Sibāᶜī's life and works are a biography of his age, for he initiated the Egyptian literary renaissance in the twentieth century.[125] Brugman reiterates the impact of al-Sibāᶜī's popular translation on the modernists' biographies of the prophet Muḥammad in the 1930s. Tageldin narrates this impact as an equivalence between secular literature and religion such that al-Sibāᶜī's *al-Abṭāl* made possible an approach to Islam as secular, 'reconcil[ing] religion to the political project of colonial modernity'.[126] Muhsin al-Musawi finds that the intellectuals' biographies normalise the colonial project by rendering Islam cultural.[127] Ḥusayn turns to religious subjects in the early 1930s, al-ᶜAqqād and Haykal write biographies of the prophet, and the Dīwān group's blasphemous poetry is repeatedly compared to Ḥusayn's *Fī al-shiᶜr al-jāhilī* (1925), a work that aroused the fury of al-Azhar by pejoratively suggesting that *jāhilī* poetry was written after Islam.[128] According to R. C. Ostle, al-ᶜAqqād and al-Māzinī's *al-Dīwān* (1921) is as controversial as the works of Ṭāhā Ḥusayn and ᶜAlī ᶜAbd al-Rāziq.[129] Nadav Safran describes the turn to Islamic subjects of Egyptian modernists as a 'reactionary phase' because they gave up on 'rationalism and a Western cultural orientation – without being able to produce viable Muslim inspired alternatives'.[130] Charles D. Smith explains Ḥusayn's and Haykal's turns to Islamic subjects as attempts to assuage their opponents and deliver their liberal agendas in a new disguise that accommodates 'the resurgence of Islamic sentiment'.[131] But all these conclusions leave out the specifics of literary adaptation and the question of genre: Why would Ḥusayn write his Islamic works in 1933, and then publish his controversial *Mustaqbal al-thaqāfa fī Miṣr* (The Future of Culture in Egypt) in 1938, a work in which he insists that Arabic and Islamic subjects not be taught in schools?[132] How does the development of literary aesthetics through translation relate to the resurgence of Islam in their works?

The secular biographies and Islamic writings, outcomes of a supposedly 'new' religion of literature arriving in translation, do not complete colonial modernity's project. Literary translation is never a straightforward process. The use of translation as a strategy to re-present Islam has to be read as a critical response to the colonial approach to religion as fundamentally translatable. Translation in its various forms does not just enable resistant alternative colonial discourses; the theorisation and practice of translation isolate the 'sacred' from the literary as they negotiate the influx of new genres in translation. Beyond domestication and foreignisation, translation exposes the formal logic of the original's representational strategies. While al-Sibāʿī's popular translation of Carlyle had a direct impact on the poet-prophet figure of modern Arabic literature (a third edition was published as early as 1930), a simple mapping of the Carlylean secular history onto the works of Arab intellectuals ignores the differences in their literary ambitions. For example, the same universalising impulse of nineteenth-century historiography that *Abṭāl Miṣr* finds in Carlyle's project emerges in the contemporaneous movement of British literary realism. A closer look at how the writers appropriated Charles Dickens's works shows the differences in their liberal agendas when we read their literature against their other pronouncements. One telling example is a comparison of al-Māzinī's and al-Sibāʿī's translations of Charles Dickens, especially since Dickens's novels capture the complex relationship between fiction and liberalism in nineteenth-century England. In the reception, transmission, and translation of English thought, the production of the secular liberal subject in the Arabic text is trapped in the promises and failures of different translation styles.

Al-Sibāʿī was the first Arabic translator of Charles Dickens, followed by al-Māzinī who adapted some of Dickens's short stories. Both were students of the New School or al-Madrasa al-ḥadītha, originally a group of intellectuals that came together in 1917, translated British, American, French, and eventually Russian literature and helped shape the modern Arabic short story.[133] While al-Māzinī engaged in outrageous plagiarising of many British texts, al-Sibāʿī at least intended to produce an accurate translation of Dickens's *A Tale of Two Cities*. Both al-Māzinī and al-Sibāʿī read Palgrave's anthology *The Golden Treasury* religiously – Muḥammad Mandūr has even said that al-Māzinī's first poetry book was entirely based on the anthology.[134] In the introduction to *al-Ṣuwar*, al-Māzinī describes al-Sibāʿī's translation style as 'precision in the commitment to the original and maintaining it' (*al-tadqīq fī iltizām al-aṣl al-mutarjam wa-l-muḥāfaẓa ᶜalayhi*).[135] Contrarily, al-Māzinī was repeatedly accused of plagiarism, presenting original texts as his own or significantly adapting large parts. In his translation of *Rubāᶜiyyāt ᶜUmar al-Khayyām*, he relies on Edward Fitzgerald's (1809–83) 1859 English rendition, making his translation a copy of a copy even further removed from the original source. He prefers Fitzgerald's to Aḥmad Rāmī's Arabic translation because the former changes the original to intensify the feeling of al-Khayyām's verse while the latter reproduces the language of the *muwashaḥḥāt*, undermining the original author's existential plight.[136] He especially praises Fitzgerald's rearrangement of lines so that the written word takes precedence over reality and becomes equal to the power of fate – meaning, as he explains, that it cannot be erased.[137] Al-Māzinī's illicit translations prescribe a literary reading practice that wants to claim both power and permanence beyond representation. Ironically, he still describes his translation method as being as 'literal' (*ḥarfiyya*) as possible when translating from one language to another.[138] He confesses that he deletes occasional lines, but only a handful, and in the extreme cases when there is no Arabic equivalent for the English original.[139] His book *Ibrāhīm al-kātib* – a disguised autobiography – also plagiarises sections from the Russian writer Mikhail Artzibashev's (1878–1927) *Sanine* (1907), which he had translated in 1920 as *Ibn al-Ṭabīᶜa* (Son of Nature).[140] In 1917, ᶜAbd al-Raḥmān Shukrī, the third member of the Dīwān group, attacked al-Māzinī's plagiarism in *al-Muqtaṭaf*, describing his critical essays on Ibn al-Rumī as stolen from Victor Hugo's 1864 *William Shakespeare* and Thomas Carlyle's *On Heroes*.[141]

In the magazine *Al-Risāla* (1937), al-Māzinī defends his plagiarism as the inevitability of influence since ideas intermarry without a writer's full awareness.[142] In '*Shaksbīr fī al-ᶜArabiyya*' (Shakespeare in Arabic), he also defends literary borrowing as inevitable, and justifies his plagiarism by relating a similar history of borrowing in Western literature: Homer himself in his quest for literary origin copied from Egyptian and other mythology.[143] Al-Māzinī's quest for cultural legitimacy is also plagiarised, for he adapts Carlyle's history as biography of great men without crediting the original, naming such biographies the only origin for a *modern* Arabic literature. Not surprisingly, in this modern literary history, the writer's narrative self figures as origin, and explains al-Māzinī's choice of Dickens's lesser known short story 'The Holly-Tree Inn: Three Branches' for translation. In '*Shajrat al-mīlād: thalāthat afruʿ*' (Christmas Tree: Three Branches), al-Māzinī is unusually faithful to the original story about a first-person narrator travelling by train from London to Yorkshire, and the translation's first section, '*Nafsī*' (Myself), foregrounds the subject's authorial account against the shifting snapshots of modern life.[144]

Al-Sibāʿī makes a different choice, but in his 1912 translation of Dickens's 1859 *A Tale of Two Cities* as *Qiṣṣat al-madīnatayn*, he is also repeatedly, even if more subtly, unfaithful to the original. In the introduction, al-Sibāʿī explains the purpose of his translation:

> [T]he third [of his publications] of the seeds of merit that we will we not hesitate to transmit despite the waterless sterility of this soil [reference to Egypt], with its dried up wealth and the lack of any hope for us to see the planting we have done with our hands turn ripe . . . yielding us its fruits. We had assumed that that will be the day when God will blow spirit into this nation and transform this grave that people call Miṣr into a country in which you encounter living people who think and reason and not mere vegetation in the image of humans who only grow and die . . . so that if God were to blow life into this dead people, the sun of feeling and emotion would shine on our buried seeds, creating around them a virtuous soil of mercy. And then the rains of humility and tenderness would come down on it, feeding its roots and growing its branches . . . and making it yield fruit.[145]

In general, as Nur Sherif and al-Māzinī note, al-Sibāʿī remains faithful to the original, occasionally making slight amendments.[146] But al-Sibāʿī inserts many footnotes to explain the original's references and almost always rewords the passages that include authorial intervention. Much like the filtering narrative voice that emerges in the translation of Carlyle's *On Heroes*, the novel's moralistic narrator is revised in the Arabic translation. In the novel's preface, Dickens credits Carlyle's *French Revolution* as the main source of his *Tale*.[147] And much like Carlyle's sage, the moralistic narrator of a *Tale* repeatedly intervenes to place events and intentions in perspective. Franco Moretti describes how English heroes, unlike French ones, hate being subjected to the external world's random tyranny. Thus, in eighteenth- and nineteenth-century English fiction, democratic stability, intended to contain the openness of fictional narrative, confines every individual to his or her particular slot in the world.[148] British realism radically separates the political sphere from the civil (private) one, and Carlyle's heroic figure who will restore order inspires the realist novel's commitment to the private individual. It is not surprising that *A Tale of Two Cities* opens with a tribute to Carlyle's account of the French Revolution. In rewriting the moralistic narrator's speech, al-Sibāᶜī's *Qiṣṣat* interrogates the realist narrator's access both to the historical event and the characters' subjectivity. Disillusioned with the moralising tendencies of the realist novel's liberal project, al-Sibāᶜī's translation is disturbed by Dickens's ironic and judgemental narrator. Many critics have discussed the realist novel's close ties with liberalism,[149] but in what follows, I focus on the ways in which the terms of this affinity are translated into Arabic in colonial Egypt.[150]

Irene Tucker finds that the realist novel's meticulous description of everyday realities creates both the author's and characters' 'condition of abstract universality'. The realist novel presents 'a formal logic', which renders 'contingent details of the material world' universally 'interpretable', much like Carlyle's secular history, because they have an author. The realist novel's characters can act, but their actions are ineffectual since 'the fictionality of the representation, the fact of its being the product of an authorial will' constitutes the 'pervasive cultural logic' of the novel. This logic promises comprehensive, detached worldviews but in fact is the only mechanism that renders 'accidental, contingent behaviors' purposeful.[151] By making the arbitrary conditions of contingency meaningful, the realist novel legitimates the contractual paradoxes of liberal ideology in nineteenth-century England – giving people freedoms while simultaneously determining their movements in the social and political spheres.[152] After all, Victorian novels also created the world they represented, offering 'interpretive possibilities for political, religious and reformist discourses'.[153] They contained 'potentially volatile discourses' and became alternate 'ways of forming', 'knowing and being in culture'.[154] The ultimate arbiter of such cultural legitimation is the realist novel's narrator who determines characters' intentions, as is the case, for instance, with *A Tale*'s narrator who critiques both the French Revolution's and liberalism's threat to human agency.[155] In a world that opposes political agents to writers, the Victorian novel embodies the division between fact and fiction, writing and doing.

In his translation, al-Sibāᶜī is acutely aware of this dichotomy and the original's metaphorical fillings for concrete actions. In literalising some of the original's metaphors and rewriting others, al-Sibāᶜī intends his translation to bring the Egyptian people to life again and instigate the semblance of human agency in a destructive history of occupation. Meanwhile, this newfound sense of agency remains bound to the promise of fiction and to an imaginary and imagined participation in political history. Like al-Māzinī, he also uses translation to authorise a new form of literary reading, here an antidote to political stagnation. In Chapter Two, I read the translation of romanticism as ultimately foiled by the writers of the realist tradition, who demonised the masses into brutes to offset the intellectuals' nationalist agenda. Dickens's 'ineffectual' characters – as mediated in al-Sibāᶜī's translation – place realism's production of abiding citizens in crisis. Curiously, and at least in its introduction, the Arabic translation approaches the original novel as a promise of triumphant individual agency. But the question remains: does the translation merely reproduce the claims of liberalism and individualism or is it conscious of the incompatibility of such claims with an Egyptian colonial context?

In the introduction, al-Sibāᶜī understands this incompatibility again in terms of narrative structure. He begins by comparing the narrative mode of the original novel's premeditated ending (the inevitable death of Sydney Carton to save his lookalike, Charles Darnay) to the tales of the *One Thousand and One Nights*. Al-Sibāᶜī explains how in all his other novels, Dickens would come up with a title as he went along but this particular novel, and especially its ending, had to be carefully planned from the outset. In a sense, al-Sibāᶜī is saying that the novel can only begin when it has already ended, since death at the guillotine punctuatues the entire story. It is stuck in a narrative that it has already told, one that moves inevitably towards death. In reading the other serialised novels of Dickens, the reader would be placed in 'an awkward position similar to that of Scheherazade in *One Thousand and One Nights*'; however, in *A Tale*, Dickens 'limited the purpose and named the object that he was marching towards . . . so his story came out harmoniously and . . . well-woven'.[156] Scheherazade tells stories to delay her death sentence and sees it annulled in the end (in the post-Galland completed version of the tale-collection). In his other novels, Dickens does not prescribe an inalterable death sentence and so the reader, like Scheherazade, continues to read the tale uncertain of the ending.

As a tale of revolution, Dickens's novel addresses all the people and enables a dynamic of identification that al-Sibāʿī describes as contagious.[157] The characters are real, as real as 'we' are, in a world exactly like 'ours'.[158] The novel is successful because of the identification it presents between Dickens, his characters, and readers.[159] The first-person pronoun 'we' echoes the 'we' that opens the original novel and the 'we' of Carlyle's secular British audience. Al-Sibāʿī tells us that because the novel turns every reader into a spectator, the characters can also reflect the Egyptian reader. Just as the novel compares revolutionary France to nineteenth-century England, al-Sibāʿī finds that, with minor adjustments, it can reflect 1912 Cairo. However, the identification between the British 'we' and the Egyptian reader cannot be absolute.

The translation makes the original speak to the Egyptian context through paratextual insertions and metatextual moments at the limits of genre. The original's multiple narratorial voices, from those of the characters to the moralist's perspectives, are condensed into the voice of the sceptical reporter. All the original metaphors that refer to the narrator's omniscience are made to refer to the only omniscient author – God – thus reframing the relationship of the novel to history within a reference to *Allāh* or al-Sibāʿī's Muslim God. For instance, in describing the female witness at the trial, the translation adds the following: 'The actor, if he comes to an exciting, suspenseful part of the story [*riwāya* –the same description he uses in *Abṭāl Miṣr*] and all eyes are on him, then on the faces of the people without even noticing would be the same meaning that is drawn on his face.'[160] The introduction of Sydney Carton is the culmination of this meta-textual moment. In the original, the narrator tells us:

> Allowing for my learned friend's appearance being careless and slovenly if not debauched, they were sufficiently like each other to surprise, not only the witness, but everybody present, when they were thus brought into comparison. . . . My Lord inquired of Mr. Stryver (the prisoner's counsel), whether they were next to try Mr. Carton (name of my learned friend) for treason? But, Mr. Stryver replied to my Lord, no; but he would ask the witness to tell him whether what happened once, might happen twice;

whether he would have been so confident if he had seen this illustration of his rashness sooner, whether he would be so confident, having seen it; and more.[161]

The first-person pronoun, which represents the ironic conflation of the narrator and lawyer into one voice, is absent in translation:

> And with what appeared on *his* legal friend of the traces of neglect in his dress and chaos in *his* aspect and also the signs of addiction to alcohol and engrossment in unemployment, there was between the two men such resemblance that it amazed upon comparison all those present for the hearing. . .. So the judge asked Mr. Stryver (the name of the lawyer) if he were asking the court with this act to double the accusation of treason on Mr. Carton (the name of his legal friend) as well? My Stryver said no. But he would ask the witness if it were not in God's power to duplicate appearance and repeat the image as things and acts are repeated, and had he seen this overwhelming evidence that is hard to break or brush over before this hour, would he still have dared to say with his own complete will that he was that sure of the truth of his testimony?[162]

The reader wonders why al-Sibāʿī would change the narratorial 'my' into 'his' but openly insist on the 'we' extending to the Egyptian reader in the introduction. The original narratorial voice becomes the detached voice of a removed and distant narrator in the translation. In other words, the reporting narrator of the translation adopts a conclusive legal language that the original novel parodies. The translation's tone confirms the likelihood of resemblance between two random characters, because God would have wanted it to be so, reminding readers that the two are not the same but merely resemble each other. By making *Allāh* the only credible witness, the translation ruptures the original novel's self-enclosed world – intended to echo Carlyle's organic whole that amends the chaos of the world outside.[163] If, as Joseph Childers describes, the Victorian novel created Victorian culture, al-Sibāʿī's translation tests the original novel's representational logic by pointing outside the narrator's authority to God the creator. [164] The original's 'what happened once, might happen twice' becomes a question as to whether 'God's power to duplicate appearance and repeat the image as things and acts are repeated' could reveal the error of the witness's human judgement. There are many such references to God in the translation: for instance, in Chapter Five of Book I, with the spilling of the wine in the Parisian suburb of Saint Antoine; Chapter 21; and Chapter 3 in Book I, the Night Shadows passage.[165] In a world ultimately authored by God, the narrator's claims to creation are void. *Qiṣṣat* exposes the mechanisms of substitution fundamental to both liberalism and realism, despite the translator's 'liberal' leanings.[166]

Even if realism and secular liberalism could be translated, the original context that has made them possible remains untranslatable into Arabic. What emerges here through al-Māzinī's and al-Sibāᶜī's different translation styles is a similar preoccupation with the narrator's absolute authority as guarantor of narrative meaning. While Samah Selim finds that narrative subjectivities emerge in Egyptian fiction only after the 1919 Revolution, I would argue that these early engagements with Dickens and Carlyle are a necessary point of departure for the study of Arabic literary subjectivity. In al-Manfalūṭī's translation, we saw a similar distrust of fictional subjectivity. Even when the Dīwān poets, Ḥusayn, and Haykal champion the writer's subjective individuality, the constitution of narrative subjectivity as the ultimate locus of truth remains contentious in their works. The various translation styles from *iqtibās* to *taᶜrīb* to *naql* reveal an essential discomfort with the generic stipulations of European literature.

## Generic Legacies: Authors and Heroes

The major legacy of al-Sibāᶜī's translations is not their influence on the production of Islamic literature (Brugman), or wholehearted reproduction of Islam in a secular British idiom (Tageldin, al-Musawi). Rather, al-Sibāᶜī's *al-Abṭāl*, *Qiṣṣat*, and *Abṭāl Miṣr* foreground the paradoxes inherent to British liberal individualism.[167] Al-Sibāᶜī's adaptations of Carlyle and Dickens both reproduce and critique the idea of the intellectual as the narrator/hero capable of changing and interpreting history. This narrative is secular to the extent that it places agency in the hands of the writer as prophet. However, this secular 'religion of literature' is also caught in the impossible task of translating liberal individualism. Al-Sibāᶜī's translations expose the tension between the liberal individual as a colonial abstraction and the poet-writer's subjective voice, between biography and autobiography in the works of al-ᶜAqqād, al-Māzinī, Ḥusayn, and Haykal. Chapter Four will deal more thoroughly with the history of biography and autobiography in the Arabic tradition before the encounter with the West. Biography as *sīra* or *tarjama* has a rich presence in the Arabic tradition, and notable scholars wrote their autobiographies mostly as biographies. The slippage becomes more problematic with the influence of Western literature in translation.

It is not surprising then that in the introduction to *ᶜAbqariyyat Muḥammad*, al-ᶜAqqād acknowledges precisely this debt to the Carlylean text: after all, the need for his book came up in a discussion of the impact of Thomas Carlyle's defence of the prophet and the need for an Arab (authentic Muslim) secular account of the prophet's life, even if thirty years later. The elitist al-ᶜAqqād finds in the modern-style biography the best means to single out the Prophet Muḥammad's singular example in order to remind people of greatness in a time when public rights have taken away from the private ones of great men.[168] Here, al-ᶜAqqād refers to the threat of democracy and enabling the masses' access to rights equal to the elites' entitlements. Al-ᶜAqqād internalises the poet-prophet figure that Carlyle develops in tandem with the English romantics that the Dīwān group was reading. However, the 'subjective' appeal of Carlyle's text – Muḥammad as human – remains a response to colonial abstractions of individuality. Ostle describes the 'subjective, egocentric tendencies' of the Dīwān group's poetry' as a reaction to the impersonal works of reformists such as Qāsim Amīn and Luṭfī al-Sayyīd, 'concerned basically with the significance of the individual in social and political terms'. Popular leaders such as Muṣṭafā Kāmil and Saᶜd Zaghlūl 'gave broad sections of the Egyptian population the conviction that they too as individuals had a part to play in the struggles and the destiny of the newly emerging nation state'.[169] That tension between the subjective expression of the poet and social expression of an abstract individualism is the major legacy of al-Sibāᶜī's translation. Even when the secular legacy of English individualism remains tangible in al-Sibāᶜī's work, this chapter has focused less on the translator's intention and more on the translation and its reception. Israel Gershoni emphasises the importance of reception to the supposed 'religious' shift of the Egyptian intellectual elites in the 1930s, focusing primarily on Haykal's *Ḥayāt Muḥammad.* Wary of public opinion, Haykal produces his biography in a form that appeals to the masses.[170] However, Gershoni argues that this conclusion ignores the text's reception, as does Tageldin in reading al-Sibāʿī's translation. Gershoni reminds us that since authorial intention can never be reconstructed, a text's reception matters most. In the context of translation, this imperative becomes even more relevant, as the original authorial intention is already adapted to the translator's whims and the cultural considerations of the reading public. It also points to the texts' reception outside the usual reading public, to the masses whose tastes determined the shape and reading of the biography.[171] The 'intellectual metamorphosis' in fact 'created the desired common ideological ground between intellectuals and broad sectors of literate society',[172] an outcome averse to the 'intention' behind al-Sibāʿī's translation as it suggests a yielding to the tastes of the public rather than the intellectual cultivating these tastes. Under the influence of al-Sibāʿī's biography, Haykal produces a 'new cultural discourse' common to intellectuals and the reading public.[173]

What Gershoni is pointing to, and which I read as a legacy of al-Sibāʿī's translation of Carlyle, is an anxiety about authorship. Chapter Four explores this anxiety in the dichotomy between author and hero in auto/biography and how it is passed on to the modern Egyptian novel. These secular biographies represent more than a questionable turn to Islamic subjects – rather, as early novels, they test the limits of fiction and subjectivity. After all, these *tarjamas* come together under the influence of translation, and the translator's voice, in choosing whether to acknowledge the original, further complicates the division between biography and autobiography. Al-Sibāʿī's particular influence is in transmitting a separation between the hero and narrator of history. In line with Stephen Sheehi, I am suggesting that *nahḍa* studies focus less on the modernists' intentions and more on their works.[174] Reading literature as a contingent act in their works suggests that their texts were not simply trapped in imposed narratives of modernity. Rather, the assumption of cultural prophecy, like the liberal project, is caught up in the movement between biography and autobiography, two discursive subject positions. Both remain trapped in the inequivalences of translation and remain necessarily incomplete.

Instead of reading this new religion of literature as an outcome of the translation of secularism that simply replaces the prophet with the poet, al-Sibāʿī's translations urge us to explore the narrative tension between author and hero. Carlyle's history as biography encounters Jean Jacques Rousseau's

(1712–78) history as autobiography in the next chapter, pointing to the complex legacies of the translation of British and French thought in the early twentieth century. The overlap between biography and autobiography manifests in al-ᶜAqqād's *ᶜabqariyyat*, Haykal's *tarājim*, al-Māzinī's sanctioned plagiarism, and Ḥusayn's self-positioning as a Mediterranean and Egyptian writer. This logic of emulation anticipates the more articulated identification of Ḥusayn and Haykal with the European writers they translate. Al-Sibāᶜī's auto/biographical approach to history paves the way for the emergence of the *faylasūf* or philosopher figure. We begin to witness the production of a different literary genre that marks a shift from the strict adherence to Western models towards a return to Islamic cultural forms and themes rather than Islam. Muhammad Siddiq notes the 'generic indeterminacy' of these authors' works, and Egyptian critic Ghālī Shukrī points out specifically the non-genre of Ḥusayn's autobiography.[175] However, Siddiq, like others, regards this early generic negotiation as a failure, because the author could not distance 'himself' enough to produce a novel. As a form, the novel requires a clear separation between author and hero that these early autobiographies and biographies were not capable of achieving.

Instead of focusing on the failure of these early efforts, I am suggesting that an engagement with translation shows how this separation between the two entities of hero and author translated the paradoxes of liberal individuality into Egypt. This legacy is forgotten in generational memory. In the introduction to al-Sibāᶜī's *al-Faylasūf* (the philosopher), Ḥusayn describes the difference between the two generations, father and son, Muḥammad and Yūsuf. The way Yūsuf completes his father's unfinished novel becomes exemplary of this generational rift: Yūsuf's generation is impatient, unable to transcend reality, while Muḥammad's was more daring and creative.[176] The *faylasūf*, Ḥasan Afandī, a stand-in for al-Sibāᶜī's ideal philosopher-hero, imagines himself a judge of the people, sentencing sinners to death and then writing them redeeming obituaries.[177] The people are 'imaginings', helpless products of their environments,[178] but the philosopher's abstract musings are offset by a servant's practical retort.[179] Ḥasan Afandī spends the whole 'novel' writing *The History of Modern Philosophy*, which he never completes. [180] Yūsuf al-Sibāᶜī, and not Muḥammad, decides, when finishing the novel, that the *History* book should remain unfinished.

The unfinished book within the unfinished novel speaks to the problem of genre arriving in translation. Naguib Mahfouz writes that the 'autobiographical works' of Ḥusayn, Haykal, and al-Ḥakīm were 'milestones on the road to the novel', but not novels. The absolute difference, comments Muhammad Siddiq, between autobiography and novel is in the writer's 'formal separation' from the text, 'the fundamental distinction between the (Arab) writer . . . and the novelist proper'. Novels become novels when the form and structure supplant the writer.[181] Siddiq nevertheless recognises their difficult task of creating 'a working sense of individuality' against Arabic literature's resistance to the 'personal' and the 'real',[182] pointing to the birth of the modern 'author'.[183] But these earlier texts negotiate the terms of personhood and the legal legitimacy of individuality in a colonial context. They may not measure up to the 'novel', but they expose precisely what goes into *making* an Egyptian novel. In the Egyptian context of translation, narratives of subjectivity should not be read merely as reproducing a foreign secularity. Rather, they complicate narrative modes and critique representational politics in ways that should remap their positions in current genealogical mappings of the Egyptian novel. Al-Sibāᶜī's translation may have facilitated the use of religion as a cultural commodity in the early twentieth century, but the more significant question addresses how such a transformation happens. To locate this transformation, I focus on his translations' dual legacy – a literary critique of both British literature's legitimating narrative modes and its separation between author and hero – and specifically on how this legacy impacts the works of the modernist giants Muḥammad Ḥusayn Haykal and Ṭāhā Ḥusayn in Chapter Four.

## Notes

1. *Shuᶜarāᵓ Miṣr* (Cairo: Maktabat al-Nahḍa, 1937), pp. 192–3.
2. Brugman, *An Introduction*, p. 98.
3. For a list of al-Sibāᶜī's works, see Brugman, *An Introduction*, pp. 104–6.
4. I owe this information to Shaden Tageldin's article 'Secularizing Islam'. Nur Sherif in *Dickens in Arabic: 1912–1970* (Chapter 3) also confirms that the translation was used in schools.
5. *'Al-ᶜustādh al-Sibāᶜī wa adabuhu'*, introduction in *al-Ṣuwar*, 1909, p. 8.
6. *Dickens in Arabic: 1912–1970*, pp. 5–6.

7. Selim, 'Nation and Translation', p. 9; emphasis mine.
8. Michael K. Goldberg attributes 'the revolution in historical estimates of Muhammed since the later part of the nineteenth century' to Carlyle's lecture (Goldberg, 'Introduction', in Thomas Carlyle, *On Heroes, Hero-Worship, and the Heroic in History* (1841), ed. by Michael K. Goldberg, Joel J. Brattin, and Mark Engel [Berkeley: University of California Press, 1993], pp. xxi–lxxx, p. xliii). Muhammed A. Al-Daᵓmi corroborates this view in an Arab context (*Arabian Mirrors and Western Soothsayers: Nineteenth-Century Literary Approaches to Arab-Islamic History* [New York: Peter Lang, 2002], p. 84). On Carlyle's contribution to improving Western perceptions of Islam, see Said's *Orientalism*, p. 152; and W. Montgomery Watt's 'Carlyle on Muhammed', *Hibbert Journal* 53 (1954–5): 247–54.
9. Carlyle, *On Heroes*, p. 5.
10. Ibid., p. 6.
11. Ibid., p. 7.
12. *Al-Bayān* later became a strictly literary journal that published translations (see Moosa, *Origins*, p. 105).
13. My quotations refer to the third edition of the complete translation, Muḥammad al-Sibāᶜī (trans.), *al-Abṭāl, taᵓlīf al-faylasūf al-akbar Tūmās Kārlayl*, 3rd edition, (Cairo: al-Maṭbaᶜa al-Miṣriyya bi al-Azhar, 1930).
14. Brugman, *An Introduction*, p. 100.
15. Since I was unable to consult a copy of ᶜAlāᵓ al-Dīn Waḥīd's *Muḥammad al-Sibāᶜī: al-Adīb alladhī sabaqa ᶜaṣrahu* [Muḥammad al-Sibāᶜī: the Writer who Preceded his Age] (Cairo: al-Hayᵓa al-Miṣriyya al-ᶜāmma li-l-kitāb, 1982), I rely on Tageldin's references in this section (see Tageldin, 'Secularizing Islam', pp. 131–2). Al-Sibāᶜī's reaction was not an isolated one: Indira Falk Gesink notes that in January 1906, Douglas Dunlop declared a new policy to expel any student failing her examinations, and his action mobilised student withdrawals from programmes and fuelled demonstrations (Gesink, *Islamic Reform and Conservatism*, p. 198).
16. Tageldin, 'Secularizing Islam', pp. 48–9.
17. Ibid., p. 127.
18. Tageldin, *Disarming Words*, pp. 173–4.
19. Ibid., p. 157.
20. Al-Sibāᶜī, '*Kalimat al-Muᶜarrib*', p. i.
21. Ibid., k.
22. Brugman, 'Muḥammad al-Sibāᶜī and the Egyptian Literary Renaissance', p. 87.

23. Tageldin, 'Secularizing', pp. 189–90.
24. Reinhard Schulze describes how printing in the nineteenth century fundamentally changed the Muslim outlook on history and mediated the cultural production of Islam between good tradition (*aṣlī*) and bad tradition (*taqlīd*), both determined by religious scholars who dictated this self-knowledge (see 'The Birth of Tradition and Modernity in 18th and 19th Century Islamic Culture: The Case of Printing', *Culture and History* 16 (1997): 29–72, p. 49).
25. See Gershoni, '"The Reader"-Another Production.
26. Carlyle, *On Heroes*, pp. 189–90; *al-Abṭāl*, p. 166.
27. Carlyle's approach to heroism arguably contributed to the rise of fascism. See J. Salwyn Schapiro's 'Thomas Carlyle, Prophet of Fascism', *Journal of Modern History* 2 (1945): 97–115 and H. F. C. Grierson's *Carlyle and Hitler* (Cambridge: Cambridge University Press, 1933).
28. In '*Rijāl al-fann wa-l-adab*' [Men of art and literature], 9 March 1928, collected in *Khawāṭir*, p. 172.
29. Ibid., pp. 172–3.
30. In '*Kutub*' (Books), published on 24 February 1928, collected in *Khawāṭir*, p. 142.
31. Ibid., pp. 182–3.
32. Maghraoui, *Liberalism without Democracy*, p. 90. Also see, Jamal Mohammed Ahmed, *The Intellectual Origins of Egyptian Nationalism* (London: Oxford University Press, 1960); Smith, *Islam and the Search*; and Nadav Safran, *Egypt in Search of a Political Community: An Analysis of the Intellectual and Political Evolution of Egypt*, 1804–1952 (Cambridge, MA: Harvard University Press, 1961), pp. 125–8.
33. Maghraoui, *Liberalism without Democracy*, p. 95. For Selma Botman, the 1923 Constitution was built to fail, especially that liberalism remained regulated by the monarchy. Political parties such as the Wafd and the Liberal Constitutionalists eventually lost hope. Young Egypt (Miṣr al-fatāt), established in 1933, and the Muslim Brotherhood, who gained more momentum in the 1930s and 1940s, formed in reaction to the failure of the liberal project and the secular programs of the Wafd and other groups (See 'The Liberal Age, 1923–1952', in *The Cambridge History of Egypt, Volume 2: Modern Egypt from 1517 to the End of the Twentieth Century*, M. W. Daly (ed.), [Cambridge University Press, 1998]), pp. 285–308, esp. pp. 286, 297).
34. Ṣidqī, 'Muqaddima', p. 4.
35. Ibid., pp. 6–7.

36. Al-Sibāᶜī, *Khawāṭir*, pp. 120–1.
37. Ibid., pp. 122–3.
38. Ḥusayn, 'Muqaddima', p. 5.
39. Ibid., pp. 7–8, 11.
40. See Anshuman A. Mondal, *Nationalism and Postcolonial Identity: Culture and Ideology in India and Egypt* (London: RoutledgeCurzon, 2003), p. 5. I am grateful to Shaden Tageldin for bringing my attention to this book.
41. The influence of Herbert Spencer's thought is also significant through al-Sibāᶜī's translation of *Education*. Spencer invests in educating the individual to serve the needs and purposes of government.
42. Asad, *Formations* (2003), p. 207. For Asad, there are two prevalent approaches to reform beyond its European intention: either as failure to modernise or as native manifestations of experiences coming from both local traditions and 'contradictory European representations of European modernity' (p. 217). Asad resists both positions and focuses on 'new institutional and discursive spaces (themselves not immutably fixed) that make different kinds of knowledge, action, and desire possible' (p. 217). In my analysis, these new discursive spaces, especially as mediated by literary discourse, do not simply authorise the secular state's new grammar. Rather, these emerging discourses historicise representation by exposing the limitations of both new and traditional literary forms and interrogate the state's tautological narrative of legitimacy.
43. Ibid., p. 218; emphasis in the original.
44. Maghraoui, *Liberalism*, p. 89.
45. See Al-Sayyid, *Egypt and Cromer*, p. 86. Cromer also signed against teaching foreign languages in rural schools so as to minimise resistance and expertise. See also Hoda A. Yousef, *Composing Egypt*, pp. 140–3.
46. Asad, *Formations*, p. 225.
47. Ibid., p. 226.
48. Gasper, *The Power of Representation*, p. 65.
49. Ibid., p. 104.
50. Ibid., p. 189.
51. Ibid., p. 191.
52. Ibid., p. 216. However, I would add that while the imagined *fallāḥ(a)* remained constitutive of both reform discourses and literary imaginaries, literary representation – specifically in borrowing Western techniques – undoes both its own and the borrowed discourse's abstractions of the collective. In

other words, literary texts from the period do not just reflect the historical reality, but also expose it.

53. See George P. Landow, *Elegant Jeremiahs: The Sage from Carlyle to Mailer* (Ithaca: Cornell University Press, 1986), p. 31.
54. Gross, 'Reading Cant, Transforming the Nation', p. 100.
55. Ibid., p. 101.
56. Ibid., p. 104.
57. Ibid., p. 108.
58. Ibid., p. 112.
59. Al-Sibāᶜī, *Abṭāl Miṣr*, p. 3.
60. Ibid., p. 5.
61. Ibid., pp. 37–8.
62. Al-Sibāᶜī, *Abṭāl Miṣr*, pp. 27–8; emphasis added.
63. Ibid., p. 30.
64. Ibid., p. 34; pp. 37–8.
65. Ibid., p. 35.
66. Ibid., p. 38.
67. Ibid., p. 214, pp. 216–17.
68. Ibid., p. 60.
69. Ibid., p. 67.
70. Ibid., p. 68.
71. Ibid., p. 70; emphasis added.
72. Jann, p. 36.
73. Ibid., p. 50.
74. Ibid., p. 52.
75. Ibid., p. 54.
76. See *Nationalism and Irony: Burke, Scott, Carlyle* (Oxford: Oxford University Press, 2004), p. 109.
77. Bossche, *Carlyle and the Search for Authority* (Columbus: Ohio State University Press, 1991), p. 107.
78. Carlyle, *On Heroes*, p. 199.
79. 'On History', p. 220.
80. Ibid., p. 222.
81. Al-Sibāᶜī, *Abṭāl Miṣr*, pp. 171, 174.
82. Ibid., pp. 104, 115.
83. Ibid., p. 16
84. Tageldin, *Empire,* p. 181.

85. *Al-Abṭāl*, p. 52
86. Carlyle, *On Heroes*, pp. 52–3.
87. Ibid., p. 53.
88. Tageldin also refers to the same moment. See Tageldin, *Disarming Words*, p. 181.
89. Tageldin, 'Secularizing Islam', p. 134.
90. Carlyle, *On Heroes*, p. 55.
91. Ibid., p. 69.
92. Ibid., pp. 70–1. The narrative address to the reader is a staple of Victorian literature. Garrett Stewart describes two such narrative strategies of Victorian novelists: direct address to the reader and staged scenes of reading. In either case, 'the invisible life of the reader' (p. 57) determines the forms of address and 'the reader' is 'spirited away from self-identity by text' (p. 10). The reader thus troubles the closed world of the text. The Arabic translations incorporate that address within an established oral tradition.
93. See *al-Abṭāl*, pp. 57, 59.
94. Carlyle, *On Heroes*, p. 76.
95. *Al-Abṭāl*, p. 74.
96. Carlyle, *On Heroes*, p. 77.
97. Ibid.
98. Ibid., p. 78; emphasis added.
99. *Al-Abṭāl*, p. 74. The 'miracle of the Qurᵓān' (*iᶜjāz al-Qurᵓān*) is the belief that the Qurᵓān cannot be imitated because it a miracle bestowed on the Prophet Muḥammad. Qurᵓānic language is the measure of excellence, the absolute literary standard when judging poetry. The text's divine origin is also bound to its place and moment of revelation, thus its association with pre-Islamic odes and the language of the Quraysh tribe. The schism between the text's divinity and its historical moment is the subject of Ṭāhā Ḥusayn's 'blasphemous' claims about the historicity of the text in *Fī al-shiᶜr al-jāhilī*, as we will see in Chapter Four.
100. *Al-Abṭāl*, pp. 74–5.
101. Ibid., p. 75.
102. Carlyle, *On Heroes*, p. 80.
103. Ibid., p. 84.
104. *Al-Abṭāl*, p. 86.
105. Carlyle, *On Heroes*, p. 94.
106. *Al-Abṭāl*, p. 86.
107. Carlyle, *On Heroes*, pp. 95–6.

108. *Al-Abṭāl*, p. 87.
109. For Dante on Islam, see Said, *Orientalism*, pp. 69–70.
110. Carlyle, *On Heroes*, p. 117.
111. *Al-Abṭāl*, pp. 105, 106.
112. *Al-Abṭāl*, p. 90.
113. Ibid., p. 117. The expression occurs in the Qurʾān 2:256 in '*Sūrat al-baqara*' (verse of the cow), which states that whoever believes in God and rejects false religions builds '*al-ʿurwatu al-wuthqā*' with God, a bond that could never be broken. It is also the title of Muḥammad Abduh and Jamāl al-Afghānī's Islamic reform journal. See al-Sayyid, *Egypt and Cromer*, pp. 87–93.
114. *Al-Abṭāl*, p. 109.
115. Tageldin, 'Secularizing Islam', p. 135.
116. Al-Sibāʿī translated several of Shakespeare's plays, which had already been in circulation for at least a decade. For more on these translations, see Mustafa M. Badawi's 'The Arabs and Shakespeare', in *Modern Arabic Literature and the West* (Oxford: Garnett Publishing, 1985); Ferial Ghazoul's 'The Arabization of Othello', *Comparative Literature* 50 (1) (1998): 1–31; Mahmoud F. Al-Shetawi's 'Arabic Adaptations of Shakespeare and Postcolonial Theory', *Critical Survey* 25(3) (2013): 4–28; and Sameh F. Hanna's 'Hamlet Lives Happily Ever After in Arabic: The Genesis of the Field of Drama Translation in Egypt', *The Translator* 11 (2) (2002): 167–92.
117. *Al-Abṭāl*, pp. 159–60.
118. Ibid., p. 162.
119. Ibid., p. 163.
120. Ibid., p. 164.
121. Ibid., p. 165.
122. *Al-Abṭāl*, p. 172.
123. Ibid., p. 179.
124. Al-ʿAqqād and al-Māzinī, *al-Dīwān*, p. 92.
125. Yūsuf al-Sibāʿī, 'Kāna Abī', p. 6.
126. Tageldin, 'Secularizing Islam', p. 127.
127. Muhsin Al-Musawi, *Islam on the Street*, pp. 23–4, also mentioned in Tageldin, 'Secularizing Islam', p. 132.
128. Some of the popular biographies and autobiographies include: Muḥammad Ḥusayn's Haykal *Ḥayāt Muḥammad* (1935) [The Life of Muhammad], *Jān Jāk Rūsū: ʾAʿmāluhu wa ḥayātuhu* [Jean Jacques Rousseau: His Works and Life] (1921; 1923); *Fī manzil al-waḥy* [In the House of Inspiration]; Ṭāhā Ḥusayn's

*al-Ayyām* [The Days] (1933), Volume 2, 1937, Volume 3, 1943 and his *ᶜAlā hāmish al-sīra* [On the Margin of Biography] (Islamic stories about the life of the prophet) (1933); Tawfīk al-Ḥakīm's (1898–1987) *Muḥammad* (1936); Maḥmūd ᶜAbbās Al-ᶜAqqād's *Anā* [Me] (1946) [autobiography]; *ᶜAbqariyyat Muḥammad* [The genius of Muhammad] (1942), *Allāh* (1947); and al-Māzinī's *Ibrāhīm al-kātib* (1933).

129. See Ostle, 'The Romantic Poets', pp. 82–131.
130. See *Egypt in Search of a Political Community: An Analysis of the Intellectual and Political Evolution of Egypt, 1804–1952* (Cambridge, MA: Harvard University Press, 1961), p. 140.
131. Charles D. Smith, 'Crisis of Orientation', p. 384.
132. In *Mustaqbal* (1938), Ḥusayn wants to remove the study of language and religion in an effort to include all the people of Egypt in his definition of citizen. Gershoni writes that Ḥusayn's political state was based on Rousseau's solution for the tension between ruler and ruled: all men should be free to rule themselves. See Gershoni, 'Liberal Democratic Legacies in Modern Egypt: The Role of the Intellectuals, 1900–1950' (2012) at https://www.ias.edu/ideas/2012/gershoni-democratic-legacies-egypt.
133. For more on the New School, see Hafez, *Genesis*, pp. 215–32.
134. Brugman, *An Introduction*, p. 99.
135. '*Al-ᵓustādh al-Sibāᵓī*', in *al-Ṣuwar*, p. 4.
136. Al-Māzinī, '*Al-taṣawwuf fī al-adab*', pp. 69–70.
137. Ibid., p. 60 and p. 64.
138. 'Muqaddima', in *Mukhtārāt min al-qiṣaṣ al-inklīzī*, p. 7.
139. Niᶜmāt Aḥmad Fūᵓād takes issue with al-Māzinī's confession: comparing his translation to her own literal rendition, she concludes that there are in fact adequate Arabic expressions for the English words that he removes (Fūᵓād, *Adab al-Māzinī*, p. 287).
140. Fūᵓād, *Adab al-Māzinī*, pp. 288–90.
141. See Brugman, *An Introduction*, p. 184.
142. Al-Māzinī, '*Al-Sariqāt al-adabiyya*', pp. 1,243–7.
143. *Ḥiṣād al-Hashīm*, p. 23.
144. 'I was stunned out of place and time, and I might have been unconscious' (*kuntu dhāhilan ᶜan al-zamān wa-l-makān, wa akād akūn fī ghayr waᶜyī*) (*Mukhtārāt min al-qiṣaṣ al-inklīzī*, p. 43).
145. Al-Sibāᶜī, 'Kalimat al-mutarjim', p. 1.
146. Sherif, p. 6.

147. See Andrew Sanders, *The Companion to* A Tale of Two Cities (London: HarperCollins, 1988); Ruth Glancy (ed.), *Charles Dickens's A Tale of Two Cities: A Sourcebook*, (London and New York: Routledge, 2006), pp. 31–37, pp. 97–101. The atypicality of the novel is also a recurring subject of its critical reception. See Taylor Stoehr, *Dickens: The Dreamer's Stance* (Ithaca: Cornell University Press, 1965), pp. 1–33.
148. See Moretti, *The Way of the World*, pp. 182, 185, 195.
149. On the relationship between British realism and liberalism, see Lauren M. E. Goodlad, *Victorian Literature and the Victorian State: Character and Governance in a Liberal Society* (Baltimore: Johns Hopkins University Press, 2003); Nancy Armstrong, *Desire and Domestic Fiction: A Political History of the Novel* (Oxford: Oxford University Press, 1987); and D. A. Miller, *The Novel and the Police* (Berkeley: University of California Press, 1988). For more on the transnational grounds for liberalism, see Uday Singh Mehta, *Liberalism and Empire: A Study in Nineteenth-Century British Liberal Thought* (Chicago: University of Chicago Press, 1999), and Jennifer Pitts, *A Turn to Empire: The Rise of Imperial Liberalism in Britain and France* (Princeton: Princeton University Press, 2006).
150. Irene Tucker, 'What Maisie Promised: Realism, Liberalism and the Ends of Contract', *The Yale Journal of Criticism* 11 (2): p. 335. Realism ironically also defined orientalist scholarship in the nineteenth century, which largely based itself on realist techniques of representation. See also Mitchell, *Colonising Egypt*, pp. 10–12.
151. Ibid., pp. 336–7.
152. See Irene Tucker, *A Probable State: The Novel, the Contract, and the Jews* (Chicago: University of Chicago Press, 2000), p. 61. While I am referring to the transnational blind spots of British realism, I am approaching the subject differently by thinking about what the translation of realism reveals about the mechanisms of realistic representation in a colonial context.
153. Childers, *Novel Possibilities*, p. 13.
154. Ibid., p. 181.
155. For more on the novel as a response to Chartism, see John Gardiner, 'Dickens and the Uses of History', in *A Companion to Charles Dickens*, David Paroissien (ed.) (London: Blackwell, 2008), pp. 31–59. Critics disagree on *A Tale of Two Cities*' stance on liberal individual freedoms and the equality of the French Revolution. For some examples, see Georg Lukács, *The Historical Novel*, pp. 243–4 and Frances Ferguson 'On Terrorism and Morals: Dickens's *A Tale*

*of Two Cities*', *Partial Answers: Journal of Literature and the History of Ideas* 3(2) (2005): 49–74, esp. p. 59.

156. '*Kalimat al-mutarjim*', in *Qiṣṣat*, p. 20.
157. Ibid., p. 19.
158. Ibid., p. 13.
159. Ibid., p. 23.
160. Al-Sibāᶜī, *Qiṣṣat*, p. 94.
161. *A Tale*, pp. 81–2.
162. Al-Sibāᶜī, *Qiṣṣat*, p. 97; emphasis added.
163. This is not a position outside of ideology, but a metatextual stance that foregrounds how the novel builds its world through rational narrative.
164. Childers, *Novel Possibilities*, p. 13.
165. *Qiṣṣat*, pp. 27, 36, and 12–13.
166. I am not suggesting that Islam figures as an absolute ahistorical outside, but that the translation is sensitive to the original's totalistic vision.
167. The confusion between the two 'genres' is also evident in *Sartor Resartus* and in *On Heroes*. See Linda H. Peterson and Neil Gray's *Victorian Autobiography: The Tradition of Self-Interpretation*, especially the chapter 'Carlyle's *Sartor Resartus*: The Necessity of Reconstruction' (New Haven: Yale University Press, 1986).
168. 'Muqaddimat al-ṭabᶜat al-ūlā' in *ᶜAbqariyyat Muḥammad*, pp. 4, 7.
169. 'The Romantic Poets', pp. 5–6.
170. Gershoni, '"The Reader"', p. 246.
171. Ibid., pp. 267, 272.
172. Ibid., p. 270.
173. Ibid., pp. 271–2.
174. See Sheehi, 'Towards a Critical'.
175. Shukrī, *Mādhā yabqā min Ṭāhā Ḥusayn*, pp. 47–8.
176. Ḥusayn, 'Muqaddima', in *al-Faylasūf*, p. 16. In 'Kāna Abī', the introduction to Muḥammad al-Sibāᶜī's *Qiṣaṣ Russiyya* (Cairo: Maktabat Miṣr, n.d.), Yūsuf al-Sibāᶜī describes his father's use of *taḍmīn* (citing classical poetry) (p. 10) and *sajᶜ* as his main legacies, even though his literature intended only to present a truthful picture of people's lives (p. 11).
177. Muḥammad al-Sibāᶜī, *al-Faylasūf*, pp. 26–7.
178. Ibid., pp. 29–30.
179. Ibid., p. 40.
180. Ibid., p. 66.
181. Ibid., p. 176.

182. Siddiq, *Arab Culture*, p. 178.
183. Susan Bassnett and Harish Trivedi describe the correlation in colonial India between the rise of print and the 'birth of the individual copyright-holding "author" . . . Such an author could no longer be simply and silently rewritten; he needed to be scrupulously, even faithfully, translated' (see 'Introduction: Of Colonies, Cannibals and Vernaculars', in Susan Bassnett and Harish Trivedi [eds.], *Postcolonial Translation: Theory and Practice*, 1989 [London: Routledge, 2002], pp. 1–18, p. 9).

# 4

# *Tarjama* as Debt: The Making of a Secular History of Arabic Literature

> You see that taking up this method is not necessary only for those who study science and write about it, but it is also necessary for those who read.
>
> Ṭāhā Ḥusayn, *Fī al-shiʿr al-jāhilī* (1926)[1]

> Egypt teeters back and forth even today, as in the past, between the Arab and Western mentalities, one of them winning at one point, the other later on. When the Western mentality triumphs, the liberal idea is reasserted, scientific ideas are published and spread about, and culture is influenced by these ideas in various institutes of learning, even the religious institutes. When the Arab mentality triumphs, sentiment takes over and dominates arbitrarily, the power of the past is revived, and culture is influenced by these ideas in various institutes, even in the secular university.
>
> Muḥammad Ḥusayn Haykal, *Mudhakkirāt fī al-siyāsa al-Miṣriyya* (Memoirs of Egyptian Politics) (1951–3)

In 1908, Ṭāhā Ḥusayn was one of the first students to enrol in the Egyptian University.[2] After completing his doctoral thesis on Abū al-ʿAlāʾ al-Maʿarrī, Ḥusayn left for Paris to study history at the Sorbonne and write his dissertation on Ibn Khaldūn under the supervision of Emile Durkheim, founder of the modern discipline of sociology.[3] He returned to Egypt in time for the 1919 Revolution and soon became its most polemical literary figure. On 10 November 1921, Ḥusayn published an article in *al-Istiqlāl* (Independence) newspaper– '*Waylun lī-l-ḥurrīya min Saᶜd [Zaghlūl]*' (No Freedom under Saᶜd), attacking Saᶜd Zaghlūl, prime minister and head of the Wafd majority party, for restricting intellectual freedom. Both Ḥusayn and Muḥammad Ḥusayn Haykal attacked the Wafdist government openly in *al-Siyāsa*.[4] The newspaper issues were banned, Haykal, then editor-in-chief, was indicted, and Ḥusayn put on trial even though his most aggressive articles remained unsigned. On 17 June 1924, Ḥusayn was summoned to court: when he denied penmanship of the articles, he was dismissed but ordered to refrain from writing political criticism.[5] In 1925, ᶜAlī ᶜAbd al-Rāziq published his controversial book *al-Islām wa-uṣūl al-ḥukm* (Islam and the Foundations of Governance), advocating for the separation of religion and politics in Islam. The Azhar *ᶜulamāᵓ* revoked his title of *ᶜalīm*. Soon after, the minister of justice, ᶜAbd al-ᶜAzīz Fahmī, who came to ᶜAbd al-Rāziq's defence, was dismissed from his government position and many liberal-constitutionalist ministers resigned. *Al-Siyāsa* also came to ᶜAbd al-Rāziq's defence, and Ḥusayn was instrumental in writing against the Azharites' attack on ᶜAbd al-Rāziq's thought. In one such defence, Ḥusayn addresses al-Rāziq: 'You have affirmed that the caliphate is not one of the foundations of Islam. Why did you not continue the study of the term and prove the theory? The caliphate is derived from Roman law.'[6] In 1926, Ḥusayn published his controversial *Fī al-shiᶜr al-jāhilī* (On *Jahili* Poetry) with the profane claim that *jahili* literature was written during Islam. From December 1926 to July 1927, Ḥusayn published the first volume of his autobiography *al-Ayyām* (The Days), the most articulate defence of his 'modernist' position.[7]

On his return from Paris, Haykal also became a significant public figure, as editor of *al-Jarīda* (The Newspaper) (with Ḥusayn), Luṭfī al-Sayyid's Ḥizb newspaper, and then editor of *al-Siyāsa al-Usbūᶜiyya*. In his Paris diaries (*Yawmiyyāt* 1909), Haykal, like Ḥusayn, expresses distrust in religion's role in the state, but writes *Ḥayāt Muḥammad* (The Life of Muḥammad) in 1934, published in book form in March 1935, selling the complete print of 10,000 copies by May,[8] and *Fī manzil al-waḥy* (In the House of Inspiration) in 1937 about his pilgrimage to Mecca. Before the two 'Islamic' texts, he wrote a biography of Jean Jacques Rousseau in two volumes (1922; 1924) – *Jān Jāk Rūsū: Aᶜmāluhu wa-ḥayātuhu* (Jean Jacques Rousseau: His Works and Life) was the first of a series of biographies that Haykal began writing after

*Zaynab* (1913) – and *Thawrat al-adab* (The Revolution of Literature) in 1933. In 1929, he published *Tarājim Miṣriyya wa-gharbiyya* (Egyptian and Western Biographies). Rousseau's biography becomes Haykal's statement on the inevitable failure of perfect translation, thus compromising Haykal's modernist account of Arabic literary history.

Ḥusayn was a very prolific translator. His translations include plays by Aeschylus and Sophocles in *Selected Pages from Greek Dramatic Poetry* (*Ṣuḥuf mukhtāra min al-shiʿr al-tamthīlī ʿind al-yūnān*) (1920), Aristotle's *The Constitution of Athens* (*Niẓām al-ʾAthīniyyīn*, 1921), Gustave le Bon's *Psychologie de l'Education* (*Rūḥ al-Tarbiya*, 1921), Jean Racine's *Andromaque* (*Andrūmāk*, 1935), Sophocles in *Min al-adab al-tamthīlī al-yūnānī* (Samples from Greek drama) (1939), André Gide's *Oedipe* and *Thesée* (*Udīb*; *Thīsyūs: min abṭāl al-ʾasāṭīr al-Yūnāniya*, 1946), and Voltaire's *Zadig ou la Destinée* (*Zadīg aw-al-qadar* in *al-Kātib al-Miṣrī*, 1947). He collaborated with Muḥammad Ramaḍān on a translation of Jules Simon's *Le Devoir* (1855) (*al-Wājib*, 1920–1). Ḥusayn used translation in his pedagogical project – in prefatory introductions, he described his translations as defective, never accurate copies, intended to illustrate the original's essential message to educate the reader.[9] In this chapter, I read his translations in line with his literary criticism and autobiographical narratives, focusing on his translations of Gide and Voltaire to explore Ḥusayn's avowedly failed translation aesthetic as revisionary of European thought.

Many critical approaches to Ḥusayn's work focus on his controversial religious views, accusing him of profaning Islam (Anwar al-Jundī), being too conciliatory, and believing unstintingly in a universalist project of translation that ignores the colonial precariousness of the Egyptian modern state (Muhsin al-Musawi, Shaden Tageldin). Ibrahim Ibrahim also condemns the equivalence in Ḥusayn's work between Islamic and non-Islamic histories as 'not sacred but profane'. Ḥusayn embraced a secular humanism that believed in 'inherited moral values' common to all cultures that can be brought into a harmonious whole.[10] Haykal has also been accused of flirting dangerously with Western liberalism. However, the two writers approach translation in ways that unsettle their commitment to both universal humanism and the Western liberal project of a modern nation-state. Reading beyond their pronounced religious and political statements, I focus on translation as paradigmatic of the literary in their works. In Arabic, *tarjama* refers to both biography and translation. Their specific *tarājim* of Western authors generate conditions of impersonation that revise and contextualise the original. As a transgressive space, their translations profane the separation between religion and literature by implicating them in the text.[11] A closer examination of how their translations both trouble and challenge European categories of selfhood and society reveals that they approach translation as failed emulation. In other words, their imitation of Western ideas never becomes absolute.[12]

These revisionary formulations are possible in their works because translation becomes a deliberately decontextualising act – it removes the original from its context while keeping it within careful citation marks. In impersonating the other text, I argue, translation produces a narrative subjectivity (*dhātiyya riwāʾiyya*) that inhabits the other's voice and complicates a simple process of speaking as the other. The *tarjama* as biography promises a model, an example of emulation. Since both Ḥusayn and Haykal saw themselves as modernist pioneers, it made sense to resort to the form. However, when this emulation is of a Western other, both Ḥusayn and Haykal replace it with a more intimate form of translation, the first asserting that the translator has to become the original author and the second adapting Rousseau's philosophy to Egypt. This intimacy also inflects their literary criticism. Haykal emphasises the author's environment; Ḥusayn begins his career with a focus on 'scientific' and objective criticism, is soon disillusioned, and turns to aesthetic criticism, later bequeathed to his student Muḥammad Mandūr (1907–65). In this intimate scene of translation, biography slips into autobiography, and the claims made about both authors' religious turns in the 1930s take form through translation as impersonation and not a simply reactionary impetus (Nadav Safran), a marketing ploy (Charles D. Smith), or a complete surrender to the secular language of the nation-state (Shaden Tageldin, Muhsin al-Musawi).

A reading of their translations, *tarājim*, and critical projects together also explains the intellectual's role specifically as *rural* and not *urban* elite. As rural elites, they believed in their unique position – superior to urban Cairenes – to respond to 'the need to modernise'.[13] Ḥusayn, more than Haykal, championed the writer's intellectual freedom and the democratisation of literature to include the masses, and hoped his translations would achieve both. Haykal maintained a more exclusive and supremacist role, but they both thought that literature could mobilise the masses and cultivated their prophetic-intellectual positions in that imagined space of address to the common Egyptian. Their modernist positions, however, unfold in the uneasy conflation between the historical author and the narrative self: these two emerge as two distinct entities in their works and revise their views on universal humanism despite themselves. Emerging from their specific historical moment, Haykal's and Ḥusayn's auto/biographies with translations of Western thought reveal that accurate *naql* of the Western auto/biographical form is not possible, especially when it encounters the traditional Arabic *tarjama*.

## Translation as Impersonation

In Arabic, *tarjama* is biographical notice, but also involves interpretation and transformation because most authors included their own literary work in their *tarājim*, and *tarjama* often fused biography and autobiography.[14] A *tarjama*, like an interpretation of the Qurʾān, is never complete: the historical account or life story and the subject's literary production appeared 'side by side',[15] so that there is an autobiographical section in the third person with literary examples. Traditionally, the drive behind an Arabic autobiography is not repentance or confession as in the Western tradition, but an expression of gratitude to God. In 'Die arabische Autobiographie' (1937), Franz Rosenthal defined Arabic autobiography as a narrative of experiences with 'applicable pedagogic content' that set an example.[16] Western criticism of Arab autobiographies finds the third pronoun to depart from the primary concern of autobiography, namely the communication of meaning through insight into the subject's inner personality. The Western tradition of autobiography is a strictly individual-focused narrative 'written by a real person concerning his own existence', writes Philippe Lejeune in his seminal *On Autobiography*.[17] Autobiography reaches its full definition in the contract of fidelity with the reader, promising an 'authentic' account of a coherent historical authorial self and his discursive 'I' (in this case, he examines a strictly white, heteronormative male corpus).[18] For Lejeune, so long as this contract is in place, the third-person narrator in autobiography is not an anomaly because it is essentially a stylistic device, used for 'internal distancing' and 'personal confrontation'.[19] As opposed to this 'inner' component of Western autobiography, the Arabic examples rely on an external relationship to God as their condition of possibility, a similar gesture to al-Sibaᶜī's reconciliation of realism with traditional Arabic narrative. In 1546, the autobiographer Ibn Ṭūlūn al-Dimashqī preferred that 'someone else writes one's biography than to write a text about oneself', not for the sake of credibility, 'but from a moral or ethical point of view; it spares the author the temptations of pride or arrogance and being accused thereof'.[20] Combined with Rosenthal's claim of the lack of personhood in Arabic autobiography, the previous quote explains why Arabic autobiography is most often read according to the characteristics of the novel or historical narrative (*sīra*). It is only in the twentieth century that *tarjama*, according to Muḥammad ᶜAbd al-Ghanī Ḥasan, begins to explore the subject's psychological state in both historical and personal contexts.[21] But translation forces us to be careful with such terms as individual, subject, and voice. The traditional imperative to write autobiography as biography, and the implication of the third person in speaking about and for the first, persists in the *tarjama* as biography and the apprenticeship novel of the early twentieth century. But when *tarjama* narrates the life of a Western author, its second meaning as translation complicates the division between biography and autobiography.

In a *tarjama*, as Haykal writes in *Jān Jāk*, the biographer 'tracks the life of his subject at every period, even those periods that the *mutarjim* [translator/biographer] would like to hide and render latent'; however, 'the subject leaves him . . . no image except fully exposed to the critical eye, and he is very keen on people identifying him when he thinks he has disappeared from sight'.[22] Haykal adheres to the Arabic tradition of biographical writing when he combines biographical details with Rousseau's works. *Jān Jāk* is a translation in two ways: it includes multiple translated citations, and also translates Rousseau's person into an exemplary figure who could guide Egypt to political emancipation. But Haykal's intimate reading of Rousseau inevitably exposes Rousseau's contradictory thought on writing, society, and culture. Rousseau's already tenuous articulation of cultural and social origins becomes doubly problematic in Haykal's *tarjama*, recalling Derrida's statement: 'From the origin of the original-to-be-translated, there is exile and fall.' Haykal fashions his translated Rousseau into a prophetic figure for the new nation, slyly inserting himself into the biography through slippages (Paul de Man's term) in translation. These slippages appear when Haykal struggles to accept Rousseau's Christian thought or his political project for society, and so Haykal inserts commentaries, changes references, or quotes from other texts. The prophetic stops being a vehement espousal of the figure of Rousseau as Egypt's emancipator and becomes a critically ironic impersonation of Rousseau's voice. The *tarjama* rather than the *mutarjim* (Haykal) exposes the deceptive equivalences assumed in colonial transactions and recasts Haykal's version of Arabic literary history in *Thawrat al-adab* (The Revolution of Literature) (1933). Ḥusayn's critical articles on Western writers and adaptations of European literature are equally experimental *tarājim* that selectively engage the originals to the extent that they *could* serve as literary origins and cultural models. However, reading his translations as intimately as he did the originals reveals generic tensions between the tradition of *tarjama* and Ḥusayn's oeuvre that undo the seemingly absolute equivalences in his modernisation project. For example, Arab critics have approached Ḥusayn's and Haykal's auto/biographical works in the language of Arabic literary genres. Yaḥyā Ibrāhīm ᶜAbd al-Dāyim uses the term *al-tarjama al-dhātiyya*, a biographical narrative about oneself that purposefully subdues excess emotion through setting an example of the perfect life.[23] In the modern period, the *tarjama* merges with the novel as in Haykal's *Zaynab* (1913) and is no longer a *tarjama dhātīyya*.[24] Haykal's later *tarājim* focus only on his ideological and political position[25] while Ḥusayn's *tarjama* uses the novel form to hide his personality.[26] What is evident in these formal labels and their shortcomings is that both Haykal and Ḥusayn find it difficult to separate the biographical from the autobiographical in copying Western literature. Their struggle with genres and the receiving context exposes the limitations and promises of one's own language, especially when compelled to translate.[27]

Jacques Derrida expresses a similar struggle in his autobiographical *Monolingualism of the Other, or, the Prosthetics of Origin* (French 1996, trans. 1998), when he writes, 'I only have one language; it is not mine since language always anticipates the "coming of the other".'[28] The lack of monopoly over his language reflects the precariousness of his identity, as Derrida recounts how his French citizenship was revoked during World War II. The paradoxical encounter between the universal and particular, the illusion of one pure language and the impossibility of a local idiom, stem from the colonial fantasy of imposing one language and culture. But if culture is 'originally colonial' – acquiring mastery through naming – then Western colonialism can only promise the colonised an illusory emancipation. If language tends towards oneness, but remains a colonial enterprise, then the worst part of its colonialism is to forget that originary moment of being always predisposed to the other. Such forgetting also explains the impossibility of translation for Derrida. The desire for origin inevitably speaks in a language predetermined by its almost forgotten anticipation of an other, and such a desire, like translation, remains impossible. Haykal and Ḥusayn struggle with a similar desire for a language that would promise its oneness. Perhaps at face value, their works pretend to have overcome the colonial trappings of their modernist tongues, but their *tarājim* as biographies and translations make such separations impossible. That their translations slip into autobiographical utterances, in which the other's words appear side by side with their reflections on them, confounds the previous desire even more.

After all, *tarjama*, as translation and biography, complicates the relationships between author, translator, and subject of the translation. From 1922 to 1924, contemporaneous with Haykal's *Jān Jāk*, Mikhail Bakhtin (1895–1975) was also thinking about the problem of author and subject in auto/biography.[29] The 'I-for-myself' (the embodied subject), writes Bakhtin, and the fictional 'hero' (the object of description) are never fully separable, for the author completes the hero by providing 'all those moments which are inaccessible to the hero himself from within himself'.[30] In autobiography, the author would have to self-objectify, but 'never coincide with myself – I-for-myself shall continue to be in the act of this self-objectification, and not in its product'.[31] Like translation, autobiography remains an impossible form because my 'own word about myself is in principle incapable of being the last word'. Since I can never complete my self-representation, autobiography and biography can never be absolutely divided, for neither 'in biography nor in autobiography does the I-for-myself (my relationship with myself) represent the organizing, constitutive moment of form'.[32] Even when Bakhtin champions this lack of control in Fyodor Dostoevsky (1821–81) as foundational to the novel, autobiography remains an impossible form, much like Derrida's resignation to the impossible mastery of his language. Bakhtin's essay exposes the conditions of Lejeune's autobiographical pact: the contract with the reader must be guaranteed from any narrative perspective by the author as *owner* of his text, a distinctly modern outcome of copyright and print culture. Bakhtin unsettles the coincidence between author and narrator, and his insight is especially relevant to the study of Arabic auto/biography. In addition to the different tradition of Arabic *tarjama*, the Egyptian author in the early twentieth century was still *becoming* the locus of copyright, and so the socio-historical context also explains Arabic auto/biography's preoccupation with defining the narrative self away from the historical author.

The modern Arabic *tarjama* as both translation and biography conflates the impossible form of the auto/biography with the equally impossible translation that remains true to one's language while anticipating the other. In-between *tarjama* and autobiography, Ḥusayn's and Haykal's translations embody both impossibilities, a legacy of al-Sibāʿī's translation of Carlyle as I argue in Chapter Three. Translation also challenges the generic features of Ḥusayn's novella *Adīb* (The Writer) (1933) and *al-Ayyām*, Haykal's *Fī manzil* and *Jān Jāk*, making them difficult to classify.[33]

Translation as *tarjama* complicates both writers' accounts of literary history and the genres they produce: the narrative voice that emerges between biography and autobiography reframes teleologies of the self in Egyptian fiction (Selim and Badr), accounts of the Egyptian self as subservient to the Western model (Tageldin), and modernist ruptures in narratives of modern Arabic literary history (Jeffrey Sacks). Similarly, the expectation of an 'inner' component in autobiography – which remains a transactional voice immersed in the other's words – parallels the expectation of fidelity to the original. However, both authors frame such 'interiority' in language within an irreconcilability between the theory and practice of translation. Accordingly, their translations do not fit into the literary histories they map and explain the lack of aesthetic criteria with which to read them. Despite their universalist assumptions, what they produce are 'contingent modernities' (Kamran Rastegar's term)[34] that continuously testify to the failed reconciliation of theory and life – a double failure of universal philosophy and translation.

## *Tarjama* as Romantic Debt: For Love of Rousseau

On the Seine, Haykal experiences the river through French literature. In 1929, when he returns to Egypt from Rome, he stands on the Nile and has an even more profound experience of identification, this time with his own history: first, the writer must reconnect with his own history, but the epitome of poetic inspiration, comes to those who are then able to 'merge with the entire human soul . . . in the unity of being'.[35] Although he was not as prolific a translator as Ḥusayn, translation is paradigmatic of a reading practice in Haykal's works, for he believed in accurate *naql*, or complete translation, as harbinger of modernity to Egypt.[36] However, such a promise of perfect translation is repeatedly compromised in *Jān Jāk* (1921; 1923) and *Thawrat al-adab* (1933). In *Jān Jāk*, Haykal delivers Rousseau's historical person framed within quotations from Rousseau's works and Haykal's commentaries. He adapts the traditional genre of *tarjama* by displacing Rousseau's life and works into his imagined Egypt. *Tarjama* as both biography and translation takes on a radical form of impersonation in *Jān Jāk*: amended correctly, Rousseau's re-presentation in Haykal's account – 'accurately' copied into Arabic – could become a model for Islamic Egypt, although such accurate translation has already failed to keep its promise.

Failed translation, recalling Derrida's and Bakhtin's impossible translation and auto/biography, resonates with the generic confusion of Haykal's *tarājim*. In the introduction to *Tarājim Miṣriyya wa gharbiyya*, he defines *tarājim* as both 'biographical sketches' (including the English term) and in the case of Shakespeare, Taine, and Shelley, 'a debt of love'.[37] Haykal's generic confusion stems from a methodological paradox that he learned from Hippolyte Taine: while the context shapes and determines a writer's thoughts, those are also original expressions of genius. If *tarjama* could refer to an autobiographical biography (with the original author's and biographer's words), then Haykal pushes that generic paradox to its limit as he rewrites Rousseau's life and works from the perspective of 1920s Cairo. Haykal's Rousseau defines the spirit of a national literature mired in that complicated translation of the Egyptian self into a European other. However, this translation is not as clear-cut as Stephen Sheehi finds in reading Buṭrus al-Bustānī's works, nor is it a product of the seduction Shaden Tageldin finds in the appeal of resemblance (see Introduction). Charles D. Smith locates Haykal as a transitional figure, adopting Luṭfī al-Sayyid's secular aspirations but also speaking to the emerging currents of religious conservatism. As a material form that negotiates these historical transitions, the adapted *tarjama* falls for the deceiving promise of translation as perfect *naql* and complicates absolute identification with the other. Haykal's incentive behind translation and his actual translation practice remain, like Ḥusayn's, at odds with each other. But the lack of correspondence between the theory and practice of translation makes room for the improved, significantly *fictional*, and prophetic Rousseau.

Rousseau's prophetic status as author of the French Revolution provides the initial grounds for emulation between him and his biographer. Haykal saw himself as 'a true Egyptian, a *fallāḥ*, of rural peasant stock uncorrupted by foreign influences, particularly Turkish' and found 'his exposure to Western ideas and education' instrumental 'to Egypt's national development and his own personal freedom to act within Egypt'.[38] His elite 'messianic' mission is based on a Darwinian belief in enabling the masses 'to act as free individuals, approaching if not equal to the elite'.[39] This theoretical social structure that Haykal inherits from Rousseau does not clash with Haykal's own prophetic mission, because he is inspired only when withdrawn from society: he receives *al-waḥy* (inspiration) in *Fī manzil* 'in those hours when man escapes into himself away from the burdens of the world'. In isolation, the writer 'reaches truths which I, with my soul enclosed in my body, in a world poisoned by imperfection and corruption, cannot'. Inspiration is possible only when 'the soul . . . [is] freed from the material so that it can reach the truths residing in the interior of the world'.[40] Like al-Manfalūṭī's *khayāl*, Haykal's *waḥy* is inspired by the imperfect translation of French romanticism. Like al-Sibāʿī, Haykal feared the uninformed masses, and his biography of Rousseau expresses the anxiety that social structures would defeat him rather than be changed by him.[41] Also like al-Sibāʿī's reader, Haykal's 'man' is imagined to be 'free by nature, civilised by disposition' for in Rousseau's words, education could help man 'return to his natural state of freedom and civilisation' through an Eastern-inspired model that champions modernity.[42] But the treatise on Rousseau failed to articulate what Haykal wanted to find in Rousseau. Quoting Ḥusayn, Smith writes that Haykal lost sight of his reader and wrote only for himself, failing to harmonise his emotional and critical responses to Rousseau.[43] In *Jān Jāk*, he fails twice: first, in believing that he is delivering perfect translation and, second, in thinking that he is practising objective critique. But Haykal's failures are also the inevitable failures of translation.

Haykal dedicates his book to the post-1919 Revolution Egypt, urging it to recognise its own history in Rousseau's words through perfect *naql*.[44] For the revolution of Rousseau's thought lies in its conviction that the old must be destroyed so the new can be installed in a return to nature. Because the return to a natural state is not originally Rousseau's, but recalls ancient Egyptian thought, Haykal intends his book:

> to show the people of Egypt and of the East an image of a vital force that arose in the West. Perhaps showing it can reveal a possible relationship between East and West based on sincere and mutual understanding, and not just on the terms of a brutal, controlling power. It can also reveal similarities, even if few, between heroes there and here.[45]

This resemblance is appended by Rudyard Kipling's famous, 'The East is East, and the West is West, and never shall the twain meet', without naming Kipling. The Kipling line also comes up in al-Manfalūṭī's translation of *Paul et Virginie*; however, in al-Manfalūṭī's text, this encounter is always impossible. Haykal seemingly contests this impossibility, insisting that the route to such a meeting begins in the correct copying of heroes' lives (the Carlylean imperative).[46] '*Naql*' regularly refers to 'translation', while *tarjama* implies interpretation. The interpretation of heroes' lives could provide an antidote to the impossibility of perfect translation, even when Haykal's translations are random extractions from Rousseau's works, framed by the biographer's critical commentary – a conversation he has with Rousseau, forgetting the reader, as Ḥusayn reprimands him. But it is precisely imperfect translation that makes possible Rousseau's resonance with the East, an initial forgetting that echoes Derrida's. The *tarjama* as translation and biography of Rousseau revels in the inevitable betrayal in translation, as the translator exposes the fictionality of Rousseau's confessional self.

Haykal romanticises Rousseau into a pre-modern heroic prophet that could thwart the harms of modernity. If Rousseau is pre-modern as he reminds us of Eastern philoshopy, then Haykal could use him to connect a pre-colonial memory to a successful anti-colonial moment that would reconcile East and West. Haykal's *tawfīqī* or conciliatory approach between East and West – namely an urge to look for commonalities and ignore unequal power dynamics – is possible only when Rousseau becomes un-Christian and un-Western. 'Rousseau's way of thinking could almost be Eastern', Haykal writes in the introduction, for it reveres nature 'and the faith that it is the origin of good and every blessing in life'.[47] However, while Rousseau advises the enjoyment of life's pleasures in moderation, Eastern thinkers advise abstinence from material pleasures. Rousseau's Eastern-inspired thought if *amended* could recall harmony between East and West, and Haykal can make such amendment precisely through adapting the *tarjama*'s form to accommodate impersonating, but not becoming, Rousseau. But this is also a result of translation's inevitable failure: the generic terms that guarantee an auto/biography's proper name do not survive in Arabic. So Haykal's proper name and narrative self are not copies of Rousseau's; rather, the *tarjama*'s critical voice promises only inconsistent and incoherent narrative subjectivities.

In this troubled relationship with Rousseau, we detect an equally troubled relationship to legitimating cultural origins. In the introduction to the later *Fī manzil al-waḥy*, Haykal modifies his position specifically through the prophet Muḥammad, the absolute model of emulation and the precondition of the Islamic nation. What Haykal perceived as perfect translation in *Jān Jāk* becomes a more articulated stance on *difference* in *Fī manzil*, where differences between East and West are insurmountable, because while the West has the Church (recalling al-Sibāʿī's translation of Carlyle's difference) and metaphysics, the East has Islam and lived practice. Thus, in his autobiographical account of pilgrimage, Haykal's narrative self never coincides with the prophet who remains a perpetual ideal of emulation.[48] While he still believes in the need for *naql* of Western intellectual thought to achieve an Arab awakening (*nahḍa* literally means rising), he now disagrees with Western thought on the source of spiritual thought: Islamic spirituality becomes the condition of this rebirth.[49] David Semah marks the shift in Haykal's thought from a Pharaonic to an Islamic phase from 1929 to 1932, after the book on Rousseau and before the publication of *Thawrat al-adab* in 1933.[50] In the Pharaonic phase, Haykal urges Egyptians to let go of the Arabic-Islamic past and reclaim a sense of distinct Egyptianness by turning to Pharaonic history, but then adopts a more reconciliatory approach since Greek thought has not been able to supersede Christian spirituality. Even though Haykal compares Islam to Christianity, and the Pharaohs to the Greeks, he adapts his idea of a modular Western civilisation to include religion.[51] Haykal's 'supposed' change of heart appears most clearly in his 1928 article 'The Culture of the East – When Will it be Reborn in Order to Dissipate the Darkness of Western Civilization?' where he argues that even Western scientists are now in agreement that every culture 'must possess a soul [*rūḥ*] and faith [*īmān*]'.[52] In his later work, *al-Sharq al-jadīd* (The New East) (1963), Haykal ascribes the impossible identification between East and West to the West's materialism.[53] Before European countries had to justify colonialism, no previous historical invasions needed to employ civilisational rhetoric.[54] He wonders how to reconcile the promise of freedom of the French Revolution with colonialism, since those were always considered impossible to translate and transplant.[55] After all, Cromer's educational reforms only aim to produce obedient citizens and not revolutionary subjects.[56] Haykal's critique again emerges from the fundamental untranslatability of context that he begins formulating in the earlier *Jān Jāk*, importantly an auto/biography, in which Rousseau's figure allows an impersonation that the prophet's figure disavows.

## Stuttering Subjects: Confessions of the Writing Self

In rewriting Rousseau's historical life, Haykal exposes the contradictions of Rousseau's 'writing self'. The *Confessions* already invites this critique, as Rousseau is constantly reimagining his choices: 'I *should have been* a good Christian, a good citizen, a good father, a good friend, a good workman, a good man in every way.'[57] Jean Starobinski finds the self's discovery in the *Confessions* to coincide with the imaginary, quoting Rousseau: 'I became the character whose life I was reading.'[58] This makes it possible for Rousseau in his autobiography to take on other proper names that resist translation. The promiscuous affair with naming poses a threat to Rousseau's singular name, one that Geoffrey Bennington locates in Rousseau's practice of reading.[59] Having followed other thinkers 'unreflectively' for years, Bennington quotes Rousseau from Book Four, 'I found myself equipped with a great enough fund of learning to be self-sufficient and to think without the help of another.' And so 'when I published my own ideas, I was not accused of being a servile disciple'.[60] Rousseau's account is just as committed to plagiaristic borrowing as Haykal's *tarjama*. The other's words undo the fantasy of self-sufficiency, as the 'pure singularity' of Rousseau's writing '*se composera toujours avec une masse d'autres énoncés portant autres signatures*' (will always be composed with multiple other utterances carrying other signatures).[61] Rousseau's text erases the boundary between quotation and signature, an erasure that Haykal's *tarjama* eagerly espouses. In *Jān Jāk*, Haykal will sign his name over Rousseau's because Rousseau has already invited him to do so. The *tarjama* of Rousseau's life, already skirting dangerously between biography and translation, slips into autobiography. This form of autobiography, however, is nothing like the *Confessions*. More than a 'biographical sketch', *Jān Jāk* lapses into harsh criticism of Rousseau's person in intimate moments of reprobation of a loved one. In a *tarjama*, as Haykal has told us, the *mutarjim* (translator/biographer) has to fully expose his subject. Moreover, Haykal was also writing in a tradition of Arabic biography, and so the confusion between his words and those of another, while reinforced by Rousseau's own plagiarism, is also a tendency within the tradition. The exchange between the tradition and Rousseau's text compromises the reliability of the writing (and confessional) self.[62]

The reason is that, as Haykal explains in Volume One, Rousseau's reimagined selves are also fictions.[63] Rousseau warns his vigilant reader: 'The further I go in my story, the less order and sequence I can put into it.'[64] Because his memory keeps failing him,[65] he can only 'remain in that happy state of knowing little enough for everything to be fresh to me'.[66] Muṣṭafā Luṭfī al-Manfalūṭī opens *al-Naẓarāt* with a similar appeal to poor memory as *proof* of prophecy, but in Haykal's *tarjama*, Rousseau's failing memory can excuse his narrative inconsistencies as outcomes of his life's circumstances.[67] In one intimate dialogic moment, Haykal will say on Rousseau's behalf, 'But he has an excuse that forgives him this and any other trespasses, and that is the gift of genius.'[68] As the biographical becomes the historical, Rousseau's genius cannot be reproduced accurately but must be supplemented, compromising Haykal's project of accurate *naql*. 'And here we leave Rousseau', writes Haykal, so that we can analyse his thought. Rousseau derives ideas from his imagination that he then names human history. But being a skilled writer, those 'images' (*ṣuwar*) become universal truths, since Rousseau's eloquent style manages to hide his errors.[69] Rousseau's language invites forgetting, but Haykal remembers.

Perfect translation is as impossible as Rousseau's universal philosophical statements. Rousseau believed that 'our selves are corrupted inasmuch as our sciences and arts progress in the direction of perfection'.[70] Because accurate translation of Western thought promises 'progress', even if Rousseau writes against that promise, Haykal is compelled to revise the terms of Rousseau's natural philosophy. To explain the measure against such corruption, Rousseau uses the example of the ancient Egyptians. Not surprisingly, Haykal's redemption of Rousseau's philosophy is soon appended with harsh rebuke of Rousseau's person: this 'son of nature' is a 'spontaneous, lustful, selfish, weak Rousseau . . . incapable of following any law except the one that inspires his heart at least momentarily. He is that old bum who knows very little about social life.' Rousseau's simple vision, Haykal continues, comes from the Swiss countryside and not from his civilisational account.[71] Haykal's hostility can be explained through a detail in the original that he does not include in the *tarjama*. Using selective translation, as al-Sibāᶜī does with Carlyle, Haykal quotes only the part on Egypt as the cradle of civilisation from the *First Discourse* but omits the derogatory reference to Muslims. Rousseau had written that only a 'few centuries ago the Peoples of this Part of the World, which is today so enlightened, lived in a state worse than ignorance', and a '*revolution* was required to *return* men to common sense'. Alas, it 'finally came from the quarter from which it was least to be expected. *The stupid Muslim, the eternal scourge of Letters, caused them to be reborn among us*.'[72] Since this opening moment of the *First Discourse* promises a return to a natural origin, made possible by the 'stupid Muslim', Haykal generalises the comparison to other civilisations for 'the same has happened to Rome, Constantinople, and every nation that has been exposed to the germs of the arts and sciences as it did to Egypt and Greece'. If these nations' 'great men', whose 'greatness' had been 'measured by remaining in the arms of ignorant nature', were to see 'what became of their nations today, they would turn their faces from them and disappear in misery'.[73] He inserts commentary in between quotations from Rousseau, and his voice merges with that of his French hero, making it difficult to tell them apart. Rousseau's solution is a return to one's self, a turn away from social corruptions, because one must 'listen to the voice of his own conscience'.[74] At this point, Haykal no longer tells us which Rousseau text he is translating. He does, however, remark in an address to the reader that there is a lot of strangeness in Rousseau's idea of a return to one's self because ultimately Rousseau will call for equality in the social sphere. Haykal reassures his reader that Rousseau eventually explains himself in *Discourse on the Origin and Basis of Inequality among Men* (Discours sur l'origine et les fondements de l'inégalité parmi les hommes), or the *Second Discourse.*

But in the *Second Discourse*, Rousseau makes no recourse to history; rather, he 'delivers himself to his imagination'.[75] Rousseau becomes the origin of his fiction and Haykal is suspicious of this origin,[76] for Rousseau's natural state, 'may never have existed, and . . . probably never will exist, yet about which we must have sound ideas if we are to judge our present state satisfactorily'.[77] The *tarjama* exposes Rousseau's fictions, since he has access to his 'original self' precisely when he claims he cannot remember. Rousseau 'had only to describe himself, to know himself intimately . . . through a process that was at once active and passive: exploring his inner nature and abandoning himself to reverie'.[78] This immediate access to 'truth' through narration is a sign of prophecy. In Starobinski's words: 'If truth is to reveal itself, it must be lived by a "witness".'[79] The autobiography becomes the fantastical record of self-coincidence, wherein the historical writer coincides fully with the narrating subject, but we know that Rousseau's visions were already tainted by the uncited words of others, much like Haykal's *tarjama* of Rousseau.[80]

From Rousseau's description of these strange origins and returns, Haykal uncovers what had always been difficult for him and other intellectuals to pinpoint, that the possibility of perfect translation of Western literature into the Islamic context demands a forgetting of pure origins. In an ideal situation of perfect translation, Islam can promote scientific enquiry and maintain a spiritual openness that guards against Western materialism; as such Islam would need no help from French philosophy. But it does, and Rousseau is necessary for Haykal's vision for the new Egypt, even though Rousseau was racist, selfish, and lustful. So Haykal has to find a form of translation that becomes the possible grounds for the impossible resemblance of East and West. To do so, he has to locate an origin for Egyptian thought that is not French. But this can only be a tainted origin, already in fall and exile, as Derrida would have it, an origin that comes about in translation. This form of translation is a *tarjama* that allows Haykal to filter Rousseau's words through Haykal's voice: Haykal will impersonate but not become Rousseau.

Haykal's ideas are not unscathed importations of European thought, especially because they recognise the impossibility of an Egypt devoid of European influence. Ironically, this is itself a version of Rousseau's problem as he at once invents and returns to 'nature' or the 'self' only to discover that they are fictions that arise from within the social progress that supposedly corrupted them. Haykal's dialogue with Rousseau demonstrates that fiction provides the terms for the work of translation. Fiction also makes possible and necessary the assumption of another's name, and speaking in that other's name, to an Egyptian cause.[81] The text internalises this doubling on two levels: one, the othering of Rousseau's name fuels Haykal's auto/biographical criticism of the former, and, second, Rousseau's replaceable proper name enables Haykal's self-presentation as a translated (amended) Rousseau. The proper name's substitutability sanctions this gesture of usurpation in Haykal's text, such that the unstable proper name conditions the rewritten *tarjama* as a record of emerging fictional modalities in modern Arabic literature.[82] While Edward Said finds an absolute distinction between Islamic literature's already completed world and the European novel's openness, Haykal's reconfigured *tarjama* posits auto/biographical fictionality as the condition of historical retelling.[83] The auto/biographical form as translation complicates the articulation of literary subjectivity in Haykal's work, especially since Rousseau and Haykal become interchangeable characters complicit in treacherous, fictional emulation. Haykal describes Rousseau's ideas as the revolution's Qurʾān because their style can stir readers,[84] much like al-Manfalūṭī's faith in the literature of tears. This political revolution is an *aesthetic* one, the subject of Haykal's 1933 *Thawrat al-adab*.

## Towards an Aesthetic of Revolution[85]

In *Thawrat al-adab*, the complex impersonation between Haykal and Rousseau translates into Arabic literature's imitation of French literature's r/evolution. While the 1881 ʿUrābī Revolt and the 1919 Nationalist uprising are the backdrops of Haykal's book, political and aesthetic revolution overlap: once literature comes in touch with revolution, it leaves its 'exclusive barn' (reference to al-Azhar) for the 'correct' Arabic language must address the masses.[86] Herein lies the revolution of literature, but it requires a point of origin, a model to emulate, so Haykal asks: if Western literature has the classics, Christianity and Descartes, 'what literature or philosophy of the past must we be associated with if we want it to have the aspect of some civilisation?'[87] The modern would have to 'fill the void . . . that separates our age from the golden ages of Arabic literature'.[88] Haykal wants to mend the hiatus in Arabic literary production through a return to a fictional origin, much like Rousseau's fictional returns.

But since 'modernisation does not stop at the simplicity of language [but] also takes up the process of research, colors of sensation, and degrees of feeling', it demands a 'new kind of prose' committed to 'realism'.[89] Haykal understands realism as methodological positivism but criticises ᶜĪsā ᶜUbayd's attack on al-Manfalūṭī, because al-Manfalūṭī was right to turn to romantic Western literature. A novel must document the 'history of the present' and demonstrate a few important facts in 'styles affected by scientific principles' as do Zola, Flaubert, and Maupassant.[90] 'We can say', he writes, 'that the story evolved in Western literature in a way that makes it represent its different epochs until the present one. If [only] *we* had some stories that reflect the spirit of an age.'[91] Haykal is not merely urging the imitation of Western realism; he is also transposing a model of literary development onto the Arabic story, and the condition of modernity becomes a story's sincere reflection of its context. Searching for an origin outside of French influence, Haykal finds Ibn Tufayl's *Ḥayy ibn yaqẓān*, the earliest 'authentic' reflection of its author's liberal age (twelfth century). After that, the Arabic story turns to myths that only reflect the psychological conditions of 'the ages of deterioration', except for the mythical tales of the *One Thousand and One Nights* that offer 'correct observations' of everyday life (Haykal dismisses all other narrative forms such as the *maqāma*). A story must point to its author's idea and ideal; 'even if the idea was inconsequential and the ideal lowly, they still *translate* the storyteller's purpose'.[92] In its return to life, the Arabic story needs the Western one, but so far has only been 'imitating it in its image', for 'if imitation is often the beginning of a resurrection [*baᶜth*], and the imitation of Greek and Roman literatures was the beginning of a European renaissance in the sixteenth century', Haykal continues, 'the right kind of renaissance' must be inspired by Arab authors' ideals.[93] As emulation, the new Arabic prose demands an ideal that transpires in imitating French examples.[94] Much like Rousseau's plagiarisms, the new prose is implicated in theft, and Haykal's literary history betrays a similar lack of pure origins.

Rousseau's fictional origins seep into Haykal's thought, when in the chapter on 'Nationalist Literature', he models his stories on a return to the

Pharaohs mediated through French realism.[95] Rousseau's fictionally devised self fuels Haykal's search for his writerly ideal and authorises Haykal's position as a 'genuine *fallāḥ*', which carries him from the Seine to Egyptian history and enables him to make '*sacred* all there is in Egypt'.[96] The *fallāḥ* legitimates Haykal's fictional role of authenticity and authority, through which he finds an origin for Arabic literature in Pharaonic mythology that confirms the unchanging qualities of modern Egyptians.[97] Translation in *Thawrat* implicates the origin in the poetics of fiction, delivering a return to something already there in Egyptian history.[98] While in *Jān Jāk*, Haykal finds Rousseau's returns too fictional, here he embraces the fiction, but only because he had found Rousseau's 'means of this return' in *al-Tarbiyya* (Education), his chosen name for Rousseau's *Émile*. In *al-Tarbiyya*, Rousseau finally articulates his theory on return with no 'fictional theories', while in his other works, Rousseau's theoretical conclusions clashed with his practical concerns.[99]

However, while Haykal ironically finds in the novel *Émile* a less fictional enterprise than in Rousseau's political works, he again faults Rousseau for not considering the context, inadvertently pointing to an impossible translation of context in Haykal's own translation project. His theory of translation clashes with his practice, signalling a failure of both translation and universal philosophy. Amending his theory on translation, Haykal comes in the end to a consideration of context. The best social setup, says Rousseau in translation, '*take[s] [one's] absolute existence from him in order to give him a relative one*', such that each 'individual believes himself no longer one but part of a unity and no longer feels except within the whole'.[100] In adaped translation Haykal quotes from Rousseau's more conservative *Considérations sur le gouvernement de Pologne, et sur sa reformation projetée* (1782) (Considerations on the Government of Poland):

> Education must imprint all people in the frame of love of the nation and direct all thoughts and tastes . . . to make them nationalist in inclination and desire . . . the child must open its eyes first to its nation, and then see nothing else until he dies. Every sincere republican must breastfeed on the love of his nation as it mixes with his mother's milk . . . this love is the foundation of his life, and if he were to be isolated, he would become nothing. If he has no nation left, he has no existence.[101]

Haykal's choice is significant here because the essay on Poland contradicts most of Rousseau's democratic ideals in *The Social Contract* – in the essay on Poland, national belonging becomes the only sure way to participatory citizenry. He again reprimands Rousseau for later giving up on the nation: Rousseau's fantasy of a nationless world, says Haykal, is not possible. He again excuses Rousseau: 'we apologise for him that he wanted to build education on the rules of nature and nature has no identifying nation'.[102] Love of nation must be superior to love of self. Any other formulation can only be in 'the realm of poetic imaginary' – to rectify this, education must be 'an exact science far from illusion and imagination' for although one hopes for 'a world that is a home to all people . . . we cannot take away from the pupil the knowledge of what things are really like with the presence of nations and their competition'.[103] Rousseau's nationalism is untenable because education must be grounded in the nation. On a practical level, love of nation must provide the basis for identification with others, for every individual may have a varied understanding of his or her own commitment to the nation. Hence, *Émile* is not free of the clash between the theoretical and the practical, the universal and the particular.

Rousseau's failure makes way for Haykal's intellectual, for it is the duty of mature minds (elite intellectuals) to lead the way.[104] The motto of equality behind the French Revolution, which originates in Rousseau, can only be an empty promise, because whether the date is 1789 or 1923, there is a threat to the intellectual under imperialism. Perfect *naql* of Rousseau's ideas is impossible because while his ideas can be rendered in Arabic, their original context cannot. Haykal relates the success of Robinson Crusoe and Ḥayy ibn Yaqẓān, as opposed to the implied failure of Émile, to their contexts. Both Crusoe and ibn Yaqẓān work with what they have, that is, the contexts of their isolation, to learn and survive. But the point is not that they are isolated; rather, it is that they make survival possible from the contexts of their isolation. After all, 'the isolated individual does not exist', and 'if Ḥayy and Crusoe were to be found together and were equally resourceful . . . one would have shared all the blessings of life with his friend without attacking him'.[105] The deterministic conditions of context relate to Haykal's broader political nationalism. Haykal's *tarājim*, argue Gershoni and Jankowski, demonstrate his conviction that one individual's actions represent only 'part of collective historic accomplishment of his group'. History is 'the study of national cultural units, with the biographies of individuals . . . of value only insofar as they reflect and personify the collective biography', for an individual author's 'specific Egyptian spirit' is a product of his environment.[106] In Haykal's own text, Egypt is already implicated in a historical affair with French literature, and so Haykal will work with what he has. Just as Crusoe and Ḥayy would work together if they ever met, so Haykal and Rousseau can do the same – so long as Rousseau's French imperial and universalist thought is contextualised in Haykal's vision for Egyptian nationalism. In narrating the French Revolution as a moment of corruption that history remembers as a lesson, Haykal names Jān Jāk its author,[107] but that moment of corruption is also the present moment of the *tarjama*, and so Haykal confounds both his and Rousseau's voices, and the French Revolution with 1920s Egypt. Haykal wants to correct Rousseau's failure through practical application of the former's ideas in the Egyptian present, which can only unfold through the duty to assert the past's continuity (under the weight of tradition). The translator's debt is no longer to the original but to the past. 'But Rousseau has his excuse', Haykal retorts, 'for he considers the efforts of the past to be wasted efforts that have corrupted humanity', when discontinuity with the past invites disconnection from reality.[108] The past is equally abstracted in Haykal's vision but provides a grounding anteriority that means to legitimate his account, only it ends up compromising his translation project. Despite his best efforts, Western progress cannot be accurately copied in translation after all.

In *Thawrat al-adab*, *Ḥayy* also figures as the 'good' kind of literature – speaking to its historical context from the isolation of the forest. While *Thawrat* ignores the context as much as Rousseau does in its recommendation to imitate French realism and naturalism, it also exposes Haykal's own failure to reconcile theory and practice, translation and context. But Haykal almost acknowledges this shortcoming, when he concludes that Rousseau ultimately fails because of his Christian background, and Haykal turns to Islam to provide the terms of continuity with the past as Islam urges a search for meaning that transcends the material world. This search is unattainable in Rousseau's work, so Haykal excuses Rousseau because few intellectuals are able to apply theory to life:

> We are forced to live under the rule of the environment against our own inclinations and desires, because the environment is where life is possible even though it is infested with corrupting germs. But we are not forced to think as the environment does. . . . humanity is able by great efforts to undo the shackles of thought and allow the thinker to go off into a world other than the material one that surrounds him and to organise in his head an image of life like he would want it to be, and create a logic for it . . . but the thinker must have another life than his material existence.[109]

This is the domain of the prophetic intellectual, and it resonates with Haykal's *waḥy* when he retreats in *Fī manzil*. Haykal's failure is not so much an absconding to Western thought but rather an inevitability of the failure of both translation and universal philosophy. Haykal repeats Rousseau's mistake in thinking he could reproduce French literary history as the path of modern Arabic literature, but reading his works together, especially the dialogue between the *tarjama* and literary history, reveals the inevitable impossibility of absolute translation. Islam provides the intellectual with that other life, and it emerges in the transaction between translation and literature.

Haykal describes the failure of the intellectual's effort to reconcile theory and life in the first-person plural pronoun, 'we', initiating a string of identifications that will ultimately seal his and Rousseau's fates. Haykal identifies with Rousseau, but Rousseau fails to reconcile theory and practice, fiction and context. Jean Starobinski finds that Rousseau redeems his failure in his literature: when 'he presented himself the first time, he failed. Now he represents himself and he succeeds.'[110] Haykal was also fond of performing his intellectual role, and always made sure he had a public audience for his political speeches.[111] Like Rousseau, if Haykal fails in his presentations (political writings), his translations reveal a more articulate political stance on the colonial encounter. Haykal's life of Rousseau captures this stance best when it concludes that fiction can in fact tell the truth, as it unveils a discontinuity in the original that prevents it from imposing its imperial narrative order on colonial Cairo. In *Émile*, Rousseau recommends *tarājim*, biographies of heroes, instead of history books, as the best means of education, but Haykal is suspicious of the individual as an origin of education or the nation. The multiple representations of Rousseau in his self-portraiture are rewritten in

Haykal's *tarjama* into the *bildungsroman* that Rousseau has failed to complete in *Émile*. In the 1920s and 1930s, Haykal takes Rousseau's dictum to heart: 'The real world has its limits; the imaginary world is infinite. Unable to enlarge the one; let us restrict the other, for it is from the difference between the two alone that are born all the pains which make us truly unhappy.'[112] Later in his life, Haykal turned to Islam in his political fight to become prime minister. Haykal died in 1956, as the British and French forces were attacking the Suez, still trapped between his Western thought and Egyptian reality, finding himself 'in death as in life suspended between ideas whose irreconcilability on an international scale was an epitaph for his own endeavors'.[113]

Haykal's work confirms that a theory of perfect translation fails in practice. Reading his work comparatively as generic revision recasts some of his more declared pronouncements on liberal democracy, modernisation, and nationalism. In rewriting Rousseau and revising the *tarjama*, Haykal also transforms the unfinished pedagogical project of *Émile* into a final metaphor for the Arabic novel in translation. The writing self, much like the abstract liberal individual, remains trapped in its own incoherent stuttering, teetering back and forth like Egypt in the epigraph. In this scene Islam emerges as the *fantasy* of unmediated and unhesitant speech, not simply a marketing tool or a response to Western representation.[114] Ṭāhā Wādī blames Carlyle for shaking Haykal's faith in religion, for Carlyle's influence made Haykal give prophets the same status as writers and poets, although he eventually resolves his guilt over such an equation in his political diaries.[115] In *Thawrat*, Haykal suggests a quick fix for modernising Arabic literature after ages of decadence through the imitation of French realist style but using 'ancient' Egyptian themes that provide continuity with the past, the imagined origin needed in the *nahḍa*. At the end of *Fī manzil*, however, Haykal excuses the materialism of the ages of decadence as a product of historical circumstances.[116] What *Jān Jāk* offers Haykal that *Fī manzil* cannot provide is a revisionary history through the insertion of the narrator-intellectual as history's *mutarjim* (interpreter). This is not a Carlylean individual hero that emerges here; rather it is a transactual narrative voice that cannot escape its predetermined complicity in another's tongue all the while recognising this complicity. Haykal's miscellaneous writings, which treat politics, religion, and literature in a similar language are not a simple testament to his succumbing to secularity. Rather, they testify to the generic experimentation that understands fiction as the condition of borrowing European thought in imperfect translation. The adapted *tarjama*, which oscillates between tradition and translation as failed emulation, places this religious turn in the same fruitless quest for origin that plagues his literary history and teleological narratives of the Arabic novel that represent *Zaynab* as the first novel. It is not fortuitous that Haykal's final work, *Qiṣaṣ Miṣriyya* (1967) (Egyptian Stories), is dedicated to *Zaynab*. The inevitable failure of translation becomes a dedication to the promise of fictionality and the hesitations of the narrative self, consolidating al-ᶜAqqād's testament that Haykal's biographies were a school of their own[117] and Ḥusayn's commemoration of Haykal's pioneering role in making literature an independent object of study in *Thawrat al-adab*.[118]

## Impersonation in Ṭāhā Ḥusayn's Translations

Much like Haykal, Ḥusayn uses translation to legitimate the cultural elite's role in transforming society. In *al-Ayyām* (Volume Two) (1939), he documents his conversion from the Azharite turban to the elite's tarbush in line with his turn from religious to literary study, and later in 'The Renaissance of Modern Arabic Literature' (1955), he describes his generation's duty to 'democratise' Arabic literature and expand the masses' access to education, a duty that motivates his translations and critical biographies of European authors.[119] As with Haykal, the 1919 Revolution is the event that must bring literature closer to the people.[120] Modernity – or the promise of a literary democracy to come – appears as an anticipated futurity in Ḥusayn's 1955 essay, but its promise is possible in its openness rather than finality, much like his imperfect translations.

Ḥusayn's translations took many forms: some were commentaries on original texts later collected in his critical books; others were biographical sketches of Western authors; and others were actual translations of originals. Through these various performances, however, Ḥusayn violated the boundary between original and translation, often impersonating the original writer as he writes in the preface to Aḥmad Ḥasan al-Zayyāt's translation of Goethe's *The Sorrows of Young Werther* (1774), *ᵓĀlām Furtur* (1929):

> And the sum of it is that the translator must do his best not only to transmit [*yanqul*] to us the meaning of words that the original author intended but

> to also copy for us [*yanqul*] the soul [*nafs*] of the author clearly and reveal without effort or labor what has affected it of sentiments and feelings.[121]

In the introduction to Muḥammad ᶜAwaḍ Muḥammad's *Hurmun wa Drūtīya* (1949), translation of Goethe's *Hermann und Dorothea* (1797), Ḥusayn also urges the translator to erase his personality and resign himself to the position of translator who is not the 'comfortable reader' nor the 'creative author' but the 'connection' between the two men. The translator's place 'between producers and consumers . . . as the economists say' is as great as it is precarious because it connects peoples and generations by removing differences between them and bringing them closer to the 'ideal' – a humanist understanding of literature.[122] The translated text, in other words, enters an exchange market as a commodity whose promoter – here the translator – intends to introduce it into a Cairene marketplace that will learn to recognise its place in a global economy. Although he continues to introduce Goethe and his works, Ḥusayn makes no mention that this humanist conception of literature and its imagined task of the translator is originally Goethe's.

Translation as impersonation recalls Haykal's project in *Jān Jāk* – but here translation is an actual *becoming* of the other, inhabiting his life and experiences. The imperative to impersonate the other is most evident in Ḥusayn's translation of Gide's *Oedipus* and *Theseus* (1946). In his earlier translation of Aristotle's *System of the Athenians* (1921), he proposes a different articulation of history, which takes full form in the lives of great men in *Qādat al-fikr* (Leaders of Thought) (1925), under the influence of Carlyle's *On Heroes*. If history is the narrative of great men's deeds, the *tarjama* both as biography and translation is its ideal form. This is not to say, however, that Egyptian intellectuals uncritically espoused Carlyle's project for the writing of history. Gershoni and Jankowski explain that Egyptian intellectuals in fact favoured 'impersonal forces' as the determining agents 'in the shaping of history'. History became the product of collective and largely impersonal dynamics determined by materialist contextual conditions, and the Egyptian people (albeit abstracted) became the primary focus of historical narration: 'In an inversion of the great-man approach of Carlyle, the Egyptian nation as a whole was the only "hero" in Egyptian history, and Egyptian history was its collective biography.'[123] We find the same impetus in Haykal's work, whose final turn to the modular prophet of Islam is a further distancing of the intellectual self from the narrative of history. Ḥusayn will turn to the belief in fate as the ultimate arbiter of cultural difference between East and West. And his thought on fate – never a metaphysical project – unfolds specifically in his literary criticism. In what follows, I discuss Ḥusayn's approach to translation, focusing on his translations of Gide and Voltaire, in relation to his literary criticism, his novella *Adīb*, and autobiography *al-Ayyām*. Reading his multiple narratives together, the chapter challenges Ḥusayn's confirmation in *Mustaqbal al-thaqāfa fī Miṣr* (The Future of Culture in Egypt) (1938) that Hellenic culture is Egypt's cultural origin.[124] If, as Derrida tells us, the origin-to-be-translated was always in a state of exile and fall, then translation as an always failed endeavour, as Ḥusayn declares in commenting on his own translations, narrates another failed endeavour, that of a quest for pure origin. As such, Ḥusayn's translation practice, much like Haykal's, is more telling when it is a *tarjama* of the lives of authors he admired. Translation as intimate biographical narration that hinges on autobiographical identification with its object compromises Ḥusayn's pronounced project of importing modernity through copying.

Ḥusayn intended his translations to educate the Egyptian reader who had no access to the original, so it is not surprising that his translation project was later generously funded by Gamal Abd el-Nasser's government in 1955.[125] However, Ḥusayn's translation work in the Thousand-Book Project was government-sponsored, and his choices of texts and translation methods (which he performed and supervised) became more literal. His earlier translations, from the 1920s until the 1940s, the concern of this study, were based on individual preferences. On 6 May 1920, in the introduction to *Ṣuḥuf mukhtāra*, for example, Ḥusayn positions his imperfect translations as filling in for the absence of translated Greek literature in the first renaissance – the Abbasid age – for the Egyptian renaissance and path to modern democracy can only happen through its Greek ancestor.[126] Greek tragedy (*trajīdyā*) matured beyond Dionysius to address and unite the people,[127] but Ḥusayn recognises the impossible task of translating poetry into prose, and one language into another, like translating Imruʾ al-Qays into French or Aeschylus into Arabic – the translation would never have the same effect on the reader.[128] He therefore adapts the original, rendering the effusive statements of the

Greek chorus in logical statements.[129] Al-Manfalūṭī does something similar when he changes the sentence structure to control the sentiment. Cachia calls these 'surprising' errors in Ḥusayn's translation of Gide's *Thésée*, as Ḥusayn's attention to the sentence over and above context makes his translations sound occasionally absurd.[130]

Ḥusayn's attention to rhetoric and his 'absurd' translation mistakes acquire new significance in what Cachia names his 'critical articles', summaries of scenes or plots of French plays, meant to introduce readers to themes and not aesthetic criteria of French literature.[131] These 'critical articles' appeared in *al-Kātib al-Miṣrī* (The Egyptian Writer), later collected in *al-Alwān* (Colours) (1945) and *Ḥadīth al-Arbiᶜāᵓ* (Wednesday's Conversation) (1926).[132] In the collection *Ḥāfiẓ wa-Shawqī* (1933), and specifically '*Al-Adab al-jadīd*' (The New Literature), Ḥusayn calls for new aesthetic criteria because of translation's demand on Arabic language and literature.[133] In '*Shuᶜarāᵓuhum*' (Their Poets), he relates the difficulties of translation to the difference between Western and Arab literary tastes, but calls for more translation until the images of Western literature become models for imitation.[134] He will translate only sections for now, he continues, and if those meet with interest, he will provide the public with longer poems. For example, he translates (and occasionally summarises) Baudelaire's '*Le Crepuscule du Soir*' as '*Khilwā ilā-l-nafs*' (Alone with the Soul),[135] appending it with a later chapter '*Baudelaire: al-ḥurriya wa-l-fann*' (Baudelaire: Freedom and Art). The added chapter celebrates Baudelaire's vehement defence of art's freedom and asks al-ᶜAqqād and Haykal if evil can be made the subject of art, when the purpose is the reader's moral edification.[136] These critical articles look very much like *tarājim*, bringing together the author's words with details about his life, both contextualised in 1930s Egypt.

Ḥusayn's aesthetic interest develops through his *tarājim*. However, inadvertently, and through a professed debt to his beloved authors, he develops a critique of Western individualism that begins with Plato and Aristotle and ends in Gide. His earliest translation of Aristotle's *System of the Athenians* (1921) precedes his controversial *Fī al-shiᶜr al-jāhilī* (1926) where the Cartesian method becomes the methodological measure of truth. Reading Aristotle and Sophocles in the 1920s, he struggles to locate Egypt's cultural origin in Greece. In Ḥusayn's introduction to *Niẓām al-Athīniyyīn* (1921)

(System of the Athenians), Plato fails to achieve his desired philosophical unity because he does not follow through with his own basic premise: every external being has an essence to it, but it also has its worldly manifestation. Plato 'left the external, material objects behind in pursuit of intangible ideals', but 'Aristotle could not distinguish between the thing and its ideal, and did not say there is a separate existence of the ideal from its external image'.[137] Aristotle's materialist philosophy produced man as a social being and not an isolated individual.[138] In *Qādat al-fikr* (1925), especially the chapter on Homer, he extends Aristotle's thought to a defence of his own project of writing *tarājim* that are not only biographies. Their main purpose is to show how the environment can transform religion from an individual choice into a *collective* need.[139] The move from epic to romance in Greek culture reflects the move from collective to individual, and marks the transition to philosophy in the West in parallel with an opposite move to religion in the East.[140] The emphasis on the collective is a critique of Western individualism, pointing to the colonial separation of religion from the public sphere and from literature. In the Indian colonial context and within the institution of literary studies, Gauri Viswanathan describes a similar situation whereby the newly installed 'homogenised conception of literature' weeds out 'religious influences' and espouses a 'language to which new cultural values are then attached'.[141] Ḥusayn's careful reading of Greek philosophy in translation – his contribution to this renaissance – becomes a paradigmatic critique of representation and collective desire. The Greek tradition amends itself through Aristotle's materialism to some extent, but in *Niẓām*, Ḥusayn speaks for Aristotle, who would not have endorsed slavery in its present forms, giving colonialism as the most evident example.[142] This implicit critique of transposing universalist values of reading from one culture into another recognises unequal power dynamics, and justifies his decision against *ta$^{c}$rīb,* keeping the Greek words that have no Arabic equivalents, appended with examples.[143] Ḥusayn was not oblivious to his colonial situation, or the mechanics of colonial representation, so he tampered with the originals, keeping foreign words in place to remind readers of their foreignness.

The translations of André Gide's *Oedipe* and *Thésée* in 1946 and Voltaire's *Zadig* in 1947 further demonstrate this critique. Ḥusayn's translations move from the philosophical to the literary, echoing a similar critical change in his literary criticism: from objective positivism to subjective impressionism and finally aesthetic critique. How does Ḥusayn's critical approach develop in relation to his translation choices? His earlier condemnation of al-Manfalūṭī, which he later revokes, is very telling in this context: Ḥusayn's initial repudiation of al-Manfalūṭī's work is a subjective evaluation of the latter's sentimentalism, but, later, Ḥusayn finds literary taste (of both author and reader) to be formative in any critical project. Taste, however, remains conditioned by the environment and not merely a personal preference. Throughout his work, Ḥusayn remains uncomfortable with European literary subjectivity (the Subject), which he read as an individualistic enterprise too self-involved to be useful in his political moment. Do Ḥusayn's translations perform his vision for how Western works should be copied into Arabic? Are they accurate transmissions of Western texts as they are, chosen on the basis that they constitute 'good' and modular works? Finally, how does his work with and on translation recast the quest for origin that is fundamental to his modernist project?

## Fated, not Freed: Ḥusayn Turns to Gide and Voltaire

Within the transition from philosophy to literature, Ḥusayn turns to André Gide's rewriting of Greek heroism in modern times, subjugating the classical heroes to modern man's endless and fruitless quest of self-discovery. Ḥusayn's motive in translating these particular tales is fuelled by the *tarjama*'s promise to provide a (fictional) model of emulation that can be duly revised. Ḥusayn is drawn to this modern quest for origin, although in the introduction to the translation he does not mention that these quests end in no discovery. Ḥusayn's modernist position – the quest for origin in modern times – unfolds in his identification with Gide's person: Ḥusayn is also defining modern Egyptian literature when he translates the French text through the Greek tradition.

Ḥusayn chooses to combine the two stories into one text prefaced by one of his exemplary introductions. The address to Gide in the dedication explains that Ḥusayn is translating drama specifically because it is the perfect space to bring together art and religion. Aesthetics promises virtue, through '*taqdīs al-āliha*' (sanctification of the gods) and '*tamjīd al-abṭāl*' (glorification of heroes),[144] reminiscent of al-Sibāʿī's original title of the Carlyle translation, *ᶜIbādat al-buṭūla* (Hero Worship). In a letter responding to Gide's association of the Qurʾān with intellectual stagnation (1946), Ḥusayn distinguishes between the Islam of *inḥiṭāṭ* (a typical gesture of his self-orientalism) and *his* Islam of radical openness to the other, as proven by the first five centuries of its appearance, when 'Islam had given a lot because it has received a lot'.[145] Taking in Judaism, Christianity, and later Greek, Persian, and Indian cultures, Islam 'made of all that an Arab culture which it then summarised and gifted to the West before the fifteenth century'. This civilisational exchange also unfolds in the language of translation: 'if Islam could carry that dangerous weight (debt), then it is capable . . . of accepting modern European education and accepting it well'.[146] Ḥusayn's Islam accommodates European thought, and his translation of Gide reconciles Gide's thought with the Egyptian context, much like the stories of Oedipus and Theseus square the inevitability of destiny with human freedom.[147] What matters most, Ḥusayn writes in the introduction, 'is that man makes an effort or tries to change destiny even if he cannot, and here the example of Oedipus is the most relevant'.[148] Reminiscent of Haykal's, Ḥusayn's project for a modernity borrowed in translation finds itself in Gide's context-driven rewriting.[149] He chooses Gide's version because unlike Jean Cocteau's modernised rewriting, it remembers the original struggle between destiny and man's limited freedom.[150] And Ḥusayn's translation of both stories together would reconcile art and life through Gide, as he tells us in the critical article '*Yawmiyyāt Andrī Jīd*' (Diaries of André Gide), we need more such translations.[151] Gide's rewriting of *Oedipus* and *Theseus*, a form of translation, speaks to man's modern condition, as Gide's Oedipus is the philosophically sophisticated man of the early twentieth century who embodies the struggle between modern man's inflated self and fate – and the chorus, representing the people, 'is concerned about such vanity [*ḍayyiqa bi-hadhā al-ghurūr*], worried about its impact on the fate of the city, and the plague that has left the city in a wretched state pushes the chorus to feel pity and fear'.[152] The function of the chorus like Ḥusayn's translation is to keep the hero's ego in check even when Oedipus himself does not renounce his egoistic contempt of all the situations he encounters.[153] In *Niẓām*, Ḥusayn also critiques individuality in favour of the collective but here he finds Gide's literary forms to be more relevant: a play (Oedipus) and a theatrical dialogue (Theseus), two impressionist pieces that use genre to communicate a message. Ḥusayn is attuned to his medium, and the aesthetics of literary reading emerge in adapting Gide.[154]

To justify his translation of the two texts together, Ḥusayn explains that, while Oedipus is the unhappier character that finds peace in death, Theseus is the happier one who does not meet a peaceful death:

> So it is not strange that André Gide thought about the two men together, as did Sophocles before him. It is also not strange that we combine the translations of both these stories in one volume, even if Gide did not do that, because he spent more than ten years in between writing these two stories.[155]

Much like al-Manfalūṭī's appropriation of *Atala* and *René* in '*al-Shuhadāʾ*', Ḥusayn's translation pulls two characters together into a single narrative to communicate a *relevant* moral, attuned to the imagined reader. The Greek Theseus was a great reformer, his name stemming from the Greek root word for 'the assembly', and he unified Attica under Athens by overcoming strenuous trials (such as slaying the Minotaur). In Sophocles' trilogy, Theseus appears as the ideal king in *Oedipus at Colonus*. Representing all Athenian virtues, Theseus is the culmination of an ideal Athens, a vision comforting for an Athenian audience caught in war. Gide's Theseus is an older man looking back on his life and addressing his now-dead son Hippolyte (much like Ḥusayn does in the first two volumes of *al-Ayyām*). The translation's combination of the Theseus and Odysseus stories reiterates Ḥusayn's similar struggles with imagining a coherent and unified Egypt. Gide rewrites Theseus's story from the latter's perspective, with all the hesitations that possessed the Greek hero. Ḥusayn identifies with Gide and his hesitant Theseus. Translation again provides the terms for an impersonation that works on multiple levels: Ḥusayn translates the rewriting or translation of Greek heroism in twentieth-century France into his desire to link Egypt to Hellenic culture.

The translation is mostly faithful to the original, with the exception of some grammatical and sentence errors and the insertion of explanatory footnotes; the most interesting errors change the active subjects of verbs. In the original, Chapter 12 describes Oedipus as the agent of his failure: '*il avait échoué dans son entreprise. . .. Même la durable bénédiction que doit apporter sa dépouille à la contrée où elle repose ce n'est pas sur sa Thèbes ingrate qu'elle agira, mais sur Athènes*' (he had failed in his endeavour . . . Even the blessing which was meant to be bestowed on the country did not act on his ungrateful Thebes, but on Athens instead).[156] In the Arabic, Oedipus fails, and the gods are the active agents who bestow the blessing on the land: 'it was written that he should fail in everything he tried [*la-qad kutiba* *ᶜalayhi al-ikhfāq*]' and 'the blessing that the gods had bestowed [*qaḍāhā*] on the land'.[157] The Arabic translation makes Oedipus's failure predetermined, attributes the blessing directly to the gods, and removes the adjective 'ungrateful' from the description of Thebes. In a translation that pretends to accuracy, these changes indicate Ḥusayn's adherence to the Greek originals against the assumptions of modern subjectivity. After all, Ḥusayn believed in fate, as his treatise on al-Maᶜarrī confirms (1914), as the ultimate mediator of great men's paths. Ḥusayn's recourse to fate compromises his declared espousal of a teleological modernity that has a maturation point, and his critique of individuality resonates with his larger project of using literature as an equalising space that forges communion with the reader. Fate appears from within divine intervention, as the Greek gods manipulate the hero's trajectory, but does not limit human agency, here a form of striving that may not reach an end goal. Fate thus allows for openness rather than a dictated finality in Ḥusayn's vision. The recourse to fate becomes the ultimate mediator of cultural difference, and the aesthetic mission of art is to reflect this conviction as it develops in his rewriting of Plato, Aristotle, and Gide, and, finally, Voltaire.

Fate or *al-Qadar* is the title of Ḥusayn's 1947 translation of Voltaire's *Zadig, ou la destinée: histoire orientale* (1747), the orientalist tale that Voltaire wrote after reading the French translation of *One Thousand and One Nights*.[158] The story's moral explains its selection for translation:

> For in the story there is an exposition of the problem of judgment [*qaḍāʾ*] and fate [*qadar*] as the Orientals imagine it, or how Voltaire envisioned the Orientals to imagine it. It has a solution for this problem that is akin to what the philosophers imagined from the earliest times, which . . . solves nothing, and . . . can be summarised in the conclusion that man is shorter-witted and not intelligent enough to understand the wisdom of the Creator who made this world and its laws.[159]

But Ḥusayn tells us that in this novella there is more to the absurdity of man's attempts to fight the world; that is the social and political critique that it leverages against contemporary Parisian society, wherein the city of Babel becomes a symbol of Paris, and the castle of Babel a symbol of the Parisian throne. He has chosen this 'entertaining' tale because it could instil similar introspection in the Arab reader.[160] In this translation, fate appears again as a mediator of cultural difference and an organising trope in Ḥusayn's translation and critical projects. M. M. Badawi reads Ḥusayn's investment in fate as a means to establish his superiority to his context,[161] but a closer examination of how fate develops in his translations indicates a critique of individual prominence and makes the aesthetic into a leveraging realm for both writer and reader. Although the editor's preface is missing from the translation, Ḥusayn includes the original dedication: 'Je vous offre la traduction d'un livre d'un ancien sage' (I offer you the translation of an ancient sage's book).[162] The original is already a translation. The quest for cultural origins motivates Ḥusayn's translations of both Gide and Voltaire, but this quest unfolds in a broader commitment to literature as the ideal (aesthetic) medium of moral cultivation. Ḥusayn read French literature for such models, and the originals became examples.

Ḥusayn, like Haykal, understands *tarjama* as both translation and biography, and his translations and criticism overlap with auto/biography through his identification with Gide, Paul Valéry, and Charles Baudelaire.[163] Ḥusayn locates the second *nahḍa*, after the Abbasid revival, initially in a return to Hellenic rationality as a shared heritage for Egypt. In 1938, Ḥusayn wrote that, while Europe moved forward, 'the East started its decline, and overdid its decline, until it almost lost its rational character. Then Egypt awoke, and with it the Near East.'[164] But this transformative 'modernity' figures as interruptions in his translation project when he intervenes in the originals and adapts them to the receiving context. Modernity, in other words, so often relegated to the author's person and statements, is in fact an imaginary performance that gets caught up in its own historical moment: displacing one's own history to impersonate the modern. Ḥusayn shows us that this displacement is impossible, since the act of *tarjama* (as translation and interpretation) must remain revisionary and critical, much like Ḥusayn's 'secular' literary history.

## Literary Criticism, Auto/Biography and Missing Origins

From the earlier *Niẓām al-Athīniyyīn* (1921) to the later *al-Qadar* (1947), we find a shift in Ḥusayn's approach to translation from a pronounced faith in acculturation through exact copying to translation as an impressionistic project that engages the original as an aesthetic ideal. This turn also mirrors Ḥusayn's critical shift from positivist (objective) to aesthetic (subjective) literary criticism. The intimacy he develops in his *tarājim* and translations frames his comparatist critical project and becomes the operative paradigm for displacement in his work.

As early as 19 October 1911, in a lecture later published as '*Hal tastaridd al-lugha al-ᶜArabīya amjādahā?*' (Will the Arabic Language Retrieve its Glory?) (March 1912), Ḥusayn begins to articulate his project for literary criticism as civilisational critique before *Fī al-shiᶜr al-jāhilī* (1926). He defends both Islam and the Arabic language against those who believe the two could only spread through force, and attributes the rise and fall of civilisations – at the boundary between the Umayyad and the Abbasid caliphates – to literature and specifically oratory prose that transforms civilisational thought. As in the Abbbasid era, the modern revival of the Arabic language must happen through copying and *tarjama* – derivation, metaphor, and Arabisation to be exact. In the lecture, Ḥusayn openly attacks al-Azhar's monopoly over the language, and enlists the revivalist efforts of Muḥammad ᶜAbduh, the translation of Western literature, and the establishment of linguistic authorities to monitor linguistic reform as the necessary measures for such a revival.[165] The revival of language through literature establishes the first main component of his critical project: an attention to textual criticism. In the Introduction to the sixth edition of *Tajdīd Dhikrā Abī ᶜAlā᾿* (1951) (Renewing the Memory of Abī ᶜAlā' al-Maᵓarrī), Ḥusayn credits his teacher al-Marṣafī with introducing textual criticism into literary study, but adds that Ḥusayn's own method, which combines historical context, influence, and textual analysis, is the antidote to the critical method popular at the time of reading the text outside of a historical context.[166]

In line with his translation project in the 1920s of Greek literature and philosophy, and the quest to reintroduce a 'familiar' Hellenic rationality, *Fī al-shiᶜr al-jāhilī* (1926) seems less controversial in claiming that 'the history of *adab* is not modern . . . but old and *natural* too', and 'the history of *adab* that we want to modernise now is not an invention or a creation but a *reformation* and *renewal* of what the ancients left behind, no more and no less'.[167] From Charles Augustin Sainte-Beuve (1804–69) – the French literary historian and critic, who applied historical methods to literary studies – he borrows the psychological state of the author. From Hippolyte-Adolphe Taine (1828–93) – a main exponent of nineteenth-century French positivism – Ḥusayn borrows the universal concern of literature, and from Ferdinand Brunetière – another French critic (1849–1906) who championed universalism – the importance of studying genres in their development.[168] In the final assessment, Ḥusayn finds that the proper method for a history of literature is midway between the scientific and aesthetic, with close reading on a formalist level. This approach would reconcile Western methodology with Arabic literature,[169] since there can be no Arabic literary history without a return to *Jahili* and classical Islamic literature.[170] This return, however, must liberate the Arabic language from its status as sacred and render it the stuff of science.[171] Ḥusayn's scientific approach to the study of Arabic language and literature develops in his reading (borrowing) of French critical paradigms, but the impetus behind his project is much larger than a desire to secularise and modernise. Read in the contexts of both its reception and Ḥusayn's oeuvre, *Fī al-shi*ᶜ*r al-jāhilī* marks a transitional phase that has already settled its debt with Greek philosophy as we saw earlier, and now begins to refine its commitment to the French tradition. Both debts can only be settled in revising one's past.

Like Haykal, Ḥusayn believed in borrowing from the past what is relevant to the present.[172] In '*al-Adab al-*ᶜ*Arabī bayn amsihi wa ghadihi*' (Arabic Literature between Past and Future) (1945), Ḥusayn finds modern Arabic literature continuous with the past: 'Its past has connected with its present in such a direct way that there has been no disruption . . . on the way.' While the tradition provides stable reference, the 'renewing elements' enable growth and mobility, keeping Arabic literature alive.[173] Jeffrey Sacks reads Ḥusayn's literary historical intervention as a repetition of the colonial violence that made his discourse possible in the first place. The assumption that the Cartesian method is the only one that works for this kind of study is also an acknowledgement that the separation between the secular and sacred instilled by the colonial legacy is organic to Arabic literature, especially since Ḥusayn's primary analytical material is the linguistic aspect of pre-Islamic and early Islamic literature.[174] Sacks's analysis recalls Derrida's point that in always anticipating the other, language forgets its colonial beginnings. Mohammed al-Nowayhi similarly finds that Ḥusayn forgets the French beginnings of his aesthetic project: 'forgetting for a while his acquired knowledge, he came back to Arabic literature, and, with his developed insight, was able to make a fresh evaluation of its distinctive aesthetic quality.'[175] Ḥusayn's controversial book and its publication history, however, 'would fragment – arguably once and for all – the harmony and syncretism that had characterized the Nahda'.[176] Ḥusayn after all does not completely forget the origin of his critical idiom because he was too aware of its reception. His translations speak to his moment, and his work remains grounded in an imaginary dialogue with an imagined Egyptian reader.

Ḥusayn's literary critic is *fated* to be a social mirror. The writer is a prophet of art, not free to choose whether to accept or reject his message and vocation, so Aristotle's rules for art can be transcended in literature's quest for freedom.[177] In '*Maᶜ udabāʾinā al-muᶜāṣirīn*' (With Our Contemporary Writers) (1933), the writer is 'a social being who cannot exist in isolation' but lives off of his connection with the people and like a 'mirror' reflects their thoughts.[178] In the 1930s and 1940s, he struggles with the critic's position as social mirror, a product of the environment who could also expose this environment through literature, in other words, between literature as a solitary creative act and commitment to a cause.[179] In his conversations with al-Manfalūṭī, *adab* becomes the literary object torn between commitment and artistic creation – a legacy of romanticism and realism coinciding in translation. For al-Māzinī, the mirror is a romantic reflection of the poet's self, while al-ᶜAqqād places the mirror halfway between the poet and the people.[180] For Ḥusayn, the literary mirror is caught in that in-between space, as he critiques al-ᶜAqqād's and al-Māzinī's over-reliance on the poet's personality. Hence, Jābir ᶜAṣfūr describes Ḥusayn's position as '*tawfīqī*' (conciliatory).[181] But beyond the conciliatory position, what develops in Ḥusayn's articulated critical approach is a discursive and displaced critical subjectivity that remains anxious about the critic's position in relation to the literary object and the social sphere. While ᶜAṣfūr finds the movement in Ḥusayn's oeuvre between author, society, and humanity a facile one, the trajectory of his works repeatedly arrests this movement. ᶜAṣfūr maps this trajectory of Ḥusayn's works: in the 1920s and 1930s, he calls for separating literature from religion; in the 1930s and 1940s he develops his critical project under the influence of French thought through literary adaptation, while in the 1950s, literature becomes more representational, moving outwards towards life.[182] In this narrative, Ḥusayn's work moves through three phases: a classical phase (reflecting an Aristotelian or Platonic reality); a romantic or 'inward' phase; and, finally, a realist phase.[183] ᶜAṣfūr also finds an alarming lack of concern with genre in Ḥusayn's writing,[184] such that all forms are determined by historical movement and literature ends up a product of its social moment.[185] But Ḥusayn's translations, which altered the original's genre, style, and intention, move in tandem with his critical project, complicating such neat classifications of his work, as his so-called 'romantic', 'realist', and 'committed' literary aesthetics overlap.

From his biographical commentaries on French authors to paratextual interventions in his translations, Ḥusayn conflates the fictional with the auto/biographical to devise a critical voice that assumes its full form in *Adīb* (1933) and *al-Ayyām*. *Adīb* narrates the story of an unnamed writer ('dead brother' in the dedication) infected by the 'disease' (*ᶜillat*) of *adab*.[186] Unlike contemporaneous novels that use titular character names such as al-ᶜAqqād's *Sara* and Haykal's *Zaynab*, *Adīb* is a fictional *tarjama* whose autobiographical references stirred critical confusion.[187] The narrator tells us the *adīb*'s story in letters, memoirs, and dialogues, for he feels obligated to share his private history: 'Since he has all those thoughts, why not record them to share his individual history?'[188] The desire to communicate is a desire for the other, for the listener and reader, a desire to move outward from the text. Reminiscent of Haykal's quibble with the many versions of Rousseau, Ḥusayn's novel incorporates the other self in a similar 'move outward' that Abdelrashid Mahmoudi finds in *al-Ayyām*.[189] The narrative self develops in this transactional literary space between writer and reader.

Moreover, the critique of absolute individuality that he develops in reading Plato, Aristotle, and Gide materialises in the narrative voices of his fictions. In *al-Ayyām*, this voice emerges in the crisis of becoming a writer.[190] An autobiographical *tarjama*, the text uses a third-person narrator that occasionally radically splits from the subject: for example, the narrator reveals secrets that Ḥusayn has told him: 'He swore to me afterwards that from that day he despised learning.'[191] He also tells Ḥusayn's daughter: 'Your mother understood, your father understood, and I also understood that you wept because.'[192] This narrative split duplicates the boy's crisis – his turn from al-Azhar to literature – through literary reading.[193] The crisis unfolds as illicit pleasure, the translations he reads in secret: 'They used to marvel at what they found in them [the translations] of pictures of life that go against what they know in their countryside and their cities.'[194] Literature records this movement outward, much like how Paul de Man implicates literary history with interpretation, both as movements that stive towards reality outside the text but then return to the text. In de Man's description, the *moi* of the writer is always threatened by the *non-moi*; that is why literature reaches out to reality but then returns to itself. In this movement, the literary becomes the absolute paradigm of a revisionary modernism: the modern always seeks to be exceptional, occurring outside of an established historical narrative that assigns its place to specific dates and epochs. However, the modern cannot escape historical time, which always reclaims it as another node on its teleological way.[195] In Ḥusayn's autobiography, this external movement of literature plays out in the address to the reader; the overlap between the two genres of autobiography and novel undoes the narrative self's solipsisim – an expectation of the autobiographical genre.[196] While Rousseau's *Confessions* inspires Ḥusayn's *al-Ayyām*, Ḥusayn's narrative voice presents less of himself as an individual.[197] In '*Fī al-ṭarīq*' (On the Road) (1935), Ḥusayn the critic reiterates that 'one should not think of oneself too much, for man does not deserve that much attention', and continues as per the traditional *tarjama*, that 'one should divert his attention from oneself by reading, conversation, work, and the enjoyment of pleasures permitted by God and morality'.[198]

What develops in Ḥusayn's work is a critique of individuality rather than a mere copying of the Western subject into an Egyptian context. His translations, which map his critical transitions and generic playfulness, speak to literature's potential threat to the writer's self and its obligation to move outside towards the reader. Much like Haykal, Ḥusayn believes in the importance of context. In 'The Modern Renaissance of Arabic Literature' (1955), he defines his generation's task as writing critique and not literature, describing *Adīb* (1933) and *al-Ayyām* as *incidental* novels.[199] Those have to be left behind and forgotten, however, because his moment requires critique in order to establish the foundations of an Egyptian modernity. Ḥusayn's oeuvre, read holistically and comparatively, exposes the paradoxical logic of modernity, especially through the literary object, as it simultaneously asserts and erases its newness. He dislikes Voltaire for being too metaphysical, a similar accusation that he levels at the Syrian immigrant writers who lagged behind writers in the Arab world by remaining too preoccupied with metaphysical problems. 'When one reads Gibran Khalil Gibran and Amin Rihani', Ḥusayn continues, she or he finds 'expatriated, thought . . . in the mold of the American concepts which surround them' and foreign forms.[200] His literature is 'only accidental' because he and other modernists 'preferred to devote ourselves to works which, rightly or wrongly, we considered more important', in other words, with 'criticism' and not 'creation'. The interplay between the scientificity of critique and openness of creation develops in tandem with his translations from the 1920s to the 1940s.

The elites, the nation's prophets, had to both free the Arab mind from tradition and fight the 'encroaching siege of Western materialism'. These writers were 'men of thought and men of action' since they were in Parliament and ministers, and they resorted to prose as the most apt medium to record the imbalance between what one is and what one hopes to be.[201] This projected futurity, however, is also only incidental to Ḥusayn's modernist project because the prose-self, the transacted narrative self, is not a decidedly finished product; rather, it fluctuates in the generic fluidity that qualifies Ḥusayn's work and critical contribution to Arabic narrative. While the conflation of auto/biography and fiction has been read as an inadequacy on Ḥusayn's part, dooming his fiction to immaturity, his incidentally *modern* hybridisation of both the autobiographical novel and fictional auto/biography recalls how the two genres historically coalesced into the modern European novel. His negotiation with literary genre through translation is precisely the critical contribution that he wanted his generation to make.[202] The literary self is a transactual being, carrying traces of the other that it has seemingly forgotten, and speaking in tongues despite itself.

## Ḥusayn and Haykal Weighed in the Balance

In the '*Muqaddima*' (introduction) to *Ḥāfiẓ wa Shawqī* (1933), Ḥusayn reiterates the writer's brave duty to speak to the people, while maintaining his opinion if it feels right.[203] In a letter to Haykal entitled '*Shiʿr wa nathr*' (Poetry and Prose), Ḥusayn gently berates the latter for not *explaining* the reasons for the modern turn to prose in Arabic literature: like Aḥmad Shawqī does in poetry, Haykal imposes on Egyptian writers what he has actually only found in Rousseau and Anatole France.[204] Ḥusayn also attacks Ḥāfiẓ for abridging and not faithfully translating Victor Hugo's *Les Misérables*, so Ḥusayn includes a translation of the neglected first page, because translation is only good when it is an exact copy of the original.[205] In the chapter on Baudelaire, he explains that the purpose of translation is demonstration by example, even though intervention is necessary since Baudelaire's self is not something with which '*we*' can identify. After all, Baudelaire, like Haykal's Rousseau, turned against fate to please others.[206] Ḥusayn's translation aesthetic leads to his view of civilisation as open, changing, and always moving. He again departs from Haykal, whose later opposition between the East's spirituality and the West's materialism ends up reifying both. Ḥusayn instead represents Western civilisation as a 'product of the imagination', a 'fertile and productive spirit' in constant motion.[207]

Reading *Mustaqbal* with *Niẓām*, and Theseus with *Adīb*, shows how Ḥusayn articulates a narrative self not easily complicit in a colonial self–other dynamic. Like Rousseau, Ḥusayn finds solace in his multiple fictional selves; unlike Rousseau, these imaginary selves are self-proclaimed transactions between Ḥusayn and his imagined reader, and they are most resonant when they move away from the writer's *moi*. Reading him against himself, even in 1955 when he claims that he is leaving literature behind, Ḥusayn's work remains deeply committed to the promise of literature in and as translation. He recognises that perfect translation is never fully achievable and bound to fail – this failure becomes most evident in the generic fluidity of his works that recasts his radical claims of absolute borrowing through translation. Shaden Tageldin finds that Ḥusayn's translation project is a universalist one, citing his exchange with al-ʿAqqād as silencing political nuances and cultural differences. Ḥusayn calls on the defeated to borrow from translation more than the conqueror, as opposed to al-ʿAqqād who is more aware of the precariousness of colonial power.[208] But a closer engagement with Ḥusayn's translations troubles his self-orientalising declarations precisely by way of the revisionary voice that emerges in his work. Because of the excess in the process of translation, identification is never absolute, and so coincidence with one's own or the other's language is equally impossible.

Abdelrashid Mahmoudi reads the shift from the religious to the literary in Ḥusayn's critical project as a transcendence of both his Arab and French interlocutors, as literature for him 'was essentially a kind of audible discourse (speech) which, by virtue of its sonorous and other aesthetic qualities', created 'a bond between speaker and listener and reinserted both into the world of men'.[209] The antagonism between culture and religion, wrote Husayn in 1938, was always due to their representatives. Religion must remain a condition of human freedom.[210] Ḥusayn explains the 'religious tendencies' in his contemporaries' and his own work as consequences of reading Western literature. In 'Tendances religieuses de la littérature égyptienne aujourd'hui' (Religious Tendencies in Contemporary Egyptian Literature) (published in French on 9 July 1946), he writes that Haykal's *Ḥayāt Muḥammad* is inspired by a French text, al-ᶜAqqād's *ᶜAbqariyyat Muḥammad* by Carlyle, and his own Islamic writings by Jules Lemaître.[211] In all these different narratives, he identifies a compromise in the form of *turāth mujaddad* – a renewed heritage.[212] Ḥusayn describes religion in the language of literature. Jacques Berque picks up on this correlation in 'Islam vu par Taha Hussein', when he reads Ḥusayn's *Mirᵓāt al-Islām* (Mirror of Islam) (1959) as political and social commentary and not religious treatise. The text invites collective responsibility and eschews doctrine since Ḥusayn's distinction between faith and religion echoes the historical spirit that defines all his works.[213] In Berque's final analysis, Ḥusayn's Islam emerges from within writing as critique, the act of reading and address to the other,[214] and parallels the nation's unresolved relationship to its past and present.[215] However, if we consider Ḥusayn's own confession of debt to European literature, and the way in which he rewrites these original models, his presentation of Islam in the language of literature becomes less secular and more profane. The profane comes from another tradition and becomes a space of appropriation and critique, such that religion as faith emerges from within the practice of translation and the literary act as communion with the reader. It restores religion as faith to the public sphere of communion, profaning the secular's historical separation between the two, especially in colonial contexts. Ḥusayn's approach to religion and literature did not escape these colonial traps, but his work holds on to the tension between the two, rather than simply allowing the facile supplanting of one by the other. It comes to document the historical moment that demanded their separation, such that religion and literature are brought back into the discursive public domain, as a transaction between writer and reader.

The elites must use the freedom of art to produce critique. However, the creative act, which Ḥusayn wants to describe as incidental, becomes the condition of possibility for this critique, the trajectory of prophecy that develops in their works.[216] The drive behind the *tarjama* is more fictional emulation than confession, and translation resists the finality of the novel form in heeding the political moment. Ḥusayn's disregard for the generic distinction between autobiography and novel makes both forms impossible in his oeuvre. This conflict unravels in failed translation, exposing the incompatibility between the novel form, liberalism, realism, and the collective: the failure of the socialist incentive to shake Egypt with al-Sibāᶜī or the expression of the self with al-ᶜAqqād and al-Māzinī. The translators' failure speaks to the impossibility of choice: alienated from both the tradition and European thought, their literature could only pretend to mend the crisis in adapted forms. Their failures teach us that, in the end, translation is most genuine when it falls short.

## Notes

1. I owe this quotation to Sacks, *Iterations of Loss*, p. 123.
2. He used to listen to Ḥusayn al-Marṣafī's lectures in the morning and Carlo Alfonso Nallino's (1872–1938) in the evening – both figures greatly shaped Ḥusayn's literary reading. The Italian Orientalist lectured at the Egyptian University – which later became King Fūᵓād I, and then Cairo University from 1909 to 1912. For more on the role of the orientalists at the Egyptian University, see Donald Malcolm Reid 'Cairo University and the Orientalists,' *International Journal of Middle East Studies*, 19 (1) (Feb., 1987): 51–75.
3. He also studied with Gustave Lanson (1857–1934), an influential theoretician of literary history.
4. In *al-Ayyām* (Volume Three, p. 349), he describes the hostility between him and Saᶜd. The trial is described in Muṣṭafā ᶜAbd al-Ghanī, *Ṭāhā Ḥusayn wa thawrat yūlyū*, pp. 12–15.
5. Ḥusayn was never going to be indicted, because his freedom of speech was guaranteed under the 1923 constitution. See Articles 12 and 14. The full

text of the constitution can be accessed at http://www.constitutionnet.org/files/1923_-_egyptian_constitution_english_1.pdf

6. Karīm, *Mādhā yabqā min fikr Ṭāhā Ḥusayn*, p. 90. Luc-Willy Deheuvels cites the same moment in 'Tâhâ Husayn et *Le livre des jours*' (para. 16).
7. Volume One was first serialised in *al-Hilāl* and published as a book in 1929; Volume Two appeared in 1939. Volume Three appeared in *Ākhir sāᶜa* (The Last Hour) between 30 May 1955 and 26 June 1955, and in book form in 1967 in Beirut and in 1972 in Cairo as *Mudhakkirāt Ṭāhā Ḥusayn* (Mémoires de Ṭāhā Ḥusayn).
8. The second edition with two extra chapters also came out in a 10,000 print later in 1935 and sold out within a year (see Gershoni, '"The Reader"', p. 251).
9. Ḥusayn campaigned for mass education throughout his career and became Minister of Education under the Wafd government (1950–2).
10. See Ibrahim, 'Taha Husayn: The Critical Spirit', pp. 105–18, 106.
11. Michael Allan has recently explored how the exchanges between Ḥusayn and Gide treat theology through literary discussion: 'This is not any simple binarism between East and West, the modern and the traditional, the religious and the secular, but instead a negotiation of the terms through which religious discussion transpires' (see Allan, *In the Shadow*, p. 122).
12. It is not my intention in this chapter to engage their relationships to Islam, but rather to explore how their translation process informs their attitude on religion and tradition. For more on Haykal's Islam, see Smith, *Islam and the Search*, and on Ḥusayn, Jamāl ᶜAskarī's *al-Ittijāhāt al-dīnīya fī adab Ṭāhā Ḥusayn* [Religious Tendencies in Ṭāhā Ḥusayn's work] (Cairo: al-Hayᵓa al-Miṣriiyya al-ᶜāmma li-l-kitāb, 2008).
13. See Smith, 'The Intellectual and Modernization', p. 525.
14. Reynolds, *Interpreting the Self*, p. 42.
15. Ibid., p. 43.
16. Ibid., p. 23.
17. Lejeune, *On Autobiography*, p. 4.
18. Ibid., p. 14.
19. Lejeune's 'Autobiography in the Third Person', pp. 28–9.
20. Reynolds, *Interpreting the Self*, p. 67.
21. My point here is not to engage with the debate on autobiography as a modern form, which is why I am not considering Jurjī Zaydān's seminal autobiography (1908). Rather I am interested in how translation conditions the narra-

tive self into the auto/biographical model that skirts between two narrative modalities of first and third person, or autobiography and novel. Suffice it to say that the study of autobiography in the Arabic tradition could benefit from a clearer distinction between autobiographical writing, autobiography, and *bildungsroman*. Ḥusayn's *al-Ayyām* with its chronological narrative of a character's life is often considered to be the first Arabic autobiography (see Philipp's 'The Autobiography in Modern Arab Literature and Culture'). In the early twentieth century, the apprentice novel that typically follows an Arab male's pedagogical journey in the West and documents his difficult return to the homeland also becomes associated with autobiography (Tawfīq al-Ḥakīm, Yaḥyā Ḥaqqī). The other important genre is the *sīra*, generally defined as a historical narrative, and Ḥusayn wrote a three-volume *ᶜAla hāmish al-sīra* (On the Margins of the *Sīra*) of prophetic tales, a literary treatise by his own declaration (see Rashīda Mihrān ᶜĪsā, *Ṭāhā Ḥusayn bayn al-sīra wa-l-tarjama al-dhātiyya* (Alexandria: Dār Maṭbaᶜ Maḥmadī, 1975), p. 33). For more on the formal distinctions between the *sīra* and *tarjama* with al-ᶜAqqād, Ḥusayn, and Haykal, see Rashīda Mehran ᶜĪsā, *Ṭāhā Ḥusayn*, pp. 329–82. Both Yaḥyā Ibrāhīm al-Dāyim and Muḥammad ᶜAbd al-Ghinā Ḥasan find no difference between the modern sense of *sīra* and *tarjama*; the first points to a long history and the second to a shorter history of the individual (see Ḥasan, *al-Tarājim wa-l-siyar*, 2nd edition (Cairo: Dār al-Maᶜārif, 1969), p. 28; Yaḥyā Ibrāhīm ᶜAbd al-Dāyim, *al-Tarjama al-dhātiyya fi al-adab al-ᶜArabī al-ḥadīth* (Beirut: Dār Iḥyāᵓ al-turāth al-ᶜArabī 1971), p. 31). On the conflation of autobiography and the bildungsroman, see Nedal Al-Moosa, 'The Arabic Bildungsroman: A Generic Reappraisal', *International Journal of Middle East Studies* 25 (2) (May, 1993): 223–40.

22. *Jān Jāk II*, p. 103.
23. *Al-Tarjama al-dhātiyya*, pp. 34–8. For more on the generic definition of *tarjama dhatiyya* especially, see Shawqī al-Ḍayf's *al-Tarjama al-shakhṣiyya* (Cairo: Dār al-maᶜārif, 1970); Anīs al-Makdisī, *al-Funūn al-adabiyya wa aᶜlāmuha fi-l-nahḍa al-ᶜArabiyya al- ḥadītha*, 3rd edition (Beirut: Dār al-ᶜilm li-l-malāyīn 1980) p. 517; Ḥasan, ibid., p. 23; ᶜAbd al-ᶜAzīz Sharaf, *Adab al-sīra al-dhātiyya* (Cairo: al-Sharika al-Miṣriyya al-ᶜālamiyya li-l-nashr, 1988), p. 27, and ᶜAbd al-Dāyim, ibid., pp. 3, 12.
24. Ibid., p. 80.
25. Ibid., pp. 191–3.
26. Ibid., pp. 447, 450, 454.

27. Many of Ḥusayn's works have been approached as autobiographical, for example, *Adīb* (1933) and *Min baᶜīd* (From Afar) (1935). Muḥammad ᶜAbd al-Ghinī Ḥasan finds that the modern *tarjama* and *sīra* require the novelistic form, giving the examples of Al-ᶜAqqād's *ᶜAbqariyyāt*, Haykal's *Ḥayāt Muḥammad*, and Ḥusayn's *ᶜUthmān*. See Ḥasan's *al-Tarājim wa-l-siyar*, 2nd edition (Cairo: Dār al-Maᶜārif, 1969), pp. 10, 16.
28. Derrida, *Monolingualism*, p. 68.
29. See Bakhtin, 'Author and Hero in Aesthetic Activity' (written ca. 1922–4; first published in the Soviet Union in 1977–8) (1990).
30. Bakhtin, 'Author and Hero', p. 14.
31. Ibid., p. 38.
32. Ibid., pp. 142–3, 151.
33. Several critics have noted the generic indeterminacy of the translators' works; on Ṭāhā Ḥusayn, see, for example, Shukrī, *Mādhā yabqā min Ṭāhā Ḥusayn?*, pp. 47–8; on al-Māzinī, see Muḥammad Mandūr, *Ibrāhīm al-Māzinī* (Cairo: Maṭbaᶜat nahḍat Miṣr, 1954), pp. 68–9; on al-Manfalūṭī, see Chapter Two.
34. See *Literary Modernity between the Middle East and Europe*, p. 5.
35. *Thawrat*, p. 113.
36. In 'Taqdīm dīwān al-Bārūdī', Haykal justifies his literary thefts from the tradition and the West as necessary to his modernising project (pp. 26–7).
37. Haykal, *Tarājim*, pp. 6–7.
38. Smith, 'Love, Passion and Class', p. 250.
39. Ibid., p. 250. Haykal refers to the Darwinian struggle for survival in his portrayal of the East–West struggle in the Middle Ages in Haykal, *al-Sharq al-jadīd*.
40. Haykal, *Fī manzil al-waḥy*, cited in Smith, *Islam and the Search*, p. 42.
41. Smith, *Islam and the Search*, p. 56.
42. Ibid., p. 40.
43. Smith, *Islam and the Search*, p. 58.
44. Israel Gershoni and James P. Jankowski describe the intellectual upsurge of the 1920s as a direct result of the 1919 revolution, which was represented as creating 'Egyptian people as a single, homogeneous national body struggling for a common goal' (pp. 84–5).
45. *Jān Jāk, I*, pp. vii, x–xi.
46. Smith confirms the influence of Carlyle's *On Heroes* on Haykal's view of history (*Islam and the Search*, p. 18), but Ṭāhā Wādī finds Carlyle's influence to

have distanced Haykal from his religion, making him present people as prophets, a guilt he compensates for in his later political memoirs (see *al-Duktūr Muḥammad Ḥusayn Haykal*, p. 16).

47. *Jān Jāk, I*, p. xiv.
48. In '*Taqdīm al-kitāb*', the introduction to *Fī manzil*, pp. 11–12; p. 16.
49. Ibid., p. 22.
50. Semah, *Four Egyptian Literary Critics*, p. 100.
51. Ibid., p. 97.
52. Ibid., p. 98.
53. Haykal, *al-Sharq al-jadīd*, p. 254.
54. Ibid., p. 258.
55. Ibid., p. 259.
56. Ibid., p. 261.
57. Rousseau, *Confessions*, pp. 50–1; emphasis mine.
58. Starobinski, *Jean Jacques Rousseau*, p. 7.
59. See Bennington, *Dudding*, pp. 55–6.
60. Rousseau, *Confessions*, p. 226.
61. Bennington, *Dudding*, p. 66.
62. Ṭāhā Wādī describes Haykal's genius as a direct result of his generically unclassifiable works and lack of specialisation. *Jān Jāk* can only be a *tarjama* if we expand our generic definition as the literary aspect overcomes the biographical and Haykal believed that translation should include adaptation and creativity (*al-Duktūr*, p. 141).
63. *Jān Jāk, I*, p. 132.
64. Rousseau, *Confessions*, p. 574.
65. Ibid., p. 328.
66. Ibid., p. 592.
67. The *Confessions*' resistance to closure resonates with the promised but never written sequel. Although the *Les Rêveries du promeneur solitaire, 1776–1778*, published posthumously in 1782 and *Les dialogues, Rousseau juge de Jean-Jacques* (1776) came out later, an actual sequel to the *Confessions* was never completed.
68. Haykal, *Jān Jāk, I*, p. 102.
69. Ibid., p. 105.
70. Ibid., p. 71.
71. Ibid., p. 72.
72. Rousseau, *First Discourse* in *The Discourses and Other Early Political Writings* (Cambridge: Cambridge University Press, 1997), p. 6; emphasis mine.

73. Haykal, *Jān Jāk, I*, p. 74; the original passage from the *First Discourse* occurs on pp. 3–4.
74. Ibid., pp. 75–6.
75. Ibid., p. 90.
76. Ibid., p. 94.
77. *Origin of Inequality*, cited in Starobinski, *Jean Jacques Rousseau*, p. 16. In *Émile*, Rousseau's fantasy of the ideal political state rests on his conviction that the general will is not at war with individual will because it is a direct outcome of a universal, a priori conscience.
78. Starobinski, *Jean Jacques Rousseau*, p. 19.
79. Ibid., p. 43.
80. Even though Haykal is writing a *tarjama* and not an autobiography, the latter in the classical Arabic tradition does not assume a confessional form; rather, it emphasises setting a moral example such that events take precedence over the autobiographical 'I'.
81. In the *tarjama*, Haykal tangentially mentions Dudding as Rousseau's chosen English name: 'And his name then was Dudding and it was the English name that he had chosen for himself' (Haykal, *Jān Jāk*, I, p. 44).
82. Wādī also finds Haykal's personal account of history in *Ḥayāt Muḥammad* to trouble the genre of Islamic writing, making it more of a literary translation than *sīra tārīkhiyya* (*al-Duktūr*, p. 145).
83. Edward Said finds that the Qurʾān becomes a character in Ḥusayn's *al-Ayyām*, but does not furnish authority in the same way that Western novelists claimed authority in fiction (Said, *Beginnings*, p. 82).
84. Haykal, *Jān Jāk, II*, p. 60.
85. Haykal was ambivalent about his relationship to the French Revolution. After the 1940s turn to Islam, he begins to emphasise the correlation between Islamic principles and the revolution consistently for the rest of his life. As Charles D. Smith summarises, 'Haykal proclaimed the Revolution's principles and ignored the sociopolitical circumstances to which they were opposed' (Smith, *Islam and the Search*, p. 186).
86. Haykal, *Thawrat*, p. 6.
87. Ibid., p. 11.
88. Ibid., p. 33.
89. Ibid., p. 48.
90. Ibid., p. 69; p. 71.
91. Ibid., p. 72; emphasis added.

92. Ibid., p. 73; emphasis added.
93. Ibid., p. 74.
94. Haykal lists several reasons for the deterioration of storytelling in the Arab world, such as lack of imagination and the vast difference between the language of literature and everyday speech. But the most important reason is the association of love with sexual desire (Haykal, *Thawrat*, p. 85). Because Arabs did not approach love as self-denial and striving for good, they could not write stories.
95. Gershoni and Jankowski discuss the formation of a nationalist literature as a four-tiered project in the 1920s and 1930s: theory, practice, genre, and language. Haykal is instrumental to this project because he insists that literature should be the product of its environment (Gershoni and Jankowski, *Egypt, Islam, and the Arabs*, pp. 191–227).
96. Haykal, *Thawrat*, pp. 117, 118, 119; emphasis added.
97. At the end of the book, he includes samples of his nationalist, Pharaonic stories.
98. In *al-Fikr al-ᶜArabī al-ḥadīth: athar al-thawra al-Faransiyya fī tawjīhihi al-siyāsī wa al-ᵓijtimāᶜī* [Modern Arab Thought: Political and Social Vestiges of the French Revolution] (Beirut: Dār al-makshūf, 1943), Raᵓīf al-Khūry describes the French Revolution's appeal to Arab intellectuals as a return to similar values, such as the resonance between revolution's ideals of equality and *sīra*s of the prophet's life.
99. Haykal, *Jān Jāk, II*, p. 57. The last, unfinished volume of *Émile* – *Émile et Sophie, ou les Solitaires* – follows Émile to Algeria where he completes his education. For more on Rousseau's relationship to Islam as related to Émile's penultimate education as a human and not citizen in Algeria, see Ian Coller, 'Rousseau's Turban: Entangled Encounters of Europe and Islam in the Age of Enlightenment', *Historical Reflections* 40(2) (2014): 56–77.
100. Haykal, *Jān Jāk, II*, pp. 39–40; emphasis mine.
101. Ibid., p. 66.
102. Ibid., pp. 66–7.
103. Ibid., p. 68.
104. Ibid., p. 69.
105. Ibid., p. 114.
106. Gershoni and Jankowski, *Egypt*, pp. 34, 35–6.
107. Haykal, *Jān Jāk, II*, pp. 101–2.
108. Ibid., pp. 173, 177.

109. Haykal, *Jān Jāk, I*, pp. 127, 141–2.
110. Starobinski, *Jean-Jacques Rousseau*, p. 176.
111. Smith, *Islam*, pp. 163–4.
112. Haykal, *Jān Jāk, II*, p. 81.
113. Smith, *Islam and the Search*, p. 180.
114. Trevor Le Gassick locates Haykal's Islamic turn in his reading of Washington Irving's representations of Islam (Le Gassick, 'The Faith of Islam', p. 99).
115. Wādī, *al-Duktūr*, p. 16.
116. Haykal, *Ḥayāt Muḥammad* (Cairo: Maktabat al-nahḍa al-Miṣriyya, 1952), p. 666. Also cited in Badawi, 'Islam in Modern Egyptian Literature', p. 164.
117. In his obituary to Haykal in *Akhbār al-yawm* (December 1956) entitled 'Haykal fī mīzān al-baqāʾ', p. 212.
118. Ibid., pp. 88–91.
119. In *Mādhā yabqā minhum li-l-tārīkh*, Ṣalāḥ Abdel Ṣabūr finds that Ḥusayn's conflicted style – formally influenced by his Azharite education but presenting French ideas – kept his stories from having a real impact on the Egyptian novel (p. 17).
120. Ḥusayn (Hussein), 'The Modern Renaissance', p. 255.
121. Ḥusayn, '*Muqaddimat al-mutarjim*', introduction to Aḥmad Ḥasan al-Zayyāt's *ʾĀlām Furtur*, p. 11.
122. Ibid., pp. 10–11.
123. Gershoni and Jankowski, *Egypt, Islam and the Arabs*, p. 149.
124. The difference between East and West for Ḥusayn unfolds in a teleological view of time: the Ottomans held the Egyptians back or else they would have been instrumental to the modern renaissance (*Mustaqbal*, pp. 38–9).
125. Cachia, *Ṭāhā Ḥusayn*, p. 133.
126. Muqaddima to *Ṣuḥuf mukhtāra*, pp. 11–12.
127. Ḥusayn, *Ṣuḥuf mukhtāra*, p. 26.
128. Ibid., p. 45.
129. Cachia, *Ṭāhā Ḥusayn*, p. 186.
130. Ibid,. p. 188. In the introduction to *The Days*, Cachia retracts his unkind appraisal of Ḥusayn.
131. Ibid,. p. 189. Those were very popular and went through multiple editions. The best example is *Ṣawt Bārīs* (The Voice of Paris) (Kutub li-l-jamīᶜ # 98, Cairo: Dār al-jumhūriyya, 1956), a collection of short narrative summaries of French plays, which Ḥusayn prefaces by saying that readers *desire* his book and he hopes with multiple publications it will urge them to Arabise (domesticate)

theatre, then still an intrusive (*dakhīl*) art. Every summarised play is prefaced by commentary that explains its relevance to the Cairene context.

132. *Ḥadīth* was published in three volumes in 1925, 1926, and 1945.
133. Ḥusayn, *Ḥāfiẓ wa Shawqī*, p. 7.
134. Ibid., pp. 49–50.
135. Ibid., pp. 50–1.
136. Ibid., pp. 60, 64.
137. Ḥusayn, *Niẓām*, p. 28.
138. Ibid., p. 30.
139. Ḥusayn, *Qādat al-fikr*, p. 9. Ḥusayn wrote his dissertation on Ibn Khaldūn at the Sorbonne under the supervision of Emile Durkheim, who approached religion as a social manifestation of society deifying itself and not an abstract realm that exists in parallel with the material sphere of existence.
140. Ibid., p. 21. In an interesting contrast, and another commentary on genre, Haykal gives the example of the impossible Homeric epic in Aḥmad Shawqī's 1894 epic poem, '*Kibār al-ḥawādith fī wādī al-Nīl*' (The Major Events of the Nile Valley). Shawqī's condensed twenty-line epic should have borrowed more from the *Iliad* and rendered Egyptian history through the author's 'poetic being' so it could approximate the Homeric epic, a potential *Egyptian* model for world literature and translation. However, Shawqī's political moment and exile made writing such a national epic impossible (see Muḥammad Ḥusayn Haykal, *al-Adab wa-l-ḥayāt al-Miṣriyya: dirāsāt fī shiʿr al-Barūdī wa shawqī wa Ḥāfiẓ* (Cairo: Dār al-Hilāl, 1992), pp.174–6).
141. Viswanthan, *Masks of Conquest*, p. 100.
142. Ḥusayn, *Niẓām*, p. 36.
143. Ibid., p. 42.
144. Ḥusayn, *Udīb; Thīsyūs*, p. 14.
145. Ḥusayn, 'Réponse de Taha Hussein à André Gide', p. 10.
146. Ibid.
147. Ḥusayn, *Udīb; Thīsyūs*, p. 21.
148. Ibid., p. 22.
149. Ibid., p. 26.
150. Ibid., p. 27.
151. Ḥusayn, *Fuṣūl fī al-adab wa-l-naqd* (1933), p. 147.
152. Ḥusayn, *Udīb; Thīsyūs*, p. 29.
153. Ibid., p. 31. Most readings of Ḥusayn's translations explain his choices as results of his infatuation with Western themes of individualism. Samīḥ Karīm,

for example, finds that Ḥusayn chose Gide's *Theseus* because of the triumph of individualism in Theseus's strong personality (Karīm, *Mādhā yabqā*, p. 236).

154. In *Min al-adab al-tamthīlī al-yūnānī*, Ḥusayn atypically does not include an introduction, but he renders many original scenes in prose inserting only episodic dramatic dialogue.
155. Ibid., p. 35. He also relates the difference in the choice of the two tales to the author's psychology and mental state – *Oedipus* preaches fighting fate and moving forwards, while *Theseus* advocates resigning oneself to the course of time (p. 36), corresponding to two phases in Gide's life from his happy optimistic sixties to his more pessimistic and fatigued seventies.
156. Gide, *Thésée*, pp. 106–7.
157. Ḥusayn, *Udīb; Thīsyūs*, p. 201.
158. In Al-Sibāᶜī, 'Kalimat al-mutarjim' (The Translator's Word), p. 8. Ḥusayn does not read the orientalist gesture of Voltaire's novel, which treats Babylonian history as a strictly Parisian moment. Ḥusayn's selective reading habits seemingly reinforce critical approaches to his work as self-orientalising. After all, Luṭfī al-Sayyīd named him the Voltaire of the Arab world, as Ḥusayn recounts in *al-Ayyām* (Volume Three, p. 333). Again, however, close reading complicates this approach.
159. Ibid., p. 9.
160. Ibid., pp. 9–10.
161. See Badawi, 'Ṭāhā Ḥusayn the Critic', p. 136.
162. Ḥusayn, *Al-Qadar*, p. 11.
163. In his 'critical article' on Valéry (Ḥusayn, *Alwān*, pp. 51–64), for example, the French poet's life and works are framed by Ḥusayn's own experience of the poet's work and life.
164. Ḥusayn, *Mustaqbal*, p. 27.
165. Found at https://ar.wikisource.org/wiki7/ مجلة_المقتبس/العدد_73/هل_تسترد_اللغة_العربية_أمجادها. See also Mahmoudi, *Ṭāhā Ḥusain's Education*, p. 87. Ḥusayn rejects the *ᶜammiyya* (colloquial) in favour of simplifying *fuṣḥā* as *ṭarīq wasaṭ* (middle way). See *Min adabinā al-muᶜāṣir*, pp. 21–9, 180–1.
166. Ḥusayn, 'al-Muqaddima', in *Tajdīd*, pp. 7–8, 12. This is also the period of Ḥusayn's harsh criticism of Jurjī Zaydān's historical novels, as those reduce literary works to mere products of their political situations. See Mahmoudi, *Ṭāhā Ḥusain's Education*, pp. 97–9.
167. *Fī al-shiᶜr*, p. 33; emphasis mine.
168. Ibid., pp. 40–2.

169. Ibid., p. 47.
170. Ibid., p. 51
171. Ibid., p. 56.
172. In *Fuṣūl fī al-adab wa-l-naqd*, he rejects Haykal's theory about the unity of Eastern nations, emphasising instead the Mediterranean origin of Egyptian, Greek, Latin, and modern French cultures. But in an interview with Maghrebi writers, Ḥusayn insists on literary *fuṣḥā* to unite Arab nations. See 'Taha Hussein et la Darija Marocaine', https://www.youtube.com/watch?v=kBZsvDPYpCU
173. *Alwān*, pp. 13, 17.
174. Sacks, *Iterations of Loss*, pp. 117–25.
175. Al-Nowaihi, 'Towards the Reappraisal', p. 203.
176. Hanssen and Weiss, p. 3.
177. Qultah, *Athar*, pp. 148–9.
178. Ḥusayn, *Fūṣūl*, p. 9.
179. ᶜAṣfūr, *Al-Marāya*, p. 32.
180. Ibid., p. 43.
181. Ibid., p. 53.
182. Ibid., p. 12.
183. Ibid., p. 34.
184. Ibid., p. 71.
185. Ibid., p. 82.
186. Ibid., p. 11.
187. Some autobiographical references that resonate with *al-Ayyām* include the blind character, references to al-Azhar, and the black servant in Paris. Rasheed El-Enany finds *Adīb* to be strictly autobiographical (El-Enany, *Arab Representations of the Occident*, p. 63).
188. Ḥusayn, *Adīb*, p. 12.
189. See Mahmoudi, *Ṭāhā Ḥusain's Education*, p. 11. Critical approaches to *al-Ayyām* have repeatedly noted the text's openness. For example, in '*Mā baᶜd* al-Ayyām: *Ayyām lam yaktibuha Ṭāhā Ḥusayn*' [After *The Days*, the days Ṭāhā Ḥusayn didn't write] ᶜUmar Miqdād al-Jimīnī considers Suzan Taha Hussein's book *Maᶜak* (With You) (Cairo: Dār al-Maᶜārif, 1979) and Muḥammad Ḥasan al-Zayyāt's *Mā baᶜd* al-Ayyām (After the *Days*) (Cairo: Dār al-hilāl, 1986), the real sequels to the unwritten last volume of *al-Ayyām* (p. 31). Abd al-Ḥamīd Yūnus reads *al-Ayyām* with *al-Shiᶜr al-jāhilī* to show that Ḥusayn's 'self' develops externally in social relations ('*Ṭāhā Ḥusayn bayn al-ḍamīr al-ghāᵓib wa-l-ḍamīr al-mutakallim*', p. 65). *Al-Ayyām* becomes the

author's personal defence against conservative readers of *al-Shi*ᶜ*r* and *Adīb*. Thus, Ḥusayn defends the story's status in the Muslim past as equivalent to that of ancient Greek poetry not to be blasphemous but to validate the literary as a legitimate form of knowledge (p. 67–8). These readings, however, although they point to the literary as a different discourse, still do not engage the literary aesthetics of works beyond their contextual and political references.

190. Ḥusayn, *al-Ayyām*, pp. 325–6.
191. Volume One, p. 116.
192. Volume One, p. 118. Stephan Guth attributes the turn from autobiographies to novels in Arabic literature until the 1970s to the writer's view of his life as a failure (See Guth, 'Why Novels – Not Autobiographies', pp. 139–47).
193. The turn from doctrinal religion to literature parallels the one from the turban to the *ṭarbūsh* and is narrated in Ḥusayn's *al-Ayyām*, Volume Two, chapters 17–20, pp. 251–306.
194. Ibid., p. 298.
195. De Man, 'Literary History', pp. 398, 401–3.
196. In Volume Three (*al-Ayyām*, pp. 452–3), the narrator describes the subject's new writing life as communication with others.
197. Qultah, *Athar*, p. 193.
198. Mahmoudi, *Ṭāhā Ḥusain's Education*, p. 13.
199. For a recent reading of Ḥusayn's article as a statement on *nahḍawī* Arabic as world literature, see May Hawass 'Taha Hussein and the Case for World Literature', *Comparative Literature Studies*, 55 (1) (2018): 66–92.
200. 'The Modern Renaissance', p. 253.
201. Ibid., pp. 254–5.
202. See Shukrī, *Mādhā yabqā min Ṭāhā Ḥusayn*, pp. 38–40.
203. Ḥusayn, 'Muqaddima', to *Ḥāfiẓ wa-Shawqī*, p. vii.
204. Ḥusayn, *Ḥāfiẓ wa-Shawqī*, pp. 128–9.
205. Ibid., pp. 86–7.
206. Ibid., pp. 62–3.
207. Ḥusayn, *Mustaqbal*, p. 66.
208. Tageldin, *Disarming Words*, pp. 276–88.
209. Mahmoudi, *Ṭāhā Ḥusain's Education*, p. 36.
210. Ḥusayn, *Mustaqbal*, p. 55.
211. Ḥusayn, '*al-Ittijāhāt al-dīniyya*', pp. 232–3.
212. Ibid., p. 235.
213. Berque, 'Islam Vu', p. 68.

214. Ibid., p. 72.
215. Ibid., p. 66. Robert Tignor makes a similar correlation between nationalism and religion: nationalism replaces Islam when the intellectuals are disillusioned with the modernisation project under colonialism (see *Modernisation and British Colonial Rule*, p. 258).
216. The prophet figure also recalls the contemporaneous influence of Nietzsche in Arabic translation. In 1920, Filīks Fāris published the first Arabic translation of Nietzsche's *Zarathustra* as *Hākadhā takallama Zarādusht* and dedicated it to Muḥammad Ḥusayn Haykal. In 1939, Abdelraḥman Badawī published *Nītcha* (Nietzsche) with another translation of *Zarathustra*. However, the translators produced a deliberately *literary* prophetic voice, which distinguishes itself from Western philosophy, as is evident in Ḥusayn's critique of Gebran.

# Conclusion
# The Prophet Today: The Novel in Distress

> And thus every translator is to be regarded as a middle-man [*Vermittler*] in this universal spiritual commerce [*allgemein geistigen Handels*], and as making it his business to promote/further this exchange [*Wechseltausch*]: for say what we may of the insufficiency of translation, yet the work is and will always be one of the weightiest and worthiest matters in the general concerns of the world. The Koran says: 'God has given to each people a prophet in its own tongue!' *Thus each translator is a prophet to his people.*
>
> Johann Wolfgang Goethe to Thomas Carlyle, 20 July 1827[1]

On 5 July 1945, in response to the forthcoming Arabic translation of *La Porte étroite*, André Gide (1861–1951) writes a letter to his Arab publisher expressing disappointment with his Arab audience.[2] He has enjoyed the company of Arabs and Muslims, and '*ne serais sans doute pas le même, si je ne m'étais jamais . . . avoir gouté jusqu'à l'extase l'âpre brulure du désert*' (would definitely have not been the same had I not tasted, to the point of ecstasy, the bitter heat of the desert).[3] '*J'ai su dépouiller alors les revêtements de notre culture occidentale et retrouver une authenticité humaine perdue*' (I then stripped the coatings of our Western culture and rediscovered a lost human authenticity), but the Arab world has not reciprocated. On 5 January 1946, Ṭāhā Ḥusayn replies, explaining that Gide has encountered not Islam but ignorant Muslims, committed to the '*lettre que de l'esprit des textes*' (the text's letter and not spirit).[4] He comforts Gide: this Arab audience welcomes his message as it has already embraced the '*maîtres de l'antiquité*' (masters of antiquity) – of course through Ḥusayn's translations.[5]

The seemingly clean conversation between two writers captures the confrontation between an uncritical orientalism and even more uncritical self-orientalism.[6] The epistolary exchange suggests a distorted equivalence, between both the French writer and his admirer, and two literary sign-systems: the Arab Orient is ready to receive French knowledge, while the French world has peeled itself to find grounds for resemblance in an orientalist ecstasy under desert suns. But having read Ḥusayn's translations of both Gide and the ancients, one pauses before committing to the 'innocence' of this exchange. Translation feigns 'innocence', promising perfect *naql*, fast-tracked literary modernisation, and intellectual freedom for the writer. We may also be tempted to read the literary as absolutely secular in this exchange, speaking to the modern concerns of the deliberately modern reader, knowing that she is not the average Egyptian, not just yet anyway. In this book, I have tried to interrupt that temptation, using translation to remap the literary as emerging from within treacherous appropriation and not accurate borrowing. Literary prophecy emerges as profane in that it becomes a narrative capacity of critical re-presentation of the original and its 'intended' meaning. Profanation is not opposed to the sacred, nor does it simply emerge from it and then repress it, as the secular would have it; rather, it works to keep both in place to disrupt political temporalities. Profanation makes possible a continuous engagement between original and translation, interrupting a secular time of reading that would habitually forget one or the other. Translation also positions the writers as cultural prophets. This position is not one of agency, but a discursive formation in the act of translation and conversation with the reader, the haunting spectre in every chapter. In holding on to profane literary prophecy, I have also tried to conceive of religion through literature and not in opposition to it: recognising that the sacred rises from within the secular in colonial Egypt, this study has tried to complicate approaching the literary as simply a secular product of colonial modernity. Rather, the profane places religion and literature in the same space – and this space is made possible by imperfect translation. While the colonial secular works to separate literature as a modern discipline from religion as the traditional sphere of private faith, treacherous translation unsettles this separation and stages the undoing of narrative categories that we have taken for granted in the study of the Arabic novel, such as subject, narrator, and realist representation. If translation can never really deliver accurate *naql*, in what language can the intellectual preserve his or her tongue?

In assuming an imagined linguistic purity, a prophetic articulation that promises social and political deliverance, the translators apparently fall for the trap. In his 1996 book *La Langue d'Adam et autres essais*, Abdelfattah Kilito names Adam's elegy for his slain son, Cain, the oldest poem in the world, and so 'Adam wasn't only the first prophet, he was also the first poet'.[7] No one wonders about Adam's language, writes Kilito,[8] but using Ibn Jinnī's account, he answers that in the Qurʾānic paradise, Arabic is the only language after the fall, a reversal of the Biblical Babel story: 'unity follows multiplicity, insofar as those who initially spoke all languages end by speaking only one'.[9] The fantasy of a unitary language that coincides with its reference is thus built into the pre-memory of Arabic literature, and the first prophet is also the first poet. In a different book about a similar language problem, Kilito redresses the history of modern Arabic literature as originating in a *mistranslation* – namely Mattā ibn Yūnus's faulty translation of Greek '"tragedy" as panegyric and "comedy" as satire',[10] since such mistranslation, according to popular critical accounts of Arabic literature, prematurely doomed Arabic literature's reach to European forms. Kilito recasts Ibn Yūnus's 'bad translation' as a saving grace: were it not for this fortuitous mistranslation, Arabs would have forgotten their literary tradition and imitated Greek literature instead. Mattā Ibn Yūnus's 'unfaithful translation . . . saved them unintentionally, accidentally and unwittingly'.[11] Kilito's sarcastic tone resonates with this book's major argument – namely, 'bad' and 'unfaithful' translation unmasks colonial prejudices of universality, even when those seem to be wholly espoused by the 'bad' translators. In 'The Modern Renaissance of Literature' (1955), Ṭāhā Ḥusayn evokes a similar problem of translation and genre: 'Not all those who adhered to Aristotle understood his books, nor could they find terms . . . to translate exactly the words tragedy and comedy. Thus, they called the former "eulogy" and the latter "satire".'[12]

Significantly, both Ibn Yūnus's mistranslation and Ḥusayn's accusation invoke theatrical genres: in 'The Stage of Modernity', Timothy Mitchell draws out the theatrical metaphor into the staging of colonial modernity.

The representation's failure to 'match the original' – already 'a multiplicity of imitations and repetitions' – is made possible by modernity's fragility, as it exposes itself to 'the possibility of some shift, displacement, or contamination'.[13] That translation is always an act of betrayal, as suggested in the introduction to this book, makes it precisely into that threatening re-presentation that exposes the impossibility of accurately translating colonial modernity. What these translations inevitably betray is the very synchronicity of their contexts with the formations of global modernity – their participation and implication in the projection of the stage of modernity and their struggle to articulate their roles on that stage.[14] Samah Selim relates the debate on 'free' and 'faithful' translation in the study of Arabic literature directly to the 'equivalence' assumed by colonial modernity, which promises its seamless *naql* (transfer) into the colonies. Both 'local reformist elites and European specialists', Selim continues, believed in Western humanist ideals from democracy to the novel as 'fixed and ideal forms to be acquired and reproduced in the backward target culture through "innocent" translation'.[15] But translation is never 'innocent'. My aim in this book has been to complicate various translation practices in the first decades of twentieth-century Egypt as a way of interrupting a narrative of modernity that confounds the 'secular' with the literary. I have explored various performances of translation as acts of profanity, beyond secularising the figure of the prophet into the 'modern' writer, and towards a profane reclamation of literary language that returns it to the public sphere. Translation as generic adaptation allows us to move away from the law of genre, from the novel as the quintessential modern form of representation, towards narrative experimentation. If we shift the focus from the novel to Clifford Siskin's 'novelism' – 'the habitual subordination of writing to the novel'[16] – we can read these various performances of translation less as failed novel experiments and more as sites of negotiation that use translation to critique the novel precisely as a 'modern' form. Each translator negotiates aspects of the text he is borrowing, momentarily recognising an indebtedness to its foreignness and then forgetting that debt, so that generic borrowing remains implicated in an act of forgetting.

Exposing the mechanics of representation helps explain two problems: first, how literary histories of the Arabic novel have been constructed retrospectively; and, second, how the novel came to antagonise Islam.[17] The translations' impact is hard to assess categorically, but these generic experiments are often remembered as endings that make possible the beginning of the post-1950s Arabic novel. Naguib Mahfouz finds that al-Manfalūṭī and Ḥusayn, for example, exhausted the use of modern themes in old forms.[18] Ḥusayn Fawzī is more gracious when, in 1968, he describes his generation's indebtedness to 'the translations of Muhammad al-Sibaᶜi, al-Manfaluti, Ahmad Hasan al-Zayyat, Anton al-Jumayyil, al-Mazini, and the sources from which these, and others, translated'.[19] But professed memories of influence are less consequential than reading how these translations profane rules of genre to offer a different narrative of the emergence of both the literary and the secular in twentieth-century Cairo.

## Rerouting the Novel into Novelism

Popular critical accounts of Arabic cultural modernity continue to dilute those memories. For example, Sabry Hafez finds that Arab writers from the 1900s to the 1960s embraced Western narrative forms to produce their expedited vision of Arab modernisation since the Arab literary tradition lacked its own adequate narrative model.[20] The desire for a 'completely new tradition' demanded an absolute break with one's tradition; however, after the 1967 defeat, or the end of the project of Westernisation, writers return to the classical tradition.[21] Abdallah Laroui comes to a different conclusion from a similar premise: he refers to a second *nahḍa* from 1963 to 1965, after independence, when Arabs developed a 'second degree' awareness of their thinking as ideological. 'A general frame of reference was achieved', Laroui continues, that 'struck a fatal blow at provincialism'.[22] This second *nahḍa* is a genuine 'adult' stage – 'unfold[ing] outside tradition' since 'it does not regard its backwardness as a virtue'.[23] Laroui's dialectical model of modernity dilutes the *nahḍa*'s impact as rupture, but still adopts a troubling developmental language that treats authors and not their works as primary agents of change.[24]

The 'rise' of the Arabic novel is an insightful intervention in this debate. Popular critical accounts have repeatedly confirmed the 'borrowed' origins of the Arabic novel, placing classical narrative forms and the European novel on two extremes and measuring the 'success' of the Arabic novel according to its place on the scale. In line with Ian Watt's 'rise' of the English novel, for example, Ṭāhā Badr writes that the 1919 Egyptian Revolution created the bourgeoisie, which in turn occasioned the rise of the artistic Egyptian novel. Selim retorts by historicising the difference between the European and Arabic novels, since the Egyptian bourgeoisie, unlike its European counterpart, never established its 'hegemony as a social class with a deeply rooted cultural and political tradition'. Moreover, its place within global structures of capitalism made forming a 'solid national hegemony' similar to the European model impossible, a situation that worsened with the Egyptian Revolution of 1952. This unfinished project of bourgeois hegemony, a legitimating narrative of the European novel, is 'inscribed into the novel genre': the romantic and realist 'narrative self' of the Egyptian novel was deterred by 'its own historical and discursive limits', for it found itself irrelevant in a history mobilised by the silenced masses.[25] It is not surprising that the narrative self in the adaptations studied here unfolds in conversation with, and often in fear of, the masses. Unlike Selim, Hafez and Laroui do not consider the imagined communities of the literary text and the challenges they pose to artificial temporal divides and analytical categories of resistance.

But did the European bourgeoisie provide a fully legitimating narrative for the European novel? Franco Moretti describes how the European novel loses its legitimacy after Waterloo. Having lost faith in society, the nineteenth-century realist novel develops a 'narrative' attitude that refrains from creating meaning, because restoration was no longer possible in the world of symbolic values.[26] The 'culture of stability and conformity' that Moretti ascribes to the eighteenth-century British *bildungsroman* and many nineteenth-century British (not European) realist novels is largely an effort to restore order in the public sphere through the false comfort of the private one. The Arabic novel in translation inherits this dysfunctional symbolic order as it searches for its own legitimating narrative in a colonial context of unequal development and rapid modernisation. The translations as narrative experiments and the pre-memory of the 'modern' Arabic novel however, openly resist this inheritance and strive to restore symbolic order through a reclamation of literary language. While the translators often 'rebel' against tradition, their complex articulations of Islam and the heritage through translation signal their awareness of colonial modernity's imposed and dysfunctional symbolic order. The reach to the prophetic, even from within the bounds of colonial ideology, mobilises a critique of the paradoxical claims of the novel form through 'bad' translation, especially when the translations recognise that the original contexts cannot be translated into their particular historical moment.

In the decades after the translations studied in this book, accounts of the 'rise' of the novel systematically frame these earlier phases of compounded literary aesthetics in translation as precisely anomalous to teleology, experimentations that do not count inasmuch as they do not 'look' like novels. In a changing Arab world with increasing factional and national divisions, socialist realism of the 1950s promised an undoing of a proto-romantic subjectivity, the domain of the elite *kātib* of previous decades, towards collective critique of a supposedly accessible and representable collective consciousness. *Prophetic Translation* revisits the 'political' promise of the previous decades by moving away from the interaction between a foreign form and local forms towards the confluence of narrative modalities. In these earlier translations, the tension between subjective and realist consciousness persists in generic experimentation, and the translators' struggles with representational methods form the most substantive part of their narratives.[27] Moretti once complained that if critics only focus on 200 novels of the roughly 8,000 produced in nineteenth-century Britain, it would be impossible to define the genre.[28] Similarly, the study of the Arabic novel demands a more serious engagement with particular archives, authorial letters, and different texts.[29]

## Religion, Literature and the Prophet

The second aim of this study has been to rethink the historically antagonistic relationship between Islam and the Arabic novel. For Muhsin al-Musawi, the hero's impotence documents the dissolution of the post-1967 novel's ties to the sacred.[30] Pierre Cachia locates two types of 'men of religion' in Arabic literature: a hindrance to be overcome in the *nahḍa* and idealised modern figures in post-1950s fiction, both incompatible with the world of the novel.[31] Richard Jacquemond, who favours the creative translations of the early twentieth century, finds that mid-century realism forfeits the identity of 'literary discourse'; after the 1967 defeat, there is a rejection of realism and the 'emergence' of a 'literature of prophecy' that found 'anomie' instead of promise in Nasserism.[32] The consequent rejection of realism in favour of experimentalism was never absolute, and in the late twentieth century, the political role of the 'citizen-artist' as messenger of truth turned 'national belonging into something sacred', making writers' betrayal of government the same as religious blasphemy.[33] In other words, the pronounced substitution of religion by the nation or state emerges at the end rather than the beginning of the twentieth century.

A more thorough archive of earlier narrative experiments, however, reframes the Arabic novel's conflicted relationship to the sacred away from the character's religious inclinations or authorial strategies towards overlapping narrative modes of representation.[34] Because these early narrative translations approach religion as interpretation – or more accurately as an epistemological paradigm that makes literary and religious reading possible – they ask how religion transforms into a theme in the novel. Islamic ideas and traditional narrative forms become cultural currencies in the translations studied in this book, transacted in the translators' vision for literature as both an aesthetic (rather than formal) experience and a historical object. However, the translations do not reassure us with 'a comfortable notion of a permissive hybridity', as Gayatri Chakravorty Spivak finds in the English translation of South Asian literature, guaranteed by a cultural translation that delivers a 'sanitized secularism of a global enforcement politics'.[35] While these translations have been used to indict their authors with the blasphemous charge of embracing liberal secularism, I have tried to show how their particular appropriations are not as 'clean'. In profaning the originals, the translations return both the literary and the sacred to the public sphere in an address to the reader. What they tell us, in other words, is that fiction and Islam are not incompatible. Muhammad Siddiq goes as far as denying the possibility of an Islamic novel.[36] *Nahḍa* intellectuals like Muḥammad Ḥusayn Haykal, Ṭāhā Ḥusayn, and ᶜAbbās Maḥmud al-ᶜAqqād, who turned from writing novels to producing Islamic literature, demonstrate this irreconcilability. But such an assumption only works if we consider the novel to have specifically defined attributes that implicate it both in realism and nationalism. *Nahḍawī* intellectuals recognised the need for 'a legitimating textual genealogy from within the corpus of Islamic sources for this act of desired appropriation'.[37] But Siddiq asks: 'How, why, and when in Arab/Islamic history did the spurious views on artistic creativity replace the "authentic" and enabling precedent bequeathed by the Prophet?'[38] The answer may be that this 'enabling precedent' was never left behind, but that emerging creative forms continued to engage earlier models precisely from within the changing landscape of literary translation from the nineteenth century to the twentieth.

Naguib Mahfouz appears as the locus of this transformation of religion in modern Arabic literature.[39] In Siddiq's account, Mahfouz figures as the other end of the spectrum from al-Jabartī's model of the religious scholar, 'two nearly identical versions of this antithesis' that today justify violence against the novelist.[40] Mahfouz had called for a philosophy of change and not prophetic teaching; once the latter loses its sovereignty it is easily compromised by political manipulation.[41] Mahfouz succeeds where the *nahḍawī* intellectuals fail, writes Muhsin al-Musawi, because he forgoes the secular language of the state and appeals instead to the masses.[42] For al-Musawi, Arabic literature until the 1950s, and specifically the work of Salāma Mūsā, was not politically engaged, but rather stuck in the *nahḍa*'s modernist rhetoric, miming the secular and aestheticising Islam. While the Islamic ideas of Ḥusayn made Islam fit the state's national language, Mahfouz in *Malḥamat al-ḥarafīsh* (The Harafish) (1977) avoided such a trap in addressing the masses and critiquing the state, and *Layālī alf layla* (Arabian Nights and Days) (1979) engages 'Islam on the street' as a site of 'difference, opposition and dissent'.[43] In this account, as with Shaden Tageldin's, Mahfouz finally manages what no one before him had: he succeeds in effecting 'a partial separation from the European model'.[44]

If the prophetic moves us away from thematising Islamic discourse to critiquing narrative representation, it can also recast the role of *nahḍawī* intellectuals away from familiar models of self-orientalism. Reading their 'Islamic' writings with their translated narrative experiments shows how their texts expose the representational mechanics of different discourses of modernity, most notably the separation between sacred and profane, the purview of the European novel.[45] By accepting the separation between literature and religion, Gauri Viswanthan writes, Indian colonial subjects relinquished the authority to decipher the text.[46] But in this context, we find that translators reclaim authority through a profanation of both theological and literary discourses when they conflate them in their translations. Al-Manfalūṭī represents religious practice in the contingent act of literary reading. Al-Sibāʿī seemingly accepts the separation between religion and literature as self-evident but then conflates them when he critiques Carlyle's false faith in perfect translation. Ḥusayn and Haykal are uncomfortable with the universal claims of both literature and philosophy, as much as they apparently champion both in the modernisation of Egyptian culture. Translation becomes a necessary response to colonial mechanics of exclusionary representation; even as those are 'repeated', they are never accurately reproduced. The generic experiments in this book reclaim the separations that colonial power establishes in propagating its truths as self-evident. In skirting the dangerous zone of 'illicit' knowledge – one that uses Islamic discourse to redefine the literary object – the translators historicise literary forms as aesthetic interruptions of a colonial modernity, and that is a form of political commitment that critics have denied them.[47]

Literature is more aesthetic than rigidly formal in their formulations, pointing to the complex interlocking of form and content. The translations remind us that literature is not necessarily narrative, and if we consider narrative in literature, we should think about its influence rather than succumb to its inevitability. Ian Watt's story of the 'rise of the Western novel' focused on fiction rather than narrative – a legacy bequeathed to studies of the Arabic novel. This critical shift encouraged the conflation of the two in the novel form. The translations, in focusing on story-telling, ask how literature uses narrative rather than derives from it. Hence, al-Manfalūṭī and al-Sibāʿī resurrect Scheherazade in their translations. In critiquing the pronouns that legitimate auto/biographical accounts, Hakyal's and Ḥusayn's translations foreground the rhetorical manipulation of narrative. If we approach emulation through these translations as varying degrees of adaptation, we can reframe Arabic fictional realism as an alienation from rather than reflection of immediate and borrowed contexts. In other words, we can focus on the literariness of these translations rather than their failed efforts to represent a reality. If, according to Timothy Mitchell, modernity produces its reality precisely through iterable representations, then the adaptations discussed here profane precisely this invisible rift between reality and its representation. Moreover, if realist narrative is not the bar against which we judge these translations, and if we consider that their treatment of religion is similar to their quest for a legitimating reality, then their 'unfaithful' translations prefigure the turn from social realism before 1967 to classical forms and religious themes in the post-1970s Arabic novel.

What persists in these translations is a narrative voice – a residue of *adab*'s moral address to the reader – not of a coherent subject but a specifically discursive construct that emerges in the critique of individuality, subjectivity, and omniscience and predisposes itself to the reader. In this inadvertent critique, which comes together in treacherous translation, the secular can no longer promise a similar incrimination of literature, enlightenment, and modernity. While al-Manfalūṭī's works adapt the subjective ideal of romantic literature and expose the failed adaptation of realism through the debate with the *nahḍawī* realists, al-Sibāʿī explodes the colonising power of narrative in rendering both Carlyle and Dickens, while Haykal and Ḥusayn adapt the auto/biography to authorise local forms of subjectivity away from the Western privileging of the individual. What these adaptations highlight is the lack of formal criteria with which to read them. In other words, they point to a dual problem: the conflation of literature and narrative, and the irreconcilability between the theory and praxis of translation. Just like Haykal's Rousseau fails to reconcile theory and life, translation 'fails' to reconcile the original and target cultures, but it is the failure that compels us to return to these texts. Using translation to push the boundaries of imitation, this book reassesses the place of these different performances of translation in modern Arabic literary history, especially when we give up the novelistic rule that fiction must successfully 'reflect' reality in narrative form.[48]

In the story of the Arabic novel, there is no legitimating reality outside or inside the novel. Unfaithful translation presents this absence as original, a lack in the original text that the translation inherits. I have read the translations as intimately as they invite, translating them closely, to situate their enunciations from within the text. In this project, the impossibility of perfect translation is not untranslatability, which can sideline the literary in homogenising narratives of how it resists the universal.[49] Translation is necessary, as all the writers confirm, but not in its promise of accurate copying; rather, it is necessary precisely in the literary knowledge that it makes possible. Reclaiming those earlier experiments outside of their incriminating self-orientalism can arrest the desire to make the Arabic novel point beyond itself, to a world that can be taught in classrooms, and compel us to read the terms of its own world, in its making and unmaking.

## Notes

1. I owe this quotation to Pheng Cheah in *What Is a World?: On Postcolonial Literature as World Literature* (Durham, NC: Duke University Press, 2016), p. 40; emphasis added.
2. 'La porte étroite' or the narrow door refers to the parable in Matthew 7:13–21 about the difficulty of entering heaven.
3. André Gide, 'Lettre d'André Gide au Traducteur', in *al-Bāb al-ḍayyiq* (pp. 7–8), translation of André Gide's *La Porte étroite* (1909) by Nazīh al-Ḥakīm, p. 7.
4. Ḥusayn, 'Réponse de Taha Hussein à André Gide', in *al-Bāb al-ḍayyiq* (pp. 9–11), translation of André Gide's *La Porte étroite* (1909) by Nazīh al-Ḥakīm, p. 9.
5. Ibid., p. 11.
6. Akef Kirecci (2008) discusses Ḥusayn's self-orientalism in his dissertation 'Invasive Translation' referenced earlier.
7. Kilito, *The Tongue of Adam*, Robyn Creswell (trans.), p. 35.
8. Ibid., p. 6.
9. Ibid., p. 30.
10. Kilito, *Thou Shalt Not*, p. 95. Both translation movements of the Abbasid age and the *nahḍa* reassess universal claims of philosophical and literary representation in light of the receiving context. One of the major differences is that the Abbasid translation movement did not include Greek literature. Some *nahḍawī* translators refer to this earlier movement. Buṭrus al-Bustānī, for example, mentions the prolific Abbasid translation of the sciences as historical fact rather than in connection with how he was using translation (see Al-Bustānī, *Udabāʾ al-ʿArab*, p. 172). But translation in the *nahḍa* relied on a modernising taxonomy within a colonial framework. Thomas Philipp refers to Jurjī Zaydān's major distinction between the two movements in *Tārīkh al-ādāb* (Volume Four): the *nahḍa* formed under the impact of European '*madaniyya*', away from Islamic civilisation, and the *nahḍawī* intellectuals 'are moved from phase to phase as they were at the beginning of Abbasid rule' when 'the sciences of antiquity' appeared in Arabic translation. In that period of growth, Arabs also took in other sciences and adapted them to the Islamic context, but 'in this Nahda the trends of modern civilization are overwhelming and its adherents are forced to follow its path', as much as they might reject and resist it initially (see Philipp, *Foundations*, pp. 82–3). For a recent discussion of the relationship between the *nahḍa* and the Classics, see Peter E. Pormann, 'The Arab "Cultural Awakening (Nahda)", 1870–1950, and

the Classical Tradition', *International Journal of the Classical Tradition* 13(1) (2006): 3–20.

11. Kilito, *The Tongue of Adam*, Robyn Creswell (trans.), p. 98.
12. Ibid., p. 246.
13. Mitchell, 'The Stage', p. 23.
14. Rebecca Johnson has recently made a similar argument about Khalīl al-Khūrī and Aḥmad Fāris al-Shidyāq being cognisant of their existence in a global market. Johnson suggests reframing the emergence of the Arabic novel against this global network rather than the nation-state (see Johnson, 'Importing the Novel', esp. pp. 243–5).
15. Selim, 'Nation and Translation', p. 9.
16. Siskin, 'The Rise of Novelism', p. 423.
17. Arabic poetry of the early twentieth century invoked the prophetic poet on a quest for self-redemption through the use of mythology (see, for example, Lūwīs ᶜAwaḍ's *Brūmīthiyūs Talīqan* (Prometheus Unbound) (1946)). For a thorough analysis of this trend, see M. M. Badawi, 'Convention and Revolt in Modern Arabic Poetry', in G. E. von Grunebaum (ed.), *Arabic Poetry: Theory and Development*, (Wiesbaden: Otto Harrassowitz, 1973), pp. 181–208. The association between poet and prophet becomes more political in the second half of the century in the poetry of Abd al-Wahhāb al-Bayyātī, Adonis, and Khalīl Ḥāwī. Contemporary Arab poets have also returned to the prophetic figure: examples include Shafīqa Waᶜīl (Algeria), Jamāl al-Ṣulayᶜī (Tunis), ᶜUmar ᶜAnnāz (Iraq), Ḥasan Shihāb El-Dīn (Egypt), Jāsim al-Ṣaḥīḥ (Saudi Arabia), and Mehdī Manṣūr (Lebanon).
18. See Siddiq, *Arab Culture*, pp. 165–6. Mahfouz admitted to the influence of his predecessors, but considered their works precursors of the novel, not actual novels. See Rajāᵓ al-Naqqāsh, *Awlād ḥāratinā bayna al-fann wa-l-dīn*, (Cairo: Dār al-Hilāl, 2008), pp. 69–78.
19. Fawzī, 'Muqaddima', to *Sindibād fī riḥlat al-ḥayāt* (Sindbad in the Journey of Life) (1968), cited in Muhammad Siddiq, *Arab Culture*, pp. 26–7. In the introduction to *Sindibād Miṣrī* (Egyptian Sindbad) (1961), Fawzī relinquishes his control as novelist to the Egyptian people, describing his use of tradition as impersonal pastiche, an obligation to document Egyptian history from outside himself (pp. 11–12).
20. Hafez, 'The Transformation of Reality', p. 96.
21. Ibid., pp. 97–8.
22. Laroui, *The Crisis of the Arab Intellectual*, p. 90.

23. Ibid., p. 91.
24. Laroui finds that the intellectuals' haphazard and abstract approach to modernity naturalised colonial teleological time instead of interrupting it (pp. 70–1). Laroui nuances his position when he situates 'retardation' in relation to Western modernity as a model for reform, while choosing an earlier Islamic era as a model would recast 'backwardness' (see esp. pp. 1–10).
25. Selim, *The Novel*, p. 14.
26. Moretti, *The Way of the World*, pp. 94–5. Moretti distinguishes between the *bildungsroman* in England and in Europe, preferring the latter's resistance to the desire for conformity and preservation (see Moretti, *The Way of the World*, p. 181). Since Dickens is the only British author studied in this book, and Dickens' novel as I show in Chapter Three is atypical of the British realist canon, I would argue that the early Arabic novel was impacted more by European than British eighteenth- and nineteenth-century fiction.
27. A familiar reading of the generational difference between Ḥusayn and Mahfouz finds that the first generation caught between romanticism and realism failed to adapt Western techniques to the historical moment but made way for the more mature nationalist realism of the second generation (see Nawfal, *al-Fann al-qiṣaṣī*, pp. 22, 233–40).
28. Moretti, 'Style, Inc.', p. 158.
29. A deeper engagement with earlier narrative experiments also contextualises the changes in literary translation post-1950s. Ṭāhā Ḥusayn was instrumental in Nasser's 1,000-book project (*Mashrūᶜ al-alf kitāb*); even though translation becomes state-sponsored, the original focus of modernist elites on works mostly by Sartre, Camus, Brecht, Kafka, Cervantes, and Dante persists (see Jacquemond, *Conscience*, p. 148). For more on contemporary translation policies, see Richard Jacquemond, 'Translation policies in the Arab world: Representations, discourses and realities', *The Translator* 15(1), (2009) pp. 15–35. Literary translation continued to increase: from 1,333 recorded translations between 1940 and 1956, to 1,873 in 1968, and 3,440 in 1984. The predominant source language from 1950 to 1984 was English, and literary translations still outnumber texts from other disciplines. See Hāshim Faraḥāt, *Ḥarakat al-tarjama fī Miṣr: dirāsa bibliyūmitrīya li-l-ittijāhāt al-adabīya wa-l-nawᶜīya* (Cairo: al-ᶜArabī li-l-nashr wa-l-tawzīᶜ, 1991), esp. pp. 44, 68, 73–4.
30. *Infirāṭ al-ᶜiqd al-muqaddas*, p. 44.
31. See Cachia's 'Freedom from Clerical Control: The Portrayal of Men of Religion in Modern Arabic Literature', *Journal of Arabic Literature* 26(1/2) (1995): 175–85.

32. Jacquemond, *Conscience*, pp. 91–2.
33. Ibid., pp. 106–7.
34. Notably more contemporary Egyptian novels have emerged from cracks in elitist culture, and young writers are redefining the political through more vulgar, cynical prose styles that Sabry Hafez describes as 'new directions' with new forms of social and political engagement (see Hafez, 'New Egyptian Novel', p. 49). Noha Radwan, on the other hand, has recently argued that there is a return to realism in Egyptian fiction, reclaiming omniscience to expose current events (see 'One Hundred Years of Egyptian Realism', *Novel: A Forum on Fic*tion 49(2) (2016): 262–77).
35. Spivak, 'Translating into English', p. 105.
36. Siddiq, *Arab Culture*, p. 104.
37. Ibid., p. 105.
38. Ibid. Michael Allan responds to Siddiq's questions: *adab* transforms into modern literature – a domain of knowledge and truth – through the establishment of the Egyptian University, the nation-state's language, and Ḥusayn al-Marṣafī literary lectures (Allan, *In the Shadow*, p. 83). Throughout, Allan reads these early literary transactions as mapping the creation and institutionalisation of literature in contexts of reception and exchange.
39. See, for example, Wen-Chen Ouyang's reading of Sufi practice in Mahfouz's *Riḥlat ibn Fattūma* (The Journey of Ibn Fattouma) and its critique of doctrinal Islam in the return to al-Ghazālī's *al-Munqidh min al-ḍāl* (Deliverer from Error) (*Politics of Nostalgia in the Arabic Novel: Nation-State, Modernity and Tradition* (Edinburgh: Edinburgh University Press, 2013), pp. 28–9). See also Ziad Elmarsafy, *Sufism in the Contemporary Arabic Novel* (Edinburgh: Edinburgh University Press, 2012).
40. Siddiq, *Arab Culture*, p. 106.
41. Altoma, 'Westernization and Islam', p. 84.
42. Al-Musawi, *Islam On the Street*, p. xxi.
43. Ibid., pp. 30, 74, 106.
44. Tageldin, *Disarming Words*, p. 273; Al-Musawi, *Islam On the Street*, p. 109.
45. Narratives that test the limits between sacred and profane underlie the early structures of the Western *bildungsroman*, while the move towards the profane ushers the birth of the novel. See Robert Epstein and William Robbins, 'Introduction: The Sacred, the Profane, and Late Medieval Literature', in Robert Epstein and William Robins (eds), *Sacred and Profane in Chaucer and Late*

*Medieval Literature: Essays in Honour of John V. Fleming* (Toronto: University of Toronto Press, 2010), pp. 3–29.

46. See Viswanathan, *Masks of Conquest*, p. 106.
47. Al-Musawi finds that the early Arabic imitations of the 'novelistic tradition in Europe may have . . . marred the prospects of addressing concrete situations, but at a later stage there is much engagement of these realties' (p. xii), an opposite conclusion to Kilito's praise of Ibn Yūnus's bad translation.
48. Mohamed-Salah Omri suggests the term 'novelization' instead of the novel as it points to process and not product (see Omri, 'The Novelization of Islamic Literatures', p. 361).
49. See Emily Apter, 'Untranslatables: A World System', *New Literary History* (2008): 581–98. For a recent response to the untranslatable from within Arabic studies, see Shaden Tageldin, 'Untranslatability', 3 March 2014, https://stateofthediscipline.acla.org/entry/untranslatability.

# Bibliography

## Arabic Sources


ʿAbbūd, Mārūn, *Ruwwād al-nahḍa al-ḥadītha* (Beirut: Dār al-ʿilm li-l-malāyīn, 1952).

ʿAbd al-Ghanī, Muṣṭafā, *Ṭāhā Ḥusayn wa thawrat Yūlyū: Ṣuʿūd al-muthaqqaf wa suqūṭuhu* (Cairo: Maktabat al-turāth al-ʾislāmī, n.d).

ʿAbd al-Ṣabūr, Ṣalāḥ, *Mādhā yabqā minhum li-l-tārīkh: Dirāsāt fī adab Ṭāhā Ḥusayn, Tawfīq al-Hakīm, ʿAbbās al-ʿAqqād, and Ibrāhīm ʿAbd al-Qādir al-Māzinī* (Cairo: Dār al-kātib al-ʿArabī li-l-ṭibāʿa wa-l-nashr, 1968).

ʿAbduh, Muḥammad, 'al-Riwāyāt al-mutarjama', in Muḥammad ʿAmāra (ed.), *al-ʾAʿmāl al-kāmila li-l-imām al-shaykh Muḥammad ʿAbduh*, Vol. 3 (Cairo: Dār al-Shurūq, 1993), pp. 53–6.

Abū al-Anwār, Muḥammad, *al-Manfalūṭī: Imām al-bayān al-ʿArabī*, 1st edition (Cairo: al-Dār al-Miṣriyya al-Lubnāniyya, 2000).

ʿAjlān, ʿAbbās Bayyūmī, *al-Manfalūṭī wa-atharuhu fī al-adab al-ḥadīth* (Alexandria: Dār Lurān li-l-ṭibāʿa wa-l-nashr, 1977).

ʿĀnūtī, Usāma, *al-Ḥaraka al-adabiyya fī bilād al-shām khilāl al-qarn al-thāmin ʿashar* (Beirut: Manshūrāt al-jāmiʿa al-Lubnāniyya, 1970).

ʿAṣfūr, Jābir, *al-Marāyā al-mutajāwira: Dirāsa fī naqd Ṭāhā Ḥusayn* (Cairo: al-Hayʾa al-Miṣriyya al-ʿāmma li-l-kitāb, 1983).

Al-ʿAqqād, ʿAbbās Maḥmūd, 'Haykal fī mīzān al-baqāʾ' (originally published in *Akhbār al-yawm*, December 1956), in Nabīl Faraj (ed.), *Muḥammad Ḥusayn Haykal fī ʿuyūn muʿāṣirīhi* (Cairo: al-Hayʾa al-ʿĀmma li-Dār al-Kutub wa-l-Wathāʾiq al-Qawmiyya, 1996), pp. 19–24.

Al-ʿAqqād, ʿAbbās Maḥmūd, *Murājaʿāt fī al-adāb wa-l-funūn*, in *al-Majmūʿa al-kāmila li-muʾallafāt al-ʾustādh ʿAbbās Maḥmūd al-ʿAqqād yaḥtawī ʿalā sāʿāt bayn al-kutub*, Vol. 25, al-Adab wa-l-naqd 2 (Beirut: Dār al-kitāb al-Lubnānī, 1983 [1966]).

Al-ᶜAqqād, ᶜAbbās Maḥmūd, *Sāᶜāt bayn al-kutub*, in *al-Majmūᶜa al-kāmila li-muᵓallafāt al-ᵓustādh ᶜAbbās Maḥmūd al-ᶜAqqād yaḥtawī ᶜalā sāᶜāt bayn al-kutub*, Vol. 26, al-Adab wa-l-naqd 3 (Beirut: Dār al-kitāb al-Lubnānī, 1984 [1929]).

Al-ᶜAqqād, ᶜAbbās Maḥmūd, *al-Lugha al-shāᶜira* (Cairo: Nahḍat Miṣr li-l-ṭibāᶜa wa-l-nashr wa-l-tawzīᶜ, 1995).

Al-ᶜAqqād, ᶜAbbās Maḥmūd, *ᶜAbqarīyat Muḥammad* (Cairo: Dār al-Nahḍa li-l-ṭibāᶜa wa-l-nashr, n.d. [1941, 1957]).

Al-ᶜAqqād, ᶜAbbās Mahmūd, 'Muqaddimat al-ṭabᶜat al-ᵓūlā', in ᶜAbbās Mahmūd al-ᶜAqqād, *ᶜAbqarīyat Muḥammad* (Cairo: Dār al-Nahḍa li-l-ṭibāᶜa wa-l-nashr, n.d.), pp. 3–9.

Al-ᶜAqqād, ᶜAbbās Maḥmūd and Ibrāhīm ᶜAbd el-Qādir al-Māzinī, *al-Dīwān: Kitāb fī al-naqd wa-l-adab*, 4th edition (Cairo: Dār al-shaᶜb, 1996 [1921]).

Badr, ᶜAbd al-Muḥsin Ṭāhā, *al-Riwāᵓī wa-l-arḍ* (Cairo: al-Hayᵓa al-Miṣriyya al-ᵓāma li al-taᵓlīf wa-l-nashr, 1971).

Badr, ᶜAbd al-Muḥsin Ṭāhā, *Taṭawwur al-riwāya al-ᶜArabiyya al-ḥadītha fī Miṣr (1870–1938)* (Cairo: Dār al-Maᶜārif, 1963).

Al-Baḥrāwī, Sayyīd, *Muḥtawā al-shakl fī al-riwāya al-ᶜArabiyya* (Cairo: al-Hayᵓa al-Miṣriyya al-ᵓāma li-l-kitāb, 1996).

Al-Bustānī, Buṭrus, *Udabāᵓ ᵓal-ᶜArab fī al-ᶜuṣūr al-ᶜabbāsiyya* (Beirut: Dār Marūn Abbūd, 1937).

Al-Bustānī, Buṭrus, *Muḥīṭ al-muḥīṭ: Qāmūs muṭawwal li-l-lugha al-ᶜArabiyya* (Beirut: Maktabat Lūbnān, n.d.) at https://archive.org/details/waq71540.

Darrāj, Fayṣal, *Naẓariyyat al-riwāya wa-l-riwāya al-ᶜArabiyya* (Beirut: al-Markaz al-thaqāfī al-ᶜArabī, 1999).

Al-Dasūqī, ᶜUmar, *Fī al-adab al-ḥadīth* (Cairo: Dār al-fikr al-ᶜArabī li-l-ṭibāᶜa wa-l-nashr, 2000 [1970]).

Al Ḍayf, Shawqī, *al-Adab al-muᶜāṣir fī Miṣr*, 10th edition (Cairo: Dār al-Maᶜārif, 2010 [1940]).

Fūᵓād, Niᶜmāt Aḥmad, *Adab al-Māzinī* (Cairo: Maṭbaᶜat Dār al-Hanā, 1954).

Ḥasan, Muḥammad ᶜAbd al-Ghanī, *Fann al-tarjama fī al-adab al-ᶜArabī* (Cairo: al-Dār al-Miṣriyya li-l-taᵓlīf wa-l-tarjama, 1986).

Haykal, Aḥmed, *Taṭawwur al-adab al-ḥadīth fī Miṣr*, 6th edition (Cairo: Dār al-Maᶜārif, 1994 [1968]).

Haykal, Muḥammad Ḥusayn, *Jān Jāk Rūsū: Ḥayātuhu wa adabuhu*, Vol. I (Cairo: al-Wāᶜiẓ Press, 1921).

Haykal, Muḥammad Ḥusayn, *Jān Jāk Rūsū: Ḥayātuhu wa adabuhu*, Vol. II (Cairo: al-Wāᶜiẓ Press, 1923).

Haykal, Muḥammad Ḥusayn, *Thawrat al-adab* (Cairo: Maṭbaᶜat Miṣr, 1948 [1933]).

Haykal, Muḥammad, Ḥusayn, *Ḥayāt Muḥammad*, 6th edition (Cairo: Maktabat al-Nahḍa al-Miṣriyya, 1952 [1935]).

Haykal, Muḥammad Ḥusayn, *Qiṣaṣ Miṣriyya* (Cairo: Dār al-Maᶜārif, 1974).

Haykal, Muḥammad, Ḥusayn, *Fī manzil al-waḥy*, 8th edition (Cairo: Dār al-Maᶜārif, 1986 [1937]).

Haykal, Muḥammad Ḥusayn, 'Taqdīm dīwān al-Bārūdī', in Maḥmūd Sāmī al-Bārūdī's *Dīwān Maḥmūd Sāmī al-Bārūdī bāshā*, ᶜAlī al-Jārim and Muḥammad Shafīq Maᶜrūf (eds) (Beirut: Dār al-ᶜawda, 1998), pp. 5–30.

Haykal, Muḥammad, Ḥusayn, *al-Sharq al-jadīd* (Cairo: Maktabat al-nahḍa al-Miṣriyya, 2001 [1963]).

Haykal, Muḥammad Ḥusayn, *Tarājim Miṣriyya wa gharbiyya* [Biographies of Western and Egyptian Personalities] (Cairo: Dār al-Maᶜārif, n.d. [1929]).

Ḥusayn, Fawzī, 'Muqaddima', Introduction to *Sindibād Miṣrī: Jawla fī riḥāb al-tārīkh* (Cairo: Dār al-Maᶜārif, 1961), pp. 9–16.

Ḥusayn, Ṭāhā, 'Muqaddima', Introduction to Aḥmad Ḥasan al-Zayyāt's *ᵓĀlām Furtur li-l-faylasūf al-ᵓalmānī jūteh* (Beirut: Dār al-qalam, 1929), pp. 9–17.

Ḥusayn, Ṭāhā, *Ḥāfiẓ wa Shawqī* (Cairo: Maktabat al-khānijī, 1958 [1933]).

Ḥusayn, Ṭāhā, *Min al-adab al-tamthīlī al-yūnānī: Sūfūklīz, ᵓIliktrā, ᵓAyyās, Antijūnā, Udībis Malakan*) (Cairo: Lajnat al-taᵓlīf wa-l-tarjama wa-l-nashr, 1939).

Ḥusayn, Ṭāhā, 'Ẓahar ḥadīthan', in *al-Kātib al- Miṣrī*, 1 February 1946, Issue 5, pp. 171–2, at http://archive.sakhrit.co/newPreview.aspx?PID=2121035&ISSUEID=222&AID=209830.

Ḥusayn, Ṭāhā, *Mustaqbal al-thaqāfa fī Miṣr* (Cairo: Dār al-Maᶜārif, 1957 [1938]).

Ḥusayn, Ṭāhā, *Min adabinā al-muᶜāṣir* (Cairo: al-Sharika al-ᶜArabiyya li-l-ṭibāᶜa wa-l-nashr, 1958).

Ḥusayn, Ṭāhā, 'al-Muqaddima li-l-ṭabᶜa', introduction to the edition of *Tajdīd dhikra abī al-ᶜalāᵓ al-maᶜarrī*, 6th edition (Cairo: Dār al-maᶜārif, 1963 [1922]), pp. 1–14.

Ḥusayn, Ṭāhā, 'Muqaddima', Introduction to *al-Faylasūf*, by Muḥammad al-Sibāᶜī, 2nd edition (Cairo: al-Sharika al-ᶜArabiyya li-l-ṭibāᶜa wa al-nashr, 1963), pp. 5–6.

Ḥusayn, Ṭāhā, *Udīb; Thīsyūs min abṭāl al-asāṭīr al-yūnāniyya, taᵓlīf Andrī Jīd, tarjamat Ṭāhā Ḥusayn*, 4th edition (Beirut: Dār al-ᶜilm li-l-malāyīn, 1980 [1946]).

Ḥusayn, Ṭāhā, *Alwān*, 6th edition (Cairo: Dār al-Maᶜārif, 1981 [1945]).

Ḥusayn, Ṭāhā, *Vūltayr Zadīg aw al-qadar: Qiṣṣa sharqiyya naqalahā ilā al-ᶜArabiyya al-Duktūr Ṭāhā Ḥusayn*, 5th edition (Beirut: Dār al-ᶜilm li-l-malāyīn, 1982 [1947]).

Ḥusayn, Ṭāhā, 'Muqaddima al-mutarjim', Introduction to Muḥammad ᶜAwaḍ Muḥammad's *Yūhān wūlfjānj vūn jūteh, Hurmun wa-Drūtīya* (Damascus: Ṭalas li-l-dirāsāt wa-l-tarjama wa-l-nashr, 1985 [1949]), pp. 7–24.

Ḥusayn, Ṭāhā, *al-Ayyām fī mujallad wāḥid*, 1st edition (Cairo: Markaz al-Ahrām li-l-tarjama wa-l-nashr, 1992).

Ḥusayn, Ṭāhā, *Adīb* (Cairo: al-Hayᵓa al-Miṣriyya al-ᶜāmma li-l-kitāb, 1998).

Ḥusayn, Ṭāhā, *Ṣuḥuf mukhtāra min al-shiᶜr al-tamthīlī ᶜind al-yunān* (Cairo: Muᵓassasat Hindāwī, 2014).

Ḥusayn, Ṭāhā, *Fī al-Shiᶜr al-jāhilī* (Tunis: Dār al-Maᶜārif, 1998 [1926]).

Ḥusayn, Ṭāhā, 'al-ᵓIttijihāt al-dīniyya fī al-adab al-Miṣrī al-Muᶜāṣir, bi-qalam Ṭāhā Ḥusayn, tarjamat Minjī al-Shimlī wa ᶜUmar Miqdād al-Jiminī', in Minjī al-Shimlī (ed.), *Silṭaṭ al-kalima: Masālik li-dirāsāt adab Ṭāhā Ḥusayn wa fikrihi* (Tunis: Dār al-nashr al-Jāmiᶜī, 2001), pp. 221–36.

Ḥusayn, Ṭāhā, *Fūṣūl fī al-adab wa-l-naqd* (Cairo: Muᵓassasat Hindāwī li-l-taᶜlīm wa-l-thaqāfa, 2013 [1933]).

Ḥusayn, Ṭāhā, *Qādat al-fikr* (Amman: Dār al-ᶜArab li-l-nashr wa-l-tawzīᶜ, 2015).

Ḥusayn, Ṭāhā, *Niẓām al-Athīniyyīn* (Cairo: Dār al-Maᶜārif, n.d.).

Al-Jimīnī, ᶜUmar Miqdād, 'Ma baᶜd *al-Ayyām*: Ayyām lam yaktibuha Ṭāhā Ḥusayn', in Minjī al-Shimlī (ed.), *Silṭaṭ al-kalima: Masālik li-dirāsāt adab Ṭāhā Ḥusayn wa fikrihi* (Tunis: Dar al-nashr al-jāmiᶜī, 2001), pp. 29–82.

Al-Jundī, Anwar, *Taṭawwur al-tarjama fī al-adab al-ᶜArabī al-muᶜāṣir* (Cairo: Maṭbaᶜat al-risāla, 1987).

Karīm, Sāmiḥ, *Mādhā yabqā min fikr Ṭāhā Ḥusayn* (Cairo: al-Hayᵓa al-Miṣriyya al-ᶜāmma li-l-kitāb, n.d.).

Al-Manfalūṭī, Muṣṭafā Luṭfī, *al-Shāᶜir* (Beirut: Dār al-Thaqāfa, 1983 [1921]).

Al-Manfalūṭī, Muṣṭafā Luṭfī, *al-Faḍīla, aw Paul wa Vīgīnī* (Damascus: Dār ᵓUsāma, 1986).

Al-Manfalūṭī, Muṣṭafā, Luṭfī, 'al-Bayān', in *Muᵓallafāt Muṣṭafā al-Manfalūṭī al-kāmila, al-mujallad al-awwāl* (Cairo: Kalimāt ᶜArabiyya li-l-tarjama wa-l-nashr, 2011), pp. 211–16.

Al-Manfalūṭī, Muṣṭafā, Luṭfī, 'al-Islām wa-l-masīḥiyya', in *Muᵓallafāt Muṣṭafā al-Manfalūṭī al-kāmila, al-mujallad al-ᵓawwāl* (Cairo: Kalimāt ᶜArabiyya li-l-tarjama wa-l-nashr, 2011), pp. 155–60.

Al-Manfalūṭī, Muṣṭafā, Luṭfī, 'al-Madaniyya al-gharbiyya' in *Muᵓallafāt Muṣṭafā al-Manfalūṭī al-kāmila, al-mujallad al-awwāl* (Cairo: Kalimāt ᶜArabiyya li-l-tarjama wa-l-nashr, 2011), pp. 117–21.

Al-Manfalūṭī, Muṣṭafā, Luṭfī, *al-ᶜAbarāt* (Cairo: Dār al-Maktaba al-ahlioyya, n.d.).

Al-Manfalūṭī, Muṣṭafā, Luṭfī, *al-Naẓarāt*, Vol. I (Cairo: al-Maktaba al-ᶜilmiyya al-ḥadītha, n.d.).

Al-Manfalūṭī, Muṣṭafā, Luṭfī, 'Madīnat al-saᶜāda', in *al-Naẓarāt* [Contemplations], Vol. I (Cairo: al-Maktaba al-ᶜilmiyya al-ḥadītha, n.d.), pp. 68–75.

Al-Manfalūṭī, Muṣṭafā, Luṭfī, *Riwāya fī Sabīl al-tāj, wa-hiya khulāṣat riwāya tamthīliyya bi-hadhā al-ᵓism li-l-kātib al-faransī al-shahīr Frānswā Kubay maᶜ baᶜd taṣṣaruf* (Beirut: Dār al-sharq al-ᶜArabī, n.d. [1920]).

Al-Māzinī, ᶜAbd el-Qādir, Ibrāhīm 'al-Sariqāt al-adabiyya', in *al-Risāla* (1937), Vol. 213, pp. 1,243–7, at http://archive.sakhrit.co/newPreview.aspx?PID=2047059&ISSUEID=12149&AID=238086.

Al-Māzinī, ᶜAbd al-Qādir, Ibrāhīm 'Al-ᵓustādh al-Sibāᶜī wa adabuhu,' in *al-Ṣuwar* by Muḥammad al-Sibāᶜī (Cairo: Maktabat Miṣr, 1946), pp. 3–10.

Al-Māzinī, Ibrāhīm ᶜAbd el-Qādir, *al-Shiᶜr: Wasāᵓituhu wa ghāyātuhu* (Beirut: Dār al-fikr al-Lubnānī, 1990 [1915]).

Al-Māzinī, Ibrāhīm ᶜAbd al-Qādir, '*al-ᶜAbarāt*: "Qiṣṣat al-yatīm"', in ᶜAbbās Maḥmūd al-ᶜAqqād and Ibrāhīm ᶜAbd el-Qādir al-Māzinī's *al-Dīwān: Kitāb fī al-naqd wa-l-adab*, 4th edition (Cairo: Dār al-Shaᶜb, 1996 [1921]), pp. 96–102.

Al-Māzinī, Ibrāhīm ᶜAbd al-Qādir, 'ᵓUslub al-Manfalūṭī', in ᶜAbbās Maḥmūd al-ᶜAqqād and Ibrāhīm ᶜAbd al-Qādir al-Māzinī's *al-Dīwān: Kitāb fī al-naqd wa-l-adab*, 4th edition (Cairo: Dār al-Shaᶜb, 1996 [1921]), pp. 103–14.

Al-Māzinī, Ibrāhīm ᶜAbd el-Qādir, 'Muqaddima', in *Mukhtārāt min al-qiṣaṣ al-inklīzī: Tshārlz Dikinz wa ᵓākharūn, tarjamat Ibrāhīm ᶜAbd al-Qādir al-Māzinī* (Cairo: Kalimāt ᶜArabiyya li-l-tarjama wa-l-nashr, 2011 [1939]), pp. 7–8.

Al-Māzinī, Ibrāhīm ᶜAbd el-Qadir, 'Shajrat al-mīlād: Thalāthat afrāᶜ', in *Mukhtārāt min al-qiṣaṣ al-inklīzī: Tshārlz Dikinz wa ākharūn, tarjamat Ibrāhīm ᶜAbd al-Qādir al-Māzinī* (Cairo: Kalimāt ᶜArabiyya li-l-tarjama wa-l-nashr, 2011 [1939]), pp. 39–70.

Al-Māzinī, Ibrāhīm ᶜAbd el-Qādir, 'Al-taṣawwuf fī al-adab', in *Ḥiṣād al-Hashīm* (Cairo: Muᵓassasat Hindāwī li-l-taᶜlīm wa-l-thaqāfa, 2012), pp. 57–74.

Al-Māzinī, Ibrāhīm ᶜAbd el-Qādir, 'Shaksbīr fī al-ᶜArabiyya', in *Ḥiṣād al-Hashīm* (Cairo: Muᵓassasat Hindāwī li-l-taᶜlīm wa-l-thaqāfa, 2012), pp. 23–32.

Al-Muḥāfaẓa, Alī, *al-Ittijihāt al-fikriyya ᶜind al-ᶜArab fī ᶜaṣr al-nahḍa (1798–1914)* (Beirut: al-Ahliyya li-l-nashr wa al-tawzīᶜ, 1961).

Al-Mūsawī, Muḥsin Jāsim, *Infirāṭ al-ᶜiqd al-muqaddas: Munᶜaṭafāt al-riwāya al-ᶜArabiyya baᶜda Maḥfūẓ* (Cairo: al-Hayᵓa al-Miṣriyya al-ᶜāmma li-l-kitāb, 1999).

Najm, Muḥammad Yūsuf, *al-Qiṣṣa fi-l-adab al-ᶜArabī al-ḥadīth (1870–1914)* [The Story in Modern Arabic Literature (1870–1914)] (Beirut: al-Maktaba al-ahliyya, 1961).

Naṣīr, ᶜĀyda Ibrāhīm, *Ḥarakat nashr al-kutub fī Miṣr fī al-qarn al-Tāsiᶜ ᶜAshar* (Cairo: al-Hayᵓa al-Miṣriyya al-ᶜāmma li-l-kitāb, 1994).

Naṣr, ᶜĀṭif Jawda, *al-Khayāl: Mafhumātihi wa waẓāᵓifihi* (Cairo: al-Hayᵓa al-Miṣriyya al-ᶜāmma li-l-kitāb, 1984).

Nawfal, Yūsuf, *al-Fann al-qiṣaṣī bayna jīlay Ṭāhā Ḥusayn wa Najīb Maḥfūẓ* (Cairo: al-Hayᵓa al-Miṣriyya al-ᶜāmma li-l-kitāb, 1988).

Qulta, Kamāl, *Ṭāhā Ḥusayn wa-athar al-thaqāfa al-Faransiyya fī adabihi* (Cairo: Dār al-Maᶜārif, n.d.).

Ṣabūr, Ṣalāḥ Abdel, *Mādhā yabqā minhum li-l-tārīkh: dirāsāt fī adab Tāhā Ḥusayn, Tawfiq al-Ḥakīm, ᶜAbbās Maḥmūd al-ᶜAqqād wa Ibrāhīm al-Māzinī* (Cairo: al-Hayᵓa al-Miṣriyya al-ᶜāmma li-l-kitāb, 2005).

Shāmī, Yaḥyā, *Muṣṭafā Luṭfī al-Manfalūṭī: Qirāᵓa fī 'Naẓarātihi' wa 'Abarātihi'* (Cairo: Dār al-fikr al-ᶜarabī li-l-ṭibāᶜa wa-l-nashr, 2003).

Al-Shayyāl, Jamāl al-Dīn, *Tārīkh al-tarjama fī Miṣr fī ᶜahd al-ḥamla al-Faransiyya* (Cairo: Dār al-fikr al-ᶜArabī, 1950).

Al-Shayyāl, Jamāl al-Dīn, *Tārīkh al-tarjama wa ḥarakat al-thaqāfa fī Miṣr fī ᶜAṣr Muḥammad ᶜAlī* (Cairo: Dār al-fikr al-ᶜArabī,1951).

Shukrī, Ghālī, *Mādhā yabqā min Ṭāhā Ḥusayn* (Beirut: Dār al-muṭawassit li-l-nashr wa-l-tawzīᶜ, 1974).

Al-Sibāᶜī, Muḥammad, 'Kalimat al-mutarjim', in *Qiṣṣat al-madīnatayn, taᵓlīf Sharlz Dikinz*, Muḥammad al-Sibāᶜī (trans.), Vol. 1 (Cairo: Maṭbaᶜat al-bayān, 1912), pp. i–s.

Al-Sibāᶜī, Muḥammad (trans.), *Qiṣṣat al-madīnatayn, taᵓlīf Sharlz Dikinz*, 3 vols (Cairo: Maṭbaᶜat al-bayān, 1912).

Al-Sibāᶜī, Muḥammad, *Abṭāl Miṣr* (Cairo: n.p., 1922).

Al-Sibāᶜī, Muḥammad (trans.), *al-Abṭāl, taᵓlīf al-faylasūf al-akbar Tūmās Kārlayl*, 3rd edition (Cairo: al-Maṭbaᶜa al-Miṣriyya bi al-azhar, 1930).

Al-Sibāᶜī, Muḥammad, 'Kalimat al-muᶜarrib', in *al-Abṭāl, taᵓlīf al-faylasūf al-akbar Tūmās Kārlayl*, 3rd edition (Cairo: al-Maṭbaᶜa al-Miṣriyya bi al-azhar, 1930 [1911]), pp. xii–xiii.

Al-Sibāʿī, Muḥammad, *al-Faylasūf*, 2nd edition (Cairo: al-Sharika al-ʿArabiyya li-l-ṭibāʿa wa-l-nashr, 1963).

Al-Sibāʿī, Muḥammad, *Khawāṭir fī al-adab wa-l-ḥayāt* [Thoughts on Literature and Life] (Cairo: al-Sharika al-Miṣrīyya li-l-ṭibāʿa wa-l-nashr, 1965).

Al-Sibāʿī, Yūsuf, 'Kāna abī', introduction to Muḥammad al-Sibāʿī (trans.), *Miʾat Qiṣṣa: Qiṣaṣ Rūsiyya* (Cairo: Maktabat Miṣr, n.d.), pp. 5–12.

Ṣidqī, ʿAbd al-Raḥmān, 'Muqaddima', in *Khawāṭir fī al-adab w-al-ḥayāt* by Muḥammad al-Sibāʿī (Cairo: al-Sharika al-Miṣriyya li-l-ṭibāʿa wa-l-nashr, 1965), pp. i–j.

Al-Ṭahṭāwī, Rifāʿa Badawī Rāfiʿ, *Takhlīṣ al-ibrīz fī talkhīṣ Bārīz*, Vol. 2 (Cairo: al-Hayʾa al-Miṣriyya al-ʿāmma li-l-kitāb, 1993 [1834]).

Al-Ṭahtāwī, Rifāʿa Rāfiʿ, *Kitāb manāhij al-albāb al-Miṣriyya fī mabāhij al-ādāb al-ʿasriyya* (Beirut: Dār al-kitāb al-Lubnānī li-l-ṭibāʿa wa-l-nashr, 2012 [1869]).

Tājir, Jāk, *Ḥarakat al-tarjama bi-Miṣr khilāl al-qarn al-tāsiʿ ʿashar* (Cairo: Dār al-maʿārif, 1945).

Wādī, Ṭāhā, ʿUmrān, *al-Duktūr Muḥammad Ḥusayn Haykal: Ḥayātuhu wa turāthuhu al-adabī* (Cairo: Maktabat al-nahḍa al-Miṣriyya, 1969).

Waḥīd, ʿAlāʾ al-Dīn, *Muḥammad al-Sibāʿī: al-Adīb alladhī sabaqa ʿaṣrahu* (Cairo: al-Hayʾa al-Miṣriyya al-ʿāmma li-l-kitāb, 1982).

ʿUbayd, ʿĪsā, *Iḥsān Hānim: Majmūʿat qiṣaṣ Miṣriyya ʿaṣriyya* (Cairo: al-Dār al-qawmiyya li-l-ṭibāʿa wa-l-nashr, 1964 [1923]).

ʿUwayḍa, Kamāl Muḥammad, *Muṣṭafā Luṭfī al-Manfalūṭī: Ḥayātuhu wa adabuhu* (Beirut: Dār al-kutub al-ʿilmiyya, 1993).

Yūnus, Abd al-Ḥamīd, 'Ṭāhā Ḥusayn bayn al-ḍamīr al-ghāʾib wa-l-ḍamīr al-mutakallim', in *Ṭāhā Ḥusayn kamā yaʿrifuhu kuttāb ʿaṣrihi* (Cairo: Dār al-Hilāl, n.d.), pp. 63–70.

Zaytūnī, Laṭīf, *Ḥarakat al-tarjama fī ʿaṣr al-nahḍa* (Beirut: Dār al-nahār, 1994).

Al-Zayyāt, Aḥmad Ḥasan, 'Muṣṭafā Luṭfī al-Manfalūṭī: bi-munāsabat dhikrā al-thālithat ʿashara', in *al-Risāla*, Issue 210 (Cairo: Dār al-Risāla, 12 July 1937), pp. 1121–2.

**English and French Sources**

ʿAbdul-Hai, Muhammad, *Tradition and English and American Influence in Arabic Romantic Poetry: A Study in Comparative Literature*, 1st edition (London: Ithaca Press, 1982).

Abu-Lughod, Ibrahim, *The Arab Rediscovery of Europe: A Study in Cultural Encounters* (Princeton: Princeton University Press, 1963).

Agamben, Giorgio, *Profanations*, Jeff Fort (trans.) (New York: Zone Books, 2007).

Allan, Michael, *In the Shadow of World Literature: Sites of Reading in Colonial Egypt* (Princeton: Princeton University Press, 2016).

Allen, Roger, 'The Beginnings of the Arabic Novel', in M. M. Badawi (ed.), *Modern Arabic Literature* (Cambridge: Cambridge University Press, 1992), pp. 180–92.

Allen, Roger, *The Arabic Novel: An Historical and Critical Introduction* (New York: Syracuse University Press, 1995 [1982]).

Allen, Roger, 'Literary History and the Arabic Novel', *World Literature Today* 75(2) (Spring, 2004): 204–14.

Allen, Roger, 'The post-classical period: parameters and preliminaries,' in Roger Allen and D. S. Richards (eds), *Arabic Literature in the Post-Classical Period* (Cambridge: Cambridge University Press, 2006), pp. 1–22.

Altoma, Salih, 'Westernization and Islam in Modern Arabic Fiction', *Yearbook of Comparative and General Literature* 20 (1971): 81–8.

Anderson, Benedict, *Imagined Communities: Reflections on the Origin and Spread of Nationalism*, revised edition (New York: Verso, 2006 [1983]).

El-Ariss, Tarek, *Trials of Arab Modernity: Literary Affects and the New Political* (New York: Fordham University Press, 2013).

Asad, Talal, *Genealogies of Religion: Discipline and Reasons of Power in Christianity and Islam* (Baltimore: Johns Hopkins University Press, 1993).

Asad, Talal, *Formations of the Secular: Christianity, Islam, Modernity* (Stanford: Stanford University Press, 2003).

Attridge, Derek, 'Literary Form and the Demands of Politics: Otherness in J. M. Coetzee's *Age Of Iron*' in Sue Kossew (ed), *Critical Essays on J. M. Coetzee*, (New York: G. K. Hall & Co., 1998), pp. 198–213.

Ayalon, Ami, *The Press in the Arab Middle East: A History* (Oxford: Oxford University Press, 1995).

Badawi, M.-M., 'Islam in Modern Egyptian Literature', *Journal of Arabic Literature* 2(1) (1971): 154–77.

Badawi, M.-M., 'Ṭāhā Ḥusayn the Critic: A Reconsideration', *Journal of Semitic Studies* 28 (Spring 1983): 129–49.

Badawi, M.-M., *A Short History of Modern Arabic Literature* (Oxford: Oxford University Press, 1993).

Badawi, M.-M. (ed.), *Modern Arabic Literature* (Cambridge: Cambridge University Press, 1992).

Al-Baghdadi, Nadia, 'Registers of Arabic Literary History', *New Literary History* 39(3) (2008): 437–61.

Bakhtin, Mikhail, 'Author and Hero in Aesthetic Activity' in *Art and Answerability: Early Philosophical Essays by M. M. Bakhtin*, Vadim Liapunov and Kenneth Brostrom (trans.), Michael Holquist and Vadim Liapunov (eds) (Austin: University of Texas Press, 1990), pp. 4–256.

Balfour, Ian, *The Rhetoric of Romantic Prophecy* (Stanford: Stanford University Press, 2002).

Bawardi, Basilius, 'First Steps in Writing Arabic Narrative Fiction: The Case of "Ḥadīqat al-Akhbār"', *Die Welt des Islams* 48(2) (2008): 170–95.

Benjamin, Walter, 'Excavation and Memory', in Marcus Paul Bullock, Michael William Jennings, Howard Eiland, and Gary Smith (eds), *Walter Benjamin: Selected Writings, Vol. 2, part 2 (1931–1934)* (Cambridge, MA: Belknap Press of Harvard University Press, 2005 [1932]), pp. 576–94.

Benjamin, Walter, 'The Task of the Translator', in *Illuminations*, Harry Zorn (trans.), Hannah Arendt (ed.) (London: Pimlico, 1999), pp. 70–82.

Bennington, Geoffrey, *Dudding: Des noms de Rousseau* (Paris: Éditions Galilée, 1991).

Berque, Jacques, 'Islam vu par Taha Hussein', *Bulletin d'études orientales* 29 (1977): 65–72.

Bhabha, Homi, 'Of Mimicry and Man: The Ambivalence of Colonial Discourse', in *The Location of Culture* (London and New York: Routledge, 1995), pp. 85–92.

Blanchot, Maurice, *The Space of Literature*, Ann Smock (trans.) (Lincoln, NE: University of Nebraska Press, 1982 [1955, French]).

Blanchot, Maurice, *The Infinite Conversation*, Susan Hanson (trans.) (Minneapolis: University of Minnesota Press, 1993 [1969, French]).

Blanchot, Maurice, *The Book to Come*, Charlotte Mandel (trans.) (Stanford: Stanford University Press, 2003).

Brugman, Jan, 'Muḥammad al-Sibâᶜī and the Egyptian Literary Renaissance', in Albert Dietrich (ed.), *Akten des VII. Kongresses für Arabistik und Islamwissenschaft: Göttingen, 15. bis 22. August 1974* (Göttingen: Vandenhoeck, 1976), pp. 86–91.

Brugman, Jan, *An Introduction to the History of Modern Arabic Literature in Egypt* (Leiden: E. J. Brill, 1984).

Cachia, Pierre, 'The Development of a Modern Prose Style in Arabic Literature', *Bulletin of the School of Oriental and African Studies* 52(1) (1989): 65–76.

Cachia, Pierre, *An Overview of Modern Arabic Literature* (Edinburgh: Edinburgh University Press, 1990).

Cachia, Pierre, 'Translations and Adaptations 1834–1914', in M. M. Badawi (ed.), *Modern Arabic Literature* (Cambridge: Cambridge University Press, 1992), pp. 23–35.

Cachia, Pierre, *Ṭāhā Ḥusayn: His Place in the Egyptian Literary Renaissance* (Piscataway, NJ: Gorgias Press, 2005 [1956]).

Carlyle, Thomas, *On Heroes, Hero-Worship, and the Heroic in History*, transcribed from the Everyman edition (London: J. M. Dent & Sons, 1908) (London: The Electric Book Company, 2001).

Carlyle, Thomas, 'On History', in *The Modern British Essayists Volume V: Thomas Carlyle*, edited by R. W. Emerson (Philadelphia: A. Hart, Late Carey & Hart, 1852), pp. 219–23.

Chatterjee, Partha, *The Nation and Its Fragments: Colonial and Postcolonial Histories* (Princeton: Princeton University Press, 1993).

Childers, Joseph W., *Novel Possibilities: Fiction and the Formation of Early Victorian Culture* (Philadelphia: University of Pennsylvania Press, 1995).

Cohn, Bernard S., *Colonialism and its Forms of Knowledge: The British in India* (Princeton: Princeton University Press, 1996).

De Man, Paul, 'Literary History and Literary Modernity', *Daedalus* 99(2), *Theory in Humanistic Studies* (Spring, 1970): 384–404.

De Man, Paul, 'Conclusions: Walter Benjamin's "The Task of the Translator," Messenger Lecture at Cornell University, March 4, 1983', printed in *Yale French Studies* 69 (The Lesson of Paul de Man) (1985): 25–46.

Deheuvels, Luc-Willy, 'Fiction, discours et généricité: autour de *Ḥadīth ᶜĪsā Ibn Hishām* d'al-Muwayliḥī et d'*al-Baᶜth* d'al-Manfalūṭī', *Middle Eastern Literatures* 13(2) (2010): 141–51.

Deheuvels, Luc-Willy, 'Tâhâ Husayn et *Le livre des jours*; Démarche autobiographique et structure narrative', *Revue des mondes musulmans et de la Méditerranée* [En ligne], 95–8 | avril 2002, mis en ligne le 12 mai 2009, consulté le 03 mars 2017, at http://remmm.revues.org/236; DOI : 10.4000/ remmm.236.

Derrida, Jacques, *Monolingualism of the Other, or, the Prosthetics of Origin*, Patrick Mensah (trans.) (Stanford: Stanford University Press, 1998).

Derrida, Jacques. 'What is a "Relevant" Translation?', Lawrence Venuti (trans.), *Critical Inquiry* 27(2) (2001): 174–200.

Derrida, Jacques, 'Des Tours de Babel' (1985), in Jacques Derrida and Gil Anidjar (ed.), *Acts of Religion* (New York: Routledge, 2002), pp.102–34.

Derrida, Jacques, 'The Eyes of Language: The Abyss and the Volcano', in Jacques Derrida and Gil Anidjar (ed.), *Acts of Religion* (New York: Routledge, 2002), pp. 189–227.

Elbarbary, Samir, 'Al-ᶜAqqād's Hardy: Essays and Translations', *Journal of Arabic Literature* 22(1) (March, 1991): 66–82.

ElKhadem, Saad, 'Early Precursors to the Egyptian Novel', *International Journal of Fiction Review* 29(1–2) (2002): 23–9.

El-Enany, Rasheed, *Arab Representations of the Occident: East–West Encounters in Arabic Fiction* (London: Taylor and Francis, 2006).

El Esnawi, Ibtessam, 'Rostand and al-Manfaluti: Between Historical Invocation and Artistic Adaptation', *Journal of Comparative Poetics* 28 (2008): 98–114.

Even-Zohar, Itamar, 'The Position of Translated Literature within the Literary Polysystem', *Poetics Today* 11(1) (1990): 45–51.

Fanon, Franz, *The Wretched of the Earth* (London: Penguin Classics, 1990 [1961]).

Gasper, Michael Ezekiel, *The Power of Representation: Publics, Peasants, and Islam in Egypt* (Stanford: Stanford University Press, 2008).

Gershoni, Israeli, '"The Reader"-Another Production: The Reception of Haykal's Biography of Muhammad and the Shift of Egyptian Intellectuals to Islamic Subjects in the 1930s', Poetics Today 15 (2) (1994): 241–77.

Gershoni, Israel and James P. Jankowski, *Egypt, Islam, and the Arabs: The Search for Egyptian Nationhood, 1900–1930* (Oxford: Oxford University Press, 1987).

Gesink, Indira Falk, *Islamic Reform and Conservatism: Al-Azhar and the Evolution of Modern Sunni Islam* (London: I. B. Tauris, 2010).

Gide, André, *Thésée* (Paris: Gallimard, 1981).

Gide, André, 'Lettre d'André Gide au Traducteur', in *al-Bāb al-ḍayyiq* (1998) by Nazīh al-Ḥakīm (trans.) translation of André Gide's *La Porte étroite* (1909) (Damascus: Al-Mada Press, 2002), pp. 7–8.

Gross, Erin M., 'Reading Cant, Transforming the Nation: Carlyle's Past and Present', in Bianca Tredennick (ed.), *Victorian Transformations: Genre, Nationalism and Desire in Nineteenth-Century Literature* (Farnham: Ashgate Publishing Limited, 2011), pp. 95–114.

Guth, Stefan, 'Why Novels – Not Autobiographies: An Essay in the Analysis of a Historical Development', in R. Ostle et al. (eds), *Writing the Self: Autobiographical Writing in Modern Arabic Literature* (London: Saqi Books, 1998), pp. 139–47.

Hafez, Sabry, *The Genesis of Arabic Narrative Discourse: A Study in the Sociology of Modern Arabic Literature* (London: Saqi Books, 1993).

Hafez, Sabry, 'The Transformation of Reality and the Arabic Novel's Aesthetic Response', *Bulletin of the School of Oriental and African Studies* 57(1) (1994): 93–112.

Hafez, Sabry, 'The New Egyptian Novel: Urban Transformation and Narrative Form', *New Left Review* 64 (2010): 47–62.

Hallaq, Boutros, 'Transgénérique et modernité dans la littérature arabe', *Arabic and Middle Eastern Literature* 4(2) (2001): 157–66.

Hallaq, Boutros, 'La littérature selon Manfaluti', *Arabica* 50(2) (2003): 131–76.

Hallaq, Boutros, 'Bildungsroman, Individual and Society', in Robin Ostle (ed.), *Sensibilities of the Islamic Mediterranean: Self-Expression in a Muslim Culture from Post-Classical Times to the Present Day* (London: I. B. Tauris, 2008), pp. 149–62.

Hassan, Wail, 'Postcolonial Theory and Modern Arabic Literature: Horizons of Application', *Journal of Arabic Literature* 33(1) (2002): 45–64.

Heuvel, J. Van Den, Préface, in *Paul et Virginie* by Bernardin de Saint-Pierre (Paris: Librairie Générale Française, 1974), pp. 7–23.

Holt, Elizabeth, 'Narrative and the Reading Public in 1870s Beirut', *Journal of Arabic Literature* 40(1) (1 May, 2009): 37–70.

Hourani, Albert, *Arabic Thought in the Liberal Age: 1798–1939* (London: Oxford University Press, 1970).

Hunter, J. Paul, *Before Novels* (New York: W. W. Norton & Co., 1994).

Hussein, Taha, 'Réponse de Taha Hussein à André Gide' (5 January 1946) in *al-Bāb al-ḍayyiq* (1998) by Nazīh al-Ḥakīm (trans.) translation of André Gide's *La Porte étroite* (1909) (Damascus: Al-Mada Press, 2002), pp. 9–11.

Hussein, Taha, 'The Modern Renaissance of Arabic Literature', *World Literature Today* 63(2) (1989 [1955]): 249–56.

Hussein, Taha, *The Days: His Autobiography in Three Parts*, 2nd edition, E. H. Paxton (trans.), Hilary Wayment (trans.), and Kenneth Cragg (trans.) (New York: American University in Cairo Press, 2001).

Hussein, Taha, 'Réponse de Taha Hussein à André Gide', in *al-Bāb al-dayyiq*, 1998 [5 January 1946], translation of André Gide's *La Porte étroite* (1909) by Nazih al-Hakim (Damascus: Al-Mada Press, 2002), pp. 9–11.

Ibrahim, Ibrahim, 'Taha Husayn: The Critical Spirit', in John P. Spagnolo (ed.), *Problems of the Modern Middle East in Historical Perspective: Essays in Honor of Albert Hourani* (Oxford: Ithaca Press, 1992), pp. 105–18.

Jacquemond, Richard, 'Translation and Cultural Hegemony: The Case of French–Arabic Translation', in Lawrence Venuti (ed.), *Rethinking Translation: Discourse, Subjectivity, Ideology* (London: Routledge, 1992), pp. 139–58.

Jacquemond, Richard, *Conscience of the Nation: Writers, State, and Society in Modern Egypt*, David Tresilian (trans.) (Cairo: American University in Cairo Press, 2008).

Jann, Rosemary, *The Art and Science of Victorian History* (Columbus: Ohio State University, 1985).

Jayyusi, Salma Khadra and Christopher Tingley, *Trends and Movements in Modern Arabic Poetry*, vol. 1, (Leiden: E. J. Brill, 1977).

Johnson, Rebecca, 'Importing the Novel: The Arabic Novel in and as Translation', *Novel: A Forum on Fiction* 48(2) (2015): 243–60.

Johnson, Rebecca C., 'Foreword', in Ahmad Faris al-Shidyaq, *Leg Over Leg*, Vols 1 and 2, Humphrey Davies (trans.) (New York: New York University, 2015), Vol. 1, pp. ix–xxxvi.

Khouri, Mounah Abdallah, *Poetry and the Making of Modern Egypt (1882–1922)* (Leiden: E. J. Brill, 1971).

Kilito, Abdelfattah, *Thou Shalt Not Speak My Language*, Wail Hassan (trans.) (New York: Syracuse University Press, 2008)

Kilito, Abdelfattah and, *The Author and His Doubles: Essays on Classical Arabic Culture*, Wail Hassan (trans.) (New York: Syracuse University Press, 2001).

Kilito, Abdelfattah, *The Tongue of Adam*, Robyn Creswell (trans.) (New York City: New Directions, 2016).

Laroui, Abdallah, *The Crisis of the Arab Intellectual: Traditionalism or Historicism?* Diarmid Cammell (trans.) (Berkeley: University of California Press, 1977 [1974]).

Le Gassick, Trevor, 'The Faith of Islam in Modern Arabic Fiction', *Religion and Literature* 20(1) (Spring, 1988): 97–109.

Lejeune, Philippe, 'Autobiography in the Third Person', *New Literary History* 9(1) (Autumn, 1977): 27–50.

Lejeune, Philippe., *On Autobiography*, Katherine M. Leary (trans.), Paul John Eakin (ed.) (Minneapolis: University of Minneapolis Press, 1989 [1975]).

Liu, Lydia, *Translingual Practice: Literature, National Culture, and Translated Modernity: China, 1900–1937* (Stanford: Stanford University Press, 1995).

Lowry, Joseph E. and Devin J. Stewart (eds), 'Introduction', in *Essays in Arabic Literary Biography, 1350–1850* (Wiesbaden: Harrassowitz Verlag, 2009), pp. 1–10.

Lukács, Georg, *The Historical Novel* (Lincoln, NE: University of Nebraska Press, 1983 [1937]).

Maghraoui, Abdeslam M., *Liberalism without Democracy: Nationhood and Citizenship in Egypt, 1922–1936* (Durham, NC: Duke University Press, 2006).

Mahmoudi, Abdelrashid, *Ṭāhā Ḥusain's Education from the Azhar to the Sorbonne* (Richmond: Curzon Press, 1998).

Matti, Moosa, *The Origins of Modern Arabic Fiction* (Washington, DC: Three Continents Press, 1997 [1983]).

Mitchell, Timothy, *Colonising Egypt* (Berkeley: University of California Press, 1991).

Mitchell, Timothy, 'The Stage of Modernity', in Timothy Mitchell (ed.), *Questions of Modernity* (Minneapolis: University of Minnesota Press, 2000), pp. 1–34.

Moreh, Shmuel, *Modern Arabic Poetry 1800–1970: The Development of its Forms and Themes Under the Influence of Western Literature*, Vol. 5 (Leiden: E. J. Brill, 1976).

Moretti, Franco, *The Way of the World: The Bildungsroman in European Culture* (London: Verso, 2000).

Moretti, Franco, 'Style, Inc. Reflections on Seven Thousand Titles (British Novels, 1740–1850)', *Critical Inquiry* 36(1) (Autumn, 2009): 134–58.

Al-Musawi, Muhsin J., *Islam on the Street: Religion in Modern Arabic Literature* (Lanham: Rowman, 2009).

Newman, Daniel, 'The Arabic Literary Language: The Nahḍa (and Beyond)', in Jonathan Owens (ed.), *The Oxford Handbook of Arabic Linguistics*, Vol. 1 (Oxford: Oxford University Press, 2013), DOI: 10.1093/oxfordhb/9780199764136.013.0021.

Niranjana, Tejaswini, *Siting Translation: History, Post-Structuralism and the Colonial Context* (Berkeley: University of California Press, 1992).

Al-Nowaihi, Mohamed, 'Towards the Reappraisal of Classical Arabic Literature and History: Some Aspects of Taha Husayn's Use of Modern Western Criteria', *International Journal of Middle East Studies* 11(2) (April, 1980): 189–207.

Omri, Mohamed-Salah, *Nationalism, Islam and World Literature: Sites of Confluence in the Writings of Maḥmūd al-Masᶜadī* (London: Routledge, 2006).

Omri, Mohamed-Salah, 'The Novelization of Islamic Literatures', *Comparative Critical Studies* 4(3) (2007): 359–78.

Ostle, Robin C., 'The Romantic Poets', in M. M. Badawi (ed.), *Modern Arabic Literature* (Cambridge: Cambridge University Press, 1992), pp. 82–131.

Ostle, Robin C. and Moor de E. Wild (eds.), *Writing the Self: Autobiographical Writing in Modern Arabic literature* (London: Saqi Books, 1998).

Ostle, Robin C. (ed.), *Sensibilities of the Islamic Mediterranean: Self-Expression in a Muslim Culture from Post-Classical Times to the Present Day* (London: I. B. Tauris, 2008).

Papazian, Mary A., 'Introduction', in *The Sacred and the Profane in English Renaissance Literature* (Newark, DE: University of Delaware Press, 2008), pp. 13–26.

Patel, Abdulrazzak, *The Arab* Nahḍah*: The Making of the Intellectual and Humanist Movement* (Edinburgh: Edinburgh University Press, 2013).

Peled, Mattityahu, 'Creative Translation: Towards the Study of Arabic Translations of Western Literature since the 19th Century', *Journal of Arabic Literature* 10 (1979): 128–50.

Peled, Mattityahu, 'Did al-Manfalūṭī Really Shed Tears for His Protagonist?', *Arabica* 38(1) (1991): 57–72.

Pérès, Henri. *Le Roman, Le Conte et La Nouvelle dans la littérature arabe moderne, extrait des Annales de l'institut d'etudes orientales* (Tome III, 1937) (Paris: Librairie Larose, 1937).

Philipp, Thomas, 'The Autobiography in Modern Arab Literature and Culture', *Poetics Today* 14(3) (Autumn, 1993): 573–604.

Philipp, Thomas, *Jurji Zaidan and the Foundations of Arab Nationalism* (Syracuse: Syracuse University Press, 2014).

Rastegar, Kamran, *Literary Modernity between the Middle East and Europe: Textual Transactions in the Nineteenth Century Arabic, English, and Persian Literatures* (London: Routledge, 2007).

Reynolds, Dwight, *Interpreting the Self: Autobiography in the Arabic Literary Tradition* (Berkeley: University of California Press, 2001).

Rousseau, Jean Jacques, *The Confessions of Jean Jacques Rousseau*, J. M. Cohen (trans.) (Harmondsworth: Penguin Books, 1960 [1950]).

Rousseau, Jean Jacques, *The Social Contract and Discourses 1913*, G. D. H. Cole (trans.) (London: Everyman's Library, 1963).

Rousseau, Jean Jacques, *Emile, Or Treatise on Education*, William H. Payne (trans.) (New York: Prometheus Books, 2003).

Rousseau, Jean Jacques, *The Discourses and Other Early Political Writings*, Victor Gourevitch (trans. and ed.) (Cambridge: Cambridge University Press, 2006 [1997]).

Sacks, Jeffrey, *Iterations of Loss: Mutilation and Aesthetic Form, al-Shidyaq to Darwish* (New York: Fordham University Press, 2015).

Said, Edward W., *Orientalism* (New York: Vintage, 1979 [1978]).

Said, Edward W., *Beginnings: Intention and Method* (New York: Columbia University Press, 1985).

Saint-Pierre, Bernardin de, *Paul et Virginie* (Paris: Librairie Générale Française, 1974).

Saint-Pierre, Bernardin de, Préambule, *Paul et Virginie* (Paris: Librairie Générale Française, 1974 [1806]), pp. 103–94.

Al-Sayyid, Afaf Lutfi, *Egypt and Cromer: A Study in Anglo-Egyptian Relations* (New York: Praeger, 1969).

Schleiermacher, Friedrich, 'On the Different Methods of Translating', Susan Bernofsky (trans.), in Lawrence Venuti (ed.), *The Translation Studies Reader*, 2nd edition (New York, Routledge, 2004 [2000]), pp. 43–63.

Selim, Samah, 'The Narrative Craft: Realism and Fiction in the Arabic Canon', *Edebiyat* 14(1) (2003): 109–28.

Selim, Samah. 'The Nahda, Popular Fiction, and the Politics of Translation', *MIT-EJMES* 4 (Fall, 2004): 71–90.

Selim, Samah, *The Novel and the Rural Imaginary in Egypt, 1880–1985* (New York: Routledge, 2004).

Selim, Samah, 'The People's Entertainments: Translation, Popular Fiction, and the *Nahḍa* in Egypt', in Brenda Schildgen (ed.), *In Other Renaissances: A New Approach to World Literature* (Basingstoke: Palgrave Macmillan, 2006), pp. 35–58.

Selim, Samah, 'Nation and Translation in the Middle East', *The Translator* 15(1) (2009): 1–13.

Selim, Samah, 'Towards a New Literary History', *International Journal of Middle East Studies* 43(4) (2011): 734–6.

Semah, David, *Four Egyptian Literary Critics*, Vol. 3 (Leiden: Brill, 1974).

Sheehi, Stephen, 'Inscribing the Arab Self: Butrus al-Bustani and Paradigms of Subjective Reform', *British Journal of Middle Eastern Studies* 27(1) (2000): 7–24.

Sheehi, Stephen, *Foundations of Modern Arab Identity* (Gainesville: University Press of Florida, 2004).

Sheehi, Stephen, 'Towards a Critical Theory of al-Nahdah: Epistemology, Ideology and Capital', *Journal of Arabic Literature* 43(2–3) (2012): 269–98.

Sherif, Nur, *Dickens in Arabic: 1912–1970* (Beirut, Lebanon: Beirut Arab University Press, 1974).

Schwarz, Roberto, *Misplaced Ideas: Essays on Brazilian Culture*, John Gledson (ed.) (London: Verso, 1992).

Siddiq, Muhammad, *Arab Culture and the Novel: Genre, Identity and Agency in Egyptian Fiction* (London: Routledge, 2007).

Siskin, Clifford, 'The Rise of Novelism', in Deidre Shauna and William Warner (eds), *Cultural Institutions of the Novel* (Durham, NC: Duke University Press, 1996), pp. 423–40.

Smith, Charles D., 'Crisis of Orientation: The Shift of Egyptian Intellectuals to Islamic Subjects in the 1930's', *International Journal of Middle East Studies* 4(4) (1973): 382–410.

Smith, Charles D., 'Love, Passion and Class in the Fiction of Muḥammad Ḥusayn Haykal', *Journal of the American Oriental Society* 99(2) (April–June, 1979): 249–61.

Smith, Charles D., 'The Intellectual and Modernization: Definitions and Reconsiderations – The Egyptian Experience', *Comparative Studies in Society and History* 22(4) (1980): 513–33.

Smith, Charles D., *Islam and the Search for Social Order in Modern Egypt: A Biography of Muhammad Husayn Haykal* (New York: State University of New York Press, 1983).

Somekh, Sasson, 'The Emergence of Two Stylistic Norms: In the Early Translation into Modern Arabic Prose', *Poetics Today (Translation Theory and Intercultural Relations)* 2(4) (Summer–Autumn, 1981): 193–200.

Spivak, Gayatri Chakravorty, 'The Politics of Translation', in Lawrence Venuti (ed.), *The Translation Studies Reader* (London: Routledge, 2000), pp. 397–416.

Spivak, Gayatri Chakravorti, 'Translating into English', in Sandra Bermann and Michael Wood (eds), *Nation, Language, and the Ethics of Translation* (Princeton: Princeton University Press, 2005), pp. 93–110.

Starobinsky, Jean, *Jean Jacques Rousseau: Transparency and Obstruction*, Arthur Goldhammer (trans.) (Chicago: University of Chicago Press, 1988 [1958]).

Stetkevych, Jaroslav, *The Modern Arabic Literary Language: Lexical and Stylistic Developments* (Washington, DC: Georgetown University Press, 2006 [1970]).

Stewart, Garrett, *Dear Reader: The Conscripted Reader in Nineteenth-Century British Fiction* (Baltimore: Johns Hopkins University Press, 1996).

Tageldin, Shaden, *Disarming Words: Empire and the Seductions of Translation in Egypt* (Berkeley: University of California Press, 2011).

Tageldin, Shaden, 'Untranslatability', 3 March 2014, accessed 9 May 2017, at https://stateofthediscipline.org/entry/untranslatability.

Tageldin, Shaden M., 'Secularizing Islam: Carlyle, al-Sibāʿī, and the Translations of "Religion"', *PMLA* 126(1) (2011): 123–39.

Tignor, Robert, *Modernisation and British Colonial Rule in Egypt, 1882–1914* (Princeton: Princeton University Press, 1966).

Tucker, Irene, 'What Maisie Promised: Realism, Liberalism and the Ends of Contract', *The Yale Journal of Criticism* 11(2) (1998): 335–64.

Tymoczko, Maria, 'Translation and Political Engagement: Activism, Social Change and the Role of Translation in Geopolitical Shifts', *The Translator* 6(1) (2000): 23–47.

Venuti, Lawrence, *The Translator's Invisibility: A History of Translation* (London: Routledge, 2008 [1995]).

Venuti, Lawrence, *The Scandals of Translation* (London: Routledge, 1998).

Venuti, Lawrence, 'Local Contingencies: Translation and National Identities', in Sandra Bermann and Michael Wood (eds), *Nation, Language, and the Ethics of Translation,* (Princeton: Princeton University Press, 2005) pp. 177–202.

Venuti, Lawrence, 'Translation as Cultural Politics: Régimes of Domestication in English', in Mona Baker (ed.), *Critical Readings in Translation Studies* (London: Routledge, 2010), pp. 65–79.

Viswanathan, Gauri, *Masks of Conquest: Literary Study and British Rule in India* (Delhi: Oxford University Press, 1998).

Waterfield, Robin, *Prophet: The Life and Times of Kahlil Gibran* (New York: St. Martin's Press, 1998).

Watt, Ian, *The Rise of the Novel: Studies in Defoe, Richardson, and Fielding*, 2nd edition (Berkeley: University of California Press, 2001 [1957]).

Yousef, Hoda A., *Composing Egypt: Reading, Writing and the Emergence of a Modern Nation 1870–1930* (Stanford: Stanford University Press, 2016).

Ze'evi, Dror, 'Back to Napoleon? Thoughts on the Beginning of the Modern Era in the Middle East', *Mediterranean Historical Review* 19(1) (2004): 73–94.

# Index

CPSIA information can be obtained
at www.ICGtesting.com
Printed in the USA
JSHW020452280920
8208JS00001B/17

9 781474 474504